anyone who cares about the rights of the LGBTQ community to be treated as equal citizens at every level, including the religious—which means it should be essential reading for *everybody*."

—Donna Freitas, author of *The End of Sex*

"Jeff Chu's dazzling debut proves being a gay Christian is no oxymoron—but it's far from easy. Wielding his reporter's tenacity and Scriptural chops, Chu travels the country to conduct fascinating interviews with other gay Christians, and those who condemn them. You will emerge from this book changed, for you will know Jeff Chu."

—Lisa Takeuchi Cullen,
author of *Pastors' Wives* and *Remember Me*

# DOES JESUS
# REALLY LOVE ME?

# DOES JESUS REALLY LOVE ME?

## A Gay Christian's Pilgrimage in Search of God in America

## JEFF CHU

HARPER

www.harpercollins.com

HarperCollins books may be purchased for educational, business, or sales
promotional use. For information, please e-mail the Special Markets
Department at SPsales@harpercollins.com.

Lyrics from "Undo Me" courtesy of Jennifer Knapp.

FIRST EDITION

Library of Congress Cataloging-in-Publication Data has been applied for.

ISBN: 978-0-06-204973-5

13  14  15  16  17   OV/RRD   10 9 8 7 6 5 4 3 2 1

To those who have endured.

"I seek an inheritance incorruptible, undefiled, and that fadeth not away, and it is laid up in heaven, and safe there, to be bestowed, at the time appointed, on them that diligently seek it. Read it so, if you will, in my book."

—PART I, THE FIRST STAGE, *THE PILGRIM'S PROGRESS*

# CONTENTS

# DOES JESUS
# REALLY LOVE ME?

# DOES JESUS LOVE ME?

If I were putting together the soundtrack of my life, I'd pick "Jesus Loves Me" to cover a big chunk of my childhood. As a boy, I believed that song, and I wanted to believe it. "Jesus Loves Me" is straightforward, in the way that children's songs often are, and faithful, in the way that children can be:

> *Jesus loves me, this I know.*
> *For the Bible tells me so.*
> *Little ones to him belong.*
> *They are weak, but he is strong.*

We sang that song often in Sunday school. And during school vacations, which my sister and I always spent with Grandma and Grandpa, the lyrics were a weekday thing, too. Religious tendencies in Berkeley, California, where they lived in a big, brown-shingled apartment building for old people, might typically lean more toward earth worship, or anti-establishmentarianism, or just standard righteous, aging-hippie narcissism. But for fifteen or twenty minutes, every morning at 2050 Delaware Street, Apt. 105, my Bible-teacher grandma stirred up some old-fashioned Baptist revival in her warbly soprano and a hailstorm of hallelujahs.

She'd read a Bible passage aloud in Cantonese—her English didn't go much beyond "Hello!" and "Bye-bye!" and, when we were at McDonald's, "Filet Fish!"—her index finger moving slowly down the columns of characters, right to left across the crinkly thin pages. My Baptist-preacher grandpa, retired from the pulpit and semi-silenced by a bad stroke, would listen, his eyes closed and his rocking chair moving pendulum-like. My sister and I would sit on the afghan-draped sofa, trying not to fidget. Then, before we said our prayers—for our family, for Jackie, who managed their apartment building, for the salvation of the president of the United States—we'd sing.

The songs came from dog-eared bilingual hymnals that emigrated with my grandparents from Hong Kong in 1969. Within the cracked, Longhorns-orange covers, the songs that my grandma gravitated toward were the straightforward, unabashed statements of faith with titles that tell you everything you need to know: "What a Friend We Have in Jesus," "Stand Up, Stand Up for Jesus," "Victory in Jesus." There was lots of Jesus, and not much subtlety or doubt. "Trust and Obey," one of the hymns regularly in my grandmother's mix, seemed always to be a warning to us: "Trust and obey, for there's no other way, to be happy in Jesus, but to trust and obey."

Of all the songs we sang when I was five, ten, fifteen, "Jesus Loves Me" is the one that has stuck with me. For a long time, its reasoning, so neatly encapsulated in the line "For the Bible tells me so," worked for me. I accepted it with a childlike faith. How could it not be true? Why should it be more complicated? But as I got older, the Bible felt more and more like reading someone else's mail—interesting, no doubt, but ultimately secondhand and indirect. The truth I had grown up with, the teaching that had been fed to me, it wasn't necessarily that I thought it was false, but I longed to hear it for myself. I wanted to know faith for myself.

Occasionally, fragments of the song still pop into my mind—sometimes in the Cantonese words I grew up with, sometimes in the English words I learned later. Often it's the chorus: "Yes, Jesus loves me! Yes, Jesus loves me! Yes, Jesus loves me! The Bible tells me so." And I think about how nice it would be if I were sure of that fact. What would it feel like if I believed that Jesus really loved me?


I went to high school in Miami. At Westminster Christian School, we had chapel weekly, pledged allegiance to the Christian flag as well as the American, and were assigned to read books like *This Present Darkness*, a novel that taught me nothing about literature and lots about how demons are everywhere, including probably digging their claws into all of us right now. The school's name derives from the Westminster Confession of Faith, a bedrock theological work written in 1646, and a snippet of the Westminster catechism ("Man's chief end is to glorify God and enjoy him for ever") was emblazoned on an outer wall of the athletics building. Judging by the school's priorities, a Westminster Warrior's chief means of glorifying God was winning baseball games. This high school of barely three hundred students won the national championship twice in my years there—an achievement that, to my mind, remains one of the great uninvestigated anomalies in American sports history.

During the fall of my freshman year, I took a class called James and Philippians to fulfill my Bible requirement. It was taught by a pale, earnest Bible-college graduate named Mr. Byers, who at twenty-four was one of Westminster's youngest teachers. He and his family, who also attended my church, were beloved on campus. His wife worked in the school office, and their toddler, Owen, could often be seen tottering around.

Mr. Byers said unexpected things in class. One day, one of my classmates raised a hand and asked, "What is heaven going to be like?" Mr. Byers got this far-off grin on his face and blurted out: "Heaven is going to be like an eternal orgasm." After a long, awkward pause, he added, "But you're not supposed to know what that is."

A couple of months into the semester, Mr. Byers did not show up for class one day. Rumors started to circulate around campus—churchy,

Christian-school moms have raised gossip to fine art—each news report prefaced, of course, by the admonition, "we should really be praying for _____, bless his heart."

A few days later, a special chapel was called to address Mr. Byers's mysterious disappearance. I have almost no recollection of what happened during the assembly, other than that our perpetually ill-at-ease principal, Mr. Adams, stood at the podium saying something bad about Mr. Byers. But my friend Shawn says he remembers that chapel "very well. Actually, I can recall what Mr. Adams said verbatim: 'Mr. Byers has been involved in an adulterous, homosexual relationship'"—awkward pause—"'with another man.' I think I recall it so well because I found it hysterical that he felt the need to include 'with another man.'" The only thing my friend Heather remembers from that chapel is that the guy next to her said, over and over and over, "I knew it! I knew it! I knew it!"

What I remember is the fear that swamped me. My palms still get tropical when I think of that chapel. At the mention of the word *homosexual*, I knew the truth: Even if I didn't have the words to define it then, I knew I had feelings like Mr. Byers's. And this was the lesson that I learned: Nobody could ever, ever find out, because if they did, I would be damned and cast out, just like he was.

The United States is the most demonstrably, demonstratively Christian nation in the developed world. About three-quarters of Americans identify as Christian, according to a wide range of recent surveys, and more than a third say they're regular churchgoers. A study done in the early 1990s by Kirk Hadaway of the United Church of Christ and Penny Marler of Samford University estimates, though, that the number of churchgoers is actually about half that, and the fact that so many Americans feel the need to tell pollsters they go to church even if they don't says a lot about how we see ourselves and how we want to be seen. Such sentiments may in fact matter more than the statistics, because they illuminate why and how we talk about our faith in the context of our politics, our courts, our communities, our relationships with neighbors. And this is where our reality gets especially messy: Even if we agree that, for better or for worse, America is a Christian nation, we disagree, often bombastically, rudely, and even violently, about what that information means and what it should mean. For some people, it is and should be no more than a demographic fact. For others, it's an indication of divine blessing and a call to action.

From time to time in recent years, I've been told that the culture wars are over. I wish they were, as I'm bored with the term, but they're not. They are still being fought not only in the courts, at the ballot box, on our political talk shows, and in our editorial pages, but also in my family and in families like mine all over the nation, and the single most explosive issue today is homosexuality. Witness our continuing fierce, often angry debates about gay marriage, gay adoption, and gay everything—debates that are infused with extra emotion because, for all their public-policy implications, these issues are inextricably, painfully personal. This issue is about sons and daughters, friends and lovers, our neighbors, ourselves. It is also about our freedom, our faith, perhaps our salvation.

I am now thirty-five. According to the blueprint I once had for my life, I should now be married to the lovely, smart, and accomplished woman I met in college. We would have four children (Alexander, called Xander, and Oliver, known as Oli, and two girls, but for some reason I never could come up with good girls' names) and one dog, all paid for by a career selected from the Official Chinese Parent List of Approved Professions (medicine, computer science, banking, law, engineering). I would drive the clan around in a Volvo. I would play tennis twice a week with a buddy. I would be a pillar of the community and a church deacon. Sometimes I would teach Sunday school or read one of the Scripture passages during the service. My life would be a shining example of the Good Christian Man.

I veered a little off plan, except I do have my Volvo. The only children in my house are my two nephews, who smile at me from a picture frame on the mantel. I'm a journalist. I barely exercise. Forget about deacon or Sunday school teacher; it's a good Sunday when I manage to get myself into a church pew and an excellent one when I can get through the sermon without daydreaming. My mother still cries herself to sleep at night, praying for her "lost" homosexual son and wondering what she did wrong. Thank goodness the lovely, smart, accomplished woman I dated during and after college found a nice Anglican priest to marry. There are still moments when I wonder whether my homosexuality is my ticket to hell, whether Jesus would love me but for that, and how good a Christian could I be if I struggle to believe that God loves me at all.

I suspect I'm not so different from many people who struggle to make sense of these matters of the soul. For most of us, it probably has nothing to do with being gay. Truth is, many of us have spiritual wedge issues—personal obstacles that stand in the way of us fully believing, topics or teachings that gnaw at us and at what faith we may have left. It may be some other disagreement with church doctrine. It could be something a church lady said once that was more hurtful than you'd ever want to admit. It might just be a gut feeling that you've never been able to translate into words and sentences. For me, that spiritual wedge issue is homosexuality.

I wish that I could go off into my own little corner of the world and figure it out on my own and with my God, but theology and church practice, public policy and civil liberties, are in play. Even if you do not care about Jesus and how he feels about the gays, how others feel about this issue has had inordinate influence on our modern, American lives. And the ramifications of the debate ripple far beyond our borders. To note just one example, the teachings of American preachers have helped inspire Uganda's ongoing infatuation with legislation to impose the death penalty on practicing homosexuals.

The issue probably isn't going away anytime soon, neither in American society nor in the American church. Tony Jones, a Minnesota theologian who likes to describe himself as an ecclesiastical proctologist, poking at the places that make the church uncomfortable, says homosexuality is such a sensitive issue because it's so primal and personal. "Abortion is one step removed for most people," he says. (True for men, in particular.) "Creation is three steps removed—it's almost theoretical. But when it comes to what you do with your penis, well, that's real."

From time immemorial, humans have been making pilgrimages. Tibetans believe that pilgrims have been traveling to their sacred Mount Kailash for fifteen thousand years; it's said that walking the trail around the mountain erases a lifetime of sins. In Old Testament times, Jews would travel to Jerusalem to worship at the temple on Mount Zion. The oracle at Delphi drew ancient Greeks in search of guidance. The hajj to Mecca is de rigueur, at least once in a lifetime, for every Muslim.

But pilgrimage isn't necessarily just about getting to and from a famous shrine. The word can refer to any journey of spiritual significance. A pilgrimage can be any trip taken with the goal of getting to a transformative place, any trip that's less about entertainment and more about enlightenment.

So in that spirit, I decided to embark on a year of travel, by plane and bus and train and brain wave, asking the questions that have long frightened me. My hope was to find some answers at last. My plan was to crisscross America as well as the spectrum of American Christianity. My goal was to understand why those who call themselves followers of Christ start from the same point—a god-man who lived two thousand years ago and left behind a church with his name on it—but end up in such radically different places on the issue of God, the church, and homosexuality. I would take this trip with the curiosity of a journalist and the searching spirit of a simple pilgrim. I'm no theologian, no crusader, just a regular guy trying to hang on to something resembling the faith I grew up with, as irrational as that may be.

I traveled with baggage: I grew up Southern Baptist. I am gay. I have a boyfriend. I'm relatively conservative (I've voted for both

Democrats and Republicans) in a relatively liberal city (I live in Brooklyn, New York), where I attend a relatively liberal church (Old First Reformed in Brooklyn, New York) in a relatively conservative denomination (the Reformed Church in America). I doubt. A lot. And yet I can't *not* believe in God.

That belief was solidified during my tortuous, torturous coming-out period in my twenties, a time when, ironically, I almost never went to church. As I told friends and loved ones about my homosexuality, I was repeatedly told what I should believe and how I should live my life. On the conservative side, I got plenty of Bible verses, including those delightful ones from the Old Testament about gay "abomination"—complete with the "they must be put to death; their blood will be on their own heads" part. On the liberal end, friends expressed not just occasional fury and disbelief but also head-shaking pity. I felt them judging me, too: What a shame that I insisted on trying to hang on to my archaic faith. How pathetic that I had so little self-worth that I insisted on maintaining relationships even with those who called me an "abomination." Yet few people ever asked me what I wanted, what I was hoping for, why I was making the choices I was making.

In that season, I clung to God. He *had* to exist in my mind, because I had to believe that someone bigger and more powerful would someday make this all okay. But I didn't push much deeper than that, either, not in earnest, until this journey. In the end, I flew more than twenty thousand miles and drove more than five thousand, visiting twenty-eight states and churches from more than a dozen denominations. I crashed on friends' and strangers' couches. I ate at church picnics. I was yelled at and hung up on and leered at and leaned on. I believed, and sometimes I didn't. I was scared, and I was emboldened. I interviewed more than three hundred people, recording their stories and seeking to grasp what they believe about whom we love and who loves us.

What I found was a country that deeply wants to love, but is conflicted about how to do so. I encountered a church that's far more divided than I imagined, led in large part by cowardly clergy who are called to be shepherds yet behave like sheep. I encountered myriad people with distinct voices—so distinct, in fact, that I've chosen to share several of their stories as oral histories, which you'll find amid the chapters of this book. I met a young man named Gideon Eads, who, while I was on my journey of faith and discovery, was going on one of his own. I heard the testimonies of resilient spirits and indefatigable souls, each seeking and struggling to do the right thing, whatever that may mean. And I saw the many, many faces of God in America.

# DOUBTING

"There ariseth in his soul fears, and doubts, and discouraging apprehensions, which all of them get together and settle in this place. And this is the reason of
the badness of this ground."

—PART I, THE FIRST STAGE, *THE PILGRIM'S PROGRESS*

# BEGINNINGS

## In the Capital of Christian America

---

*Nashville, Tennessee*

When I land in Nashville little creatures resembling tiny brown turbo-props whir through the air, slapping the airplane windows. The air thrums with the hum of their wings, and their corpses litter the tarmac. Cicadas, millions of them, have invaded, as they do once every seventeen years. They're harmless. Yet they look terrifying, and perceptions matter: Early Americans mistook them for the locusts of biblical-plague renown, and the mini-beasts, with their bulging red eyes and W-shaped wing markings, have often been seen as omens of war. In 1919, one Tennessee newspaper recorded the cicadas' arrival with the headline SEVENTEEN YEAR LOCUSTS APPEAR IN BATTLE ARRAY.

For me, the cicadas are a good omen: Nashville's status as a battle-ground is one of the main reasons I've come. A blue city in a purple metropolitan area in a red state, Nashville sits atop cultural and religious fault lines that define much of the debate about homosexuality in America. And Tennessee, a conservative state that has clung to the fighting frontier spirit of Davy Crockett and Andrew Jackson, has been at the epicenter of battles over social change for two centuries. Its legislature repeatedly debated the abolition of slavery before the Civil War (emancipation was defeated every time), and during that war, more battles were fought here than in any state save Virginia. Then came Jim Crow, and the Scopes Trial, and tussles over women's suffrage and civil rights.

In each case, faith came into play. "You can't do anything here without involving the church," says Chris Sanders, who leads the Nashville chapter of the Tennessee Equality Project. "You just can't." (Sanders's brand of church: Episcopal.) Indeed, this city is totally churchy. Several major Protestant denominations call Nashville home, including the United Methodist Church, the African Methodist Episcopal Church, the National Baptist Convention, and the Southern Baptist Convention. Nashville is also the capital of Christian culture in America. Thomas Nelson, the world's largest Christian publisher, is based in Nashville, as are the Gideons, the hotel room Bible supplier. Word Music, the world's number one gospel recording house, is headquartered here, as is TBN, the world's biggest Christian broadcaster, and Salem Communications, America's top Christian radio network. As the T-shirts I find in one souvenir shop testify, Nashville is the Protestant Vatican.

I land in Nashville at a contentious moment. The previous December, Belmont University, a private Christian institution in town, ousted its varsity-soccer coach, Lisa Howe, after she came out to her players and told them that her partner, Wendy Holleman, was pregnant. The furor over Howe's forced resignation inspired the Davidson County Council, which oversees Nashville, to forbid the local government from contracting with any company or organization that discriminates based on sexual orientation. This decision was too much for conservative state legislators, who responded with a bill prohibiting local antidiscrimination ordinances that are stricter than statewide law. When I visit, they are in the midst of debating an encore, a proposal to restrict schoolteachers from speaking about homosexuality in class. (Opponents dubbed it the "Don't Say Gay" bill.)

But here's the truth of why I've come to Nashville: I spent much of my childhood in Southern Baptist churches, using Sunday school materials that originated here and listening to Christian music that was recorded here and reading Christian books that were published here. If there's any place to begin the quest to understand not only American Christianity's struggle over homosexuality but also my own troubled faith, to confront the ghosts who still haunt my heart, it's here.

Lisa Howe is the opposite of a firebrand. When we meet at her lawyer's office, she is shy, and her voice, surprisingly soft for a coach, is almost eerily free of modulation. I ask her what it's like to be an activist, and befuddlement fills her face. "I never expected this," she says. "I never wanted any of it. But suddenly I was on the front page of the newspaper and I was all over the Internet. At first, I read all the comments. Some of them defended the LGBT lifestyle, and it felt good to have as much support as we did. I remember one really passionate, long comment that said we're not here to judge and Lisa was a great coach. And the very next comment was short: 'Why doesn't she like men?' It was funny!" She smiles wanly.

Because of her legal settlement with Belmont, Howe can't discuss her departure from the university, but she speaks freely about its wake, especially the attacks on her daughter, which began even before the child was born. "To call her a sinner when she's not even here yet? To pick on an unborn child?" Howe says, "I definitely didn't like that."

Howe, who grew up in the South, didn't expect a full embrace of her sexuality, not in a part of the country where, as the cliché goes, one of the first things people ask about you is what church you attend. In fact, until she told her players about Wendy's pregnancy, at work she kept almost all personal data encrypted. "I never talked about being a lesbian. If you're in the break room at lunch, talking about Thanksgiving, I would never tell the whole truth about whose family we were with," she says. "You expect—I know it's bad to say 'expect,' but you think people will say lesbians are going to hell. And they did."

Though Belmont, the alma mater of the country music megastar Brad Paisley and the award-winning poet and author H. L. Hix, now identifies as a nondenominational Christian university, it is historically Baptist and only broke from the Tennessee Baptist Convention in 2007. "When I got to Belmont, I definitely felt it was a faith-based university. I never felt any fundamentalist Baptist stuff. But on the job application, it said, 'Are you Christian?' and you had to mark yes or no," Howe says. "It doesn't say you have to be a Christian, though."

This much I know about Baptists: Their roots run deep, and whatever the official rules say, there are often stubborn, invisible standards, too. Nobody ever told me this—it was in my blood. My family is the closest thing out of China to devoutly Southern Baptist. My great-grandfather was a Baptist missionary in Southeast Asia and in 1931 helped start Kowloon City Baptist Church, which, with nearly twelve thousand members, is one of Hong Kong's biggest Christian congregations. My grandfather was a Baptist preacher, and two of my uncles still are. Our extended family on both sides includes many more pastors, deacons, church organists, Sunday school teachers, and alumni of Baptist institutions on both sides of the Pacific (Go Oklahoma Baptist Bison!).

I'll never forget the only conversation about my homosexuality I've ever had with my taciturn father. Here is the full transcript:

ME: Why is me being gay so hard for Mommy?
MY FATHER: We're not just Christian. We're Baptist.

He seemed surprised that I had to ask.

————

The Southern Baptist Convention is America's biggest Protestant denomination in membership. If you count by the number of congregations—forty-five thousand—it's the biggest Christian denomination, period, beating out even Roman Catholicism. A quarter of Tennessee's population is Southern Baptist—the fourth-highest proportion in the nation, behind Mississippi, Alabama, and Oklahoma. The Southern Baptist Convention looms as large over the downtown Nashville cityscape as it does over my psyche. The massive office block at 901 Commerce, with a brick-and-mirror facade that looks like a giant Transformers mask, houses the denomination's headquarters. An even larger building, with a ten-story cross on its side, is home to the church's LifeWay division, which publishes Sunday school material and runs a nationwide chain of Christian bookstores.

Richard Land is the human embodiment of today's Southern Baptist Convention—large, imposing, a little loud, not a lot subtle, unapologetically political. America's most influential Southern Baptist, Land serves as president of the denomination's Ethics & Religious Liberty Commission. He is the Southern Baptists' public voice, chief advocate, and top lobbyist.

The first of the ERLC's two main roles—and by extension, Land's—is "prophetic and prescriptive," he declares one evening over Texas barbecue. (Land grew up in Houston.) "It's to call the nation's leaders to be where they ought to be on the moral and social issues facing the nation." His approach to this is multimedia. He hosts a Christian radio show, pens op-eds, appears on the Sunday morning political shows, and authors books about Christianity in the public square, including *The Divided States of America? What Liberals and Conservatives Get Wrong About Faith and Politics* and, perhaps obviously, *Christians in the Public Square.*

While Land has long lived in Nashville, he seems equally at home in the grand halls of power in Washington, D.C. And while he has talked his way to prominence in right-wing Republican politics—in

2005, *Time* named him one of America's twenty-five most influential evangelicals—he and the ERLC are supposed to speak only on issues "on which there is consensus within the convention," he says. "There is no vertical structure in Southern Baptist life," no top-down decision-making structure, no directives from on high on any particular topic. So he typically shies from opining on, say, school vouchers or tax policy—two issues on which Baptists are "deeply divided."

The ERLC's second role "is descriptive," Land says. "We describe where Southern Baptists are." That, he makes clear, "is not necessarily where I would like us to be. Abortion is a good example. Our pastors are more conservative than the convention, the general laity, is." While Southern Baptists may be seen nowadays as monolithically right-wing Republican, it wasn't always this way. In the 1960s and the 1970s, many more theological moderates and liberals taught at seminaries and worked in top denominational positions. Land, part of a group including Texas judge Paul Pressler and theologian Paige Patterson that sought to purify the denomination, claims he was one of the only officials at headquarters who didn't vote for Jimmy Carter in 1976 and 1980, and four years later, "I was the only person in the building who didn't vote for Mondale."

Beginning in the 1970s, the conservatives systematically worked to elect like-minded men—and they were always men—to the denominational leadership. By the end of the 1980s, their takeover of nearly all the denomination's high offices and committees as well as the six Southern Baptist seminaries was complete, a rightward move that foreshadowed the denomination's rise as a political force.

Land has led the ERLC since 1988, calling for repentance on everything from materialism to academic cheating to racism. But he has put a special emphasis on sexual morality, decrying widespread acceptance of divorce and warning that our failings in this area, while not theologically more grave than other sin, produce tragic consequences. "Probably the greatest damage that is being done to the church today is through the degradation of sexuality," he writes in his 2004 book, *Real Homeland Security: The America God Will Bless.* "We live in a sexually pagan culture, in which it is far more difficult to have a healthy, mutually monogamous relationship than was the case for our parents and grandparents. . . . Our culture has spawned a great sexual rebellion, which has permeated the church."

On homosexuality, Land is particularly fierce (he might prefer "faithfully biblical"). He has advocated a constitutional amendment that would state, "Marriage in the United States shall consist only of the union of a man and a woman." He has accused gay activists of "recruiting people for homosexual clubs." And he says that the "gay agenda" is part of an effort to promote "full-blown paganization" in America.

"There is no crueler trick played by the devil than to have it called 'gay,'" he tells me with a shrug. "My observation is that it's obviously a pretty sad lifestyle." In *Real Homeland Security*, in which all references to homosexuality are indexed under "homosexualism," Land equates homosexuality with promiscuity: "Is AIDS a judgment of God on homosexuality and sexual immorality? Not directly, but there are few male homosexuals living an active homosexual lifestyle who don't have a suppressed immune system. God never intended us to have scores of sexual partners in casual encounters. That's going to suppress anyone's immune system." An America that God would bless would "define homosexuality and lesbianism as deviant and unhealthy, not just another lifestyle choice."

The roots of those sentiments run back to his childhood. The night before he left for Boy Scout camp when he was eleven, his father sat him down. He had a warning: "You need to understand, son, that there are some men that like boys." "I was aghast," Land says. After graduating from Princeton University in 1969—he was delighted to learn that we attended the same church there, a nondenominational congregation called Westerly Road Church, thirty years apart—he attended New Orleans Seminary and pastored Vieux Carre Baptist Church, a block from Bourbon Street. "My wife and I, we'd walk to Bible study and *I'd* get whistled at! That was different!" he says,

chortling. "I must confess, there are very few sins that I have diffi-
culty understanding. This is one of them. I just don't understand it."

I've interviewed many pastors over the years. They tend to be
eager talkers, requiring only an occasional nudge to steer their mini-
sermons and allowing few silences, awkward or otherwise. They usually give good quote, thanks perhaps to the weekly need to leave
their congregations with something to remember after the last
"amen." Land, who, when we meet, is serving as interim pastor of a
church in Chattanooga, Tennessee, is no exception. In between bites
of ribs and corn bread, I ask him: Why has homosexuality become
such a flashpoint issue now, especially in Tennessee? Interestingly,
his answer blames both the gay rights movement and the church.
"The homosexual community is trying to sell this live-and-let-live
sensibility. They're after normalizing their behavior and denormal-
izing the lifestyle that's been affirmed as healthy. And we have not
done as good a job at explaining the issues involved with homosexuality as we did with abortion.

"There is a huge difference between what we are willing to tolerate and what we're willing to have paraded before us and shoved
down our throats as acceptable lifestyles for our children," he declares with his customary understatement. "They have tried to
abnormalize those who disagree with them, to the level of Klans-
men. Well, they pushed a bridge too far in Nashville, and Tennessee
pushed back."

The next morning, I drive to Nashville's southern suburbs to meet
another Baptist pastor, David Shelley, who has helped in the political
pushback against liberals. If Richard Land is a general in the right-
wing political-evangelical movement, Shelley is a battalion com-
mander; he is a leader of an advocacy group called the Family Action
Council of Tennessee, an affiliate of the Family Research Council
and Focus on the Family that has become one of the state's main
drivers of family values legislation. Shelley helped rally opposition

to Nashville's nondiscrimination ordinance and has publicly called homosexuality "abhorrent" and "unnatural."

Shelley asked me to meet him at Panera Bread in Brentwood, a haven for many of the area's nouveau riche, including a constellation of country music stars and many Tennessee Titans football players. (When Bravo does *Real Housewives of Nashville*, Brentwood should figure prominently.) If the Southern Baptist Convention is the Republican Party at prayer, then Panera, at 8 a.m. on a Tennessee Wednesday, is the Republican Party at Bible study. Small clusters of men huddle over asiago cheese bagels, cups of coffee, and Scripture, talking a little too loudly about their prayer requests (their marriage struggles, their woebegone friends, their problems at work, etc.).

I am one of the only people without a Bible in hand, "and if you don't have a Bible in here, then you're an oddball," Shelley says with a grin. While he doesn't have an extra Bible, Shelley has brought other reading material for me: his own book, *Church & State: Being Salt and Light in the Public Square*, and a Family Research Council pamphlet titled *Homosexuality Is Not a Civil Right*. The culture wars, he tells me, aren't over. "Right now, it's small skirmishes and local battles. It's like the American Revolution, which was fought in backyards and cornfields. The battle to preserve marriage and traditional values is being fought all over our country," he says. "Homosexuality is going to be a wedge that drives traditional Christianity apart from politically correct Christianity! It's a mighty big deal. It's a sign that if we don't believe in God's word and all that it promises and distance ourselves from God, we also distance ourselves from natural law. I see it as the biggest threat to our civilization!"

Shelley is unfailingly cheery, jesting with the utter confidence of someone with unshakable faith. "Truth tends to win out," he says. Even as he excoriates our never-so-evil society, his speech is weirdly gee-whiz, punctuated with exclamation points. It's as if he's marveling at a particularly bad—but still fun!—fantasy football draft, not the moral decay of the generations. "I don't know where exactly you draw the line—under fifty? Under forty? Anyway, that generation and younger has been raised to believe a worldview that's basically secular humanism! It's in the media! It's in the schools! It's in entertainment!" he says. "Even if a kid does go to church, they get one to two hours a day—probably twenty hours a week—of Internet, MTV, TV. There's such a disproportionate presence of gay characters on television! It's a worldview that's really, really successfully preached. I do credit the media. It's easier to mobilize the masses when they feel threatened. If they don't feel an imminent threat, it's not on their radar screen—and they don't." (His own kids watch *Glee*, he admits, though he adds, "They know right from wrong.")

Shelley sees it as the pastor's duty to declare moral threats—and his colleagues' failure to do so disappoints him. "Traditional moral values are really what made America great, but if you defend them now, you're targeted as a black sheep. If I could get a couple dozen pastors, black and white, to show up, we could really stop the homosexual agenda. But only one in ten pastors really gives a rip anymore," he says. "They don't want to offend people. They don't want to lose members. If you want to fill a room, you don't really want to talk about gay marriage."

Shelley has little to lose—attendance at his church averages twenty to twenty-five people most Sundays. And he reads Scripture as replete with examples of God's servants suffering for their activism. "All the Old Testament prophets were called by God to lobby the king for political purposes. The first political lobbyist in recorded history was Moses! Moses was called by God to go to the pharaoh to lobby for the abolition of slavery!" he exclaims. He also cites the Prophet Elijah, who confronted King Ahab and Queen Jezebel about their worship of the god Baal. "All of that was political! All of it!"

I assume I know his political leanings, but I ask anyway. He surprises me. "I am not a fan of Sarah Palin. I am not a fan of Glenn Beck. I definitely don't call myself a Republican. And I was never a big fan of George W. Bush." He seems to notice a quizzical look on my face, because he begins to explain: "It's not about personality or party—it's really about principle, and I think Bush was as much a tax-and-spend liberal as anybody else." Then he smiles broadly. "You know, there are reporters at the *Tennessean* who call me whenever they want a quote from a right-wing religious nutjob!"

I make note of the societal trend lines as he sees them, which are moving in a more liberal, less devout direction, but just when I see a straight shot, somehow he makes out the beginnings of a boomerang trajectory. "Young people will grow up and want to get family right," he says. "They will want to get married and stay married."

But who wants to get family wrong when they grow up—and how do you define "wrong"? Who gets married without the hope of staying married? Didn't he say, just a few minutes earlier, that people under fifty (or maybe it was under forty) had bought into a worldview different from his own? What about them? When can we expect them to grow up and get family right, too?

Maybe it's timidity, or perhaps it's the assumed pointlessness of debating him, but I let my questions go unasked, and instead explain to Shelley that one reason I'd come to Nashville was to explore the dividing lines between urban, suburban, and rural. Why, I wondered, was the city so much more liberal than the rest of Tennessee? Where did these cultural, theological, and political splits come from?

He doesn't pause for a second. "When an inner city strikes God out of the culture, it fills the void with godlessness," he says, leaning forward as if to press his point physically. "You drive God out of the culture, and Satan fills the void. And that is why conservatives live in the suburbs."

Land and, to a lesser degree, Shelley, discuss homosexuality—and homosexuals—in a cold, clinical, almost dehumanizing way. They tell me that human identity is about more than sexuality. Ideally, they say, it should be found entirely in Christ. But from there they reduce gays and lesbians to godless, sexualized objects, as if because of homosexuality, full personhood is forfeited. What's left are just vessels of depravity.

This is what I hear them say, and I know this is as much about my ears as it is about their lips. This is what *I* hear them say. And it's complicated, because I have my own context for hearing their words. To hear them is to hear my parents' disapproval. To hear them is to hear the disdain of friends and relatives who are too timid to say what they really think about my sexuality, except when I'm not around. To hear them is to hear the echoes of my own fears of damnation.

But in addition to their reduction of gay men and women, they layer on their belief in the need to elevate their Christianity, not just in society but also in government. They devote much more time talking about legislation than about love. They seem more focused on winning elections than they do about saving souls, and they're obsessed with their rule. At one point, Land says to me, "We're not uncomfortable with power and we are not used to being in the minority. Southern Baptists still aren't convinced this culture can be turned around, but we are convinced it can't be turned around without Southern Baptists." I hear smugness and self-satisfaction, but where is God in all this?

To be fair to Shelley, I feel in my gut that he wants to do the right thing, that he's genuinely worried about civilization's downfall, and that he's truly fearful that his world is crumbling morally. This makes him not at all unique. Every society in every age has had professional worriers, and maybe with good reason, given that no empire, no kingdom, ever breaks the sinusoidal pattern of the ages— rise and fall, rise and fall. The Christian church was born amid such tumult.

Early in the fifth century, as the Roman Empire was under assault by Goths and Vandals, Augustine of Hippo wrote *De Civitate Dei contra Paganos*—literally, "Of the City of God against the Pagans," better known as *City of God*. It's a massive work, and St. Augustine's masterwork, contrasting, over twenty-one books and hundreds of chapters, the two "cities"—the heavenly and the earthly, the divine and the profane. The idea of a City of God appears several times in

Scripture, including the images of a heavenly realm in Revelation as well as in a metaphor used by Jesus in the Sermon on the Mount: "A city set on a hill cannot be hidden. . . . Let your light shine before men in such a way that they may see your good works and glorify your Father who is in heaven." Though it may insult Augustine's memory to paraphrase it so crudely, let me summarize his use of the imagery this way: The Christian ought to live in pursuit of the eternal wisdom and joys of the next world (the City of God), not the ephemeral powers and pleasures of this one (the City of Man). The locus of activity might be—sometimes must be—here, but the focus should be there.

One tricky thing about Augustine's time, as with ours, is that the church was an integral part of the establishment. When he wrote *City of God*, Christianity had been the Roman Empire's state religion for nearly a century, and for all the talk of separation of church and state today, Christianesque civil religion prevails in America. While Augustine isn't entirely clear about the practical specifics—about what the Christian should *do*, rather than what the Christian should *think* and *hope*—he's firm on a kind of spiritual separation from the rest of society. As the historian Peter Brown writes, it was not Augustine's interest "to inveigh against Roman society as a whole: It was his first duty to look after his own, to maintain the identity and the morale of his 'people,' the Catholic congregation."

Augustine was more deeply engaged with the internal life of the church than with "secular" politics, and so I wonder whether he would be somewhat more interested in the ministry of a pastor like Pete Wilson.

I knew I wanted to meet a megachurch pastor while I was in Nashville, and so, one day, on the website of the local alt-weekly, the *Scene*, I clicked across one of its annual "best of" issues. It says something about Nashville that, along with best breakfast, best bookstore, and that sort of thing, there are usually two or three church categories.

In 2009, the paper named Cross Point "best church for hipsters"; "Forget the flowered dresses and three-piece suits—at CrossPoint Community Church in Sylvan Park, you'll find tattoos, body piercings, fedoras and carefully-styled bedheads everywhere you turn," the *Scene* said. "Pastor Pete Wilson's funky hairdo has become iconic here in Nashville; rumor has it that Music City's holiest hipsters show up at Trim simply requesting 'The Pete.'" In 2010 and 2011, *Scene* readers voted Cross Point, which has eight services on six campuses and draws six thousand churchgoers on a typical weekend, "best place to worship" and "best church music"; in 2011, Wilson also came out tops in the awkwardly named, poorly defined category of "best religious leader."

I emailed Wilson, hoping for a look at that hair. He agreed to lunch, and I can testify that it's indeed a funky and carefully messy arrangement that seems to be part bedhead, part product-driven. Wilson, who founded Cross Point in 2003 when he was in his mid-twenties, is who Central Casting would send if you requested a young evangelical megachurch pastor: that hair; soul patch; tight, red microplaid shirt (with epaulets); distressed jeans; buoyant "hey, bro!" aura.

"Every generation thinks the next generation is worse and that they have no morals," Wilson says with a sigh when we sit down at a café near Cross Point's main campus. "It's always these doomsday statements: *It's worse than it's ever been!*" He grew up Baptist, but he declines to comment on anything political, broaching another, more personal possibility: that society might simply be more open and confessional. "The thing today is that authenticity is very important. But the more authentic you are, the less you tend to live up to people's expectations," he says. "When you share your struggles, you don't live up to the image."

Wilson, who attended Southern Baptist Theological Seminary in Louisville, Kentucky, says he never speaks publicly about homosexuality. So why did he agree to talk to me? "I guess you caught me at a weak moment," he says with a sheepish smile. Also, a critical one:

"Every year that goes by, this becomes a bigger issue. In the next ten years, it could be the most talked-about issue in the church."

Homosexuality certainly has become one of the most talked-about issues in Wilson's church. A few years ago, a close friend of his who was also on Cross Point's leadership team came out. "I had not had a single friend who was gay," Wilson says, before correcting himself. "Or at least who told me. I had to be honest with him and say, 'I don't know what I think.' I guess I just assumed it was wrong. And I do believe God's design is not gay relationship. What made this interesting is that this friend, he is more Christlike than me in every aspect of his life—the way he loves people, the way he helps people, the way he has served the church. And he is the one who helped me realize: He isn't an issue. He is a person."

Wilson's gay friend has since left Cross Point, which has a significant gay population for a church with a standard only-within-traditional-marriage stance on sex, but the issue of homosexuality recently arose again. A lesbian couple who regularly attend services at the church's Bellevue campus approached Wilson and the elders: They wanted to dedicate their newborn child before the congregation.* "It was a great question. We'd never thought about that at all," he says. "This couple loves our church. They want their children to be there. They know what I believe—I'd done a series recently in which I said I believe God created marriage to be between a man and a woman. So what do we do? How do we respond in a Christlike way to a family who is seeking guidance from the church?"

Wilson and the elders asked the couple for a few weeks to think and pray. "We definitely didn't all agree at first. We had to be honest and say that this was a gray issue. There is nothing in the Bible to help us deal with this," he says. *Nothing?* Whether or not you're pro-gay, it's difficult to argue that the Bible is silent on sexuality. But that's not what Wilson means. Rather, he and the elders chose to

---

* The dedication is the Baptist alternative to infant baptism, a waterfree way to pledge publicly that you'll raise your child in the faith.

answer a different question. "We weren't debating whether homosexuality was wrong or what the Bible says about homosexuality," he says. "The question was how to respond in a Christlike way to a family who is seeking guidance from the church."

At first, I take Wilson's tack as a particularly artful dodge: Let's not make this about sexuality, but let's also not miss a teachable moment. I can't imagine that Cross Point could say anything but no to the lesbians. But to my surprise, in the end the church said yes. "It was unanimous: We want to partner with this couple to raise their children in a Christlike environment," Wilson says. "The real question was, 'Who are we to turn that child away from the church?'"

"What kind of feedback did you get on that decision?" I ask.

Wilson smirks. "We got a lot of feedback, if you will, in all caps. Some people called me and said, 'We're proud to be part of a place that encourages community.' Some people were very disappointed and even hurt." But most of those people—and, as far as Wilson knows, all of those who left Cross Point over this incident—didn't attend the Bellevue campus. They had no personal connection with the family.

"People may say, 'You are condoning this couple's sinful behavior.' I don't think so. They know exactly how I feel about what the Bible teaches. If there's something to be convicted of, the Holy Spirit will do that work. I always try to be clear: I could be wrong. Let's be honest! Christians have been wrong about many things over the years, and they've used the Bible to back up their wrongness. So I tell people what I think Scripture says, but I also tell them I could be wrong. And I do believe that it's possible to have a grace-filled, intelligent conversation about it," Wilson says. He shakes his head. "When did the church become a place where we had to believe the exact same thing on everything or else we couldn't be in community together?"

Nashville surprises me in three significant ways. First, so many people told me that it's the sort of town where you're immediately asked where you go to church, but of the dozens of people I meet there, only two or three ask. Even more oddly, nobody wants to know why I'm poking around about faith and sexuality. They just talk as if they'd been waiting for someone to ask.

The other surprise? Lisa Howe. Because there's more to her story.

Howe's dad was Baptist and her mom Methodist, "but I was not raised in church," she says. "When I was growing up, I was exposed to Bible stories, but I was also exposed to Jerry Falwell and Jim Bakker and the other people on the TV. Just the general vibe of it gave me a bad taste in my mouth about organized religion. It just seemed like a business. I wanted nice, normal values, not a business spiel every Sunday."

And if anything, her views of homosexuality were even less positive. "In college, I didn't even identify as a lesbian. There were lesbians on my soccer team. They brought a lot of drama and there were things in their lifestyle, like drugs, that I definitely didn't agree with," she says. "Looking back, it was just that they were being college kids, but I was labeling it 'the lesbian lifestyle.' I am a perfectionist, and trying to be perfect all the time did not allow me to be a lesbian. I always wanted to be a good role model. But then I fell in love."

For the longest time, Howe told nearly no one. Part of it was her fear that the relationship would affect her work as a collegiate soccer coach and especially recruiting. "There are things that a parent thinks. When I came out to my mom, for example, she was looking for someone to blame it on. Of course she was going to blame it on Wendy," Howe says. "I didn't want it to be like that for the girls on my team: Was it Coach Howe's fault? Was it another girl on the soccer team?"

Howe moved from Mississippi State to Belmont in 2007, and her team quickly became her Nashville world. The worst thing for Howe about being forced to leave Belmont was being separated from her team—her all-in-one passion, work, and community. Losing all of that left a void. But none of the many newspaper articles I read before my interview with Howe mentioned what she found to fill the space: faith.

After her departure from Belmont, churches and priests inundated Howe with letters, emails, and calls of support. St. Augustine Episcopal Church, which sits on the Vanderbilt University campus here, even threw a baby shower for her and her partner; 120 people showed up—only twenty of whom Howe knew. The gifts, the hugs, the unconditional love: It shocked Howe.

"After that, we started visiting churches. We called it church surfing, and we did it for a few months," she says. "It actually got so easy. There was just a comfort level with every church we walked in, and we never walked and out and thought, Gosh, we don't belong. People—especially pastors—were so welcoming and so supportive."

She reviews her mental list of churches she visited: A Methodist one. (Pro: "The pastor was great—I believe she had a gay son." Con: "The average age of that church was just . . . old.") Covenant of the Cross, which focused on gays and lesbians. (Pro: Gays and lesbians. Con: Too many gays and lesbians. "I wanted more diversity at church. I didn't want people telling me I'm all accepted when we're all the same.") Pete Wilson's megachurch, Cross Point. (Pro: "My gaydar definitely was going off." Con: "It was too much, like a rock concert, and everyone was dressed all hip and trendy.")

Finally, they ended up at Holy Trinity, a United Church of Christ congregation. "The first Sunday we were there, I felt the pastor could have started every sentence: 'Lisa, . . .' The sermons just speak to me. The messages just hit home."

In May, her daughter, Hope Janice Holleman Howe, was born. ("I know it could be read as 'Ho Ho Ho,' poor child," she says, laughing.) Since the baby was born, Howe's church attendance has been less regular, but her faith is strengthening. "Maybe it's ironic, because most people come out and ditch the church. But I never ran away from Christianity. It was never that I didn't belong because I was lesbian," she says. "Something about the timing here was just right. I'm not a real deep thinker. I don't overanalyze anything. I can pretty easily keep things on the surface, whether it's myself or my relationships. But now I do try to include God in the way that I solve problems and make decisions. It used to just be, 'Lisa decided to do that.' Now I really think about God. I know it's so cliché to say WWJD, but I do have that in the back of my head, now more than ever."

She gets quiet for a moment. Then she says, more confidently than she has said anything all afternoon: "Yes, I do believe God had a hand in all this."

# THE AGNOSTICS

*New York; Bangor, Maine*

In 1601, Caravaggio painted *The Conversion on the Way to Damascus,* the most celebrated depiction of the most notable conversion in church history. The painting, which decorates a chapel in Rome's Church of Santa Maria del Popolo, shows Saul of Tarsus, a Pharisee who, according to Acts, was known for "breathing threats and murder against the disciples of the Lord," stunned and sprawled on the road to Damascus. In Caravaggio's interpretation, Saul, who would soon become the Apostle Paul, is petrified, reaching his arms desperately toward the heavens. The critic and Caravaggio biographer Andrew Graham-Dixon has called the painting "beautifully poetic and humane" and "a drama of light and dark."

Those words apply to the best conversion stories, which juxtapose sinful humanity and divine redemption, darkness and light, capturing the often inexplicable light-switch moment when skepticism yields to belief. There is, however, another genre of spiritual story that's less likely to be told: loss of faith. It's understandable why many Christians would be reluctant to dwell on these accounts, but it's important for a couple of reasons. First, any half-decent business book will tell you that failure matters; we learn from it. Second, in the context of my journey, I want to understand how gay people may have been pushed out of the church.

Belief grows or dies for all different reasons; the ecosystem of personal faith is rich and difficult terrain, a spiritual jungle as dense as the Amazon. Sexuality—and the discrimination, confusion, doubt that often accompany it—may provide some reasons, but not always. John Corvino, the self-proclaimed "Gay Moralist" and a philosopher at Wayne State University, grew up Roman Catholic and once planned to enter the priesthood but now identifies as an atheist. "This was about separate philosophical reasons, philosophical questions, like the problem of evil. I used to think I could solve that problem, but eventually I reached a point where I believed people did not have good reasons to believe in God," Corvino says. While he acknowledges that he's "not sure anything is entirely unrelated to my sexuality," he also asserts that ultimately, the loss of his Catholic faith "was an intellectual thing unrelated to being gay."

In many other cases, however, the church and its treatment of those who are wrestling with their sexuality are central to the decline of belief for gay people. I sought out three openly gay men, two in New York and one in Maine. Each was born in a different decade and comes from a different church tradition. Their commonalities are their sexuality and their journeys from faith—two no longer identify as Christians, while one equivocates about his religious identity. But that's where the similarities end.

John Hauenstein's upbringing was unremarkable: Working class. Mom, dad, and sister. Public school on the weekdays, Methodist church on Sundays.

The Methodists are America's largest mainline denomination, with nearly eight million members, with roots in the teaching of brothers Charles and John Wesley, who, in the eighteenth century, preached what John (Wesley) called "plain, old Bible Christianity." John (Hauenstein) says his childhood Methodism was passed down from his mother's side. "My mother took my sister and myself to the same church she grew up in," he tells me when I visit him in his Manhattan apartment. The church was your standard quiet-in-the-pews, organ-accompanied Protestant congregation, full of stolid, stiff-upper-lip families like his own.

"From an early age, I had this sense of self-reliance. I didn't feel like I could talk to my mother or my father," he says. "My family was never a very expressive family. Things like 'I love you' were not said." As he entered his teen years, his parents' marriage faltered, which only accentuated his loneliness. "Now they were too busy with their own problems," he says, "so why would they want to hear from me?"

At church camp, he found people who both listened to him and became the religious role models he'd never had. "They really seemed to be walking the walk. They seemed like genuine people of faith who weren't just going through the motions," John says. There, in the hills of eastern Pennsylvania, he felt at home in a way he never had at home. "It was a beautiful, rural, woodsy setting, and it all felt very unforced. It didn't feel like I was being led down the garden path, being given the juice. I had one of those life-changing mountaintop experiences—literally."

The summer crush is a childhood commonplace, and it applies to religion as much as to romance. Often it fades with the onset of autumn, with the reality of school and the turning of the trees, but John's faith only grew. "I studied my Bible because I wanted to study my Bible. I prayed because I wanted to pray," he says. "My outward actions reeked of straight—I studied a lot, I played soccer. But dances, prom—when it was expected of me to ask a girl, it was, like, total anxiety. Clammy hands. No desire whatsoever to go there."

At college, he got involved with the Navigators, an interdenominational organization that works in more than one hundred countries. He became particularly close to several dorm mates who attended Navigators Bible studies, and sophomore year, he confided in one of the guys, a senior. "I needed help. I needed somebody to tell me I was okay. I needed somebody to affirm that it was okay that I struggled with this. And I hoped they'd be able to tell me there was an answer, a resolution," John says. "I think I said something to the effect of 'I struggle with homosexual feelings' or 'attraction to other men.' I didn't use the word *gay*. It didn't have the right ring to it." He laughs.

The subsequent years were spent "trying to do the work and figure this out," John says. Counseling; individual Bible study; group Bible study; lots of prayer, "especially after the trips to the convenience store where I bought porn magazines, jerked off, proceeded to feel guilty and put the porn in the Dumpster, promising never to do it again," he says. For five and a half years, he never acted out physically with another man, even as the feelings became more intense. Then he moved to New York.

John made his move by the book, which is to say he immediately connected with the local Navigators rep and found a church—a Nazarene congregation more conservative than the Methodist one of his childhood. "The more I absorbed myself in church and Bible study and evangelism," he says, "that would take away time for me to be tempted and act out."

But New York also became for John what many small-town parents fear: a place where he met another guy—lots of other guys, in fact. He began exploring "the underbelly of New York City—clubs, porn theaters, places where I could seek out other men." Then fear of HIV helped send him "back in the closet," he says. "I joined an ex-gay ministry. I needed to be around people who were free of being gay. And I ended up having sex with one of the guys in my support group. I felt *really* guilty about that." He dated a woman for several years, a relationship that ended in a bad breakup and "a moment of self-acceptance," he says. "I realized, I am not going to change. *This is not going to change.*"

John's choice of the term *self-acceptance* is apt on two levels. There's the obvious—his acknowledgment that his sexuality could not be prayed away. But he also accepted himself in another way: He knew his decision would have social and spiritual consequences. "When you're in that environment, you know if you come out and say, 'I am gay and I'm going to live as a gay person in every sense of that term,' you will be effectively excommunicated," John says.

We're sitting at a round table in his living room, and as I parse John's words, I search his face for self-pity. There is none. "If they're going to be obedient to the Bible, that's what they have to do," he says, with matter-of-factness befitting the systems-minded engineer that he is. "They are going to try to change my mind first, and if I don't change, they have to cut me off."

When he moved in with his first boyfriend, John told his pastor, adding that he hoped to continue attending church. "He said, 'That's fine, but if you want your boyfriend to come, that's a nonstarter,'" John says. "That decided things for me. I said, 'I guess it's time to end this conversation.' And from there, nearly every relationship I had in the church community virtually stopped overnight, with a few exceptions of people who tried to change my mind. Not a call. Nothing. It was like I ceased to exist."

That signal moment prompted John to walk away from the church. However, it's equally true to say that the church walked away from John. Remarkably, he still refuses to blame his religious friends. In fact, he almost apologizes for them; "that's what the Bible said the procedure should be," he insists. Yet the hurt remains—I can hear the pain in his voice, which is never angry but at times halting as he sifts the memories of how he lost his relationship not only with nearly all his friends but also with God.

One could say that his faith wasn't mature enough, or that he should have been able to separate the church from God, or that he should have found another church, or that he should have done something else differently. But that's not what happened. The soul and spirit don't necessarily bend to reason and logic, even for an engineer. "I was thirty-three, and I was basically starting my life again," John says softly. "I decided to put the whole thing on the back burner. I said, inside and outside, to God and to myself, if in time it feels like it's time to reapproach this part of my life, I'm open to that—but not now."


Paul Bartoloni, John's boyfriend of twelve years, a self-described cultural Catholic who is as sharp-tongued as John is gentle, says: "Johnny doesn't talk about faith that much. I think that goes back to his mainstream Protestant upbringing. That culture does not wear their faith on their sleeve. In some way, it's considered vulgar. It's not my lack of interest—he just doesn't bring it up, and when I do ask him, he will talk about it—but I think there's a lot of pain from being rejected by so many people who were supposed to have these Christian values."

John still attends his childhood church when he visits his mom, but he would no longer mark "Christian" if he were filling out a form that asked his religion. "There was a time when I believed 'once saved, always saved.' Then I went to the Nazarene church, which believes you can lose your salvation," he says. "Now I don't know that the term *Christian*, as it's traditionally defined, should be the term I use."

"Do you miss God as you knew him?" I ask John, who is forty-eight.

He thinks for a moment. "The key operative there is 'as I knew him,'" he says. "'As I knew him' was not fully informed."

This phrasing perplexes me. When it comes to belief in God, is one ever "fully informed"? My understanding of faith is that it is sedimentary—layer upon layer of belief and experience, one atop another, the accumulating weight reinforcing what has piled up below.

John continues: "I do believe in a higher being. I do believe that a higher being makes things work together as they do, particularly in nature." He smiles. "It's something as simple as seeing a butterfly close up. Or a hummingbird taking nectar from a plant. I think about how everything is so interconnected in life."

Later, he points to a bookcase just inside the front door of the tidy, ground-floor Hell's Kitchen apartment he and Paul have long shared. The top shelf is filled with Bibles and religious books. "I virtually have not touched them for years," he says, "except to dust them off." But they're still there, remnants of his faith. "I guess it's a symbol of where I am that I haven't gotten rid of them. And there's going to be a place and time for looking at that stuff up there."

Not everyone has as direct a trajectory out of faith as John Hauenstein. Just after eleven o'clock on a Sunday morning, a fashion designer named Andrae Gonzalo and I push into the throng at Irving Plaza, a Manhattan music venue, and we're quickly swept up into the balcony. The odor—equal parts disinfectant, stale beer, and sweat—takes me back to my post-college days, as do the floors, which are still sticky from the previous night's wasted drinks. The club is standing-room-only, packed with a stereotypically downtown mix of hipsters and oxford-wearing, ribbon-belted preppy types. We wiggle into a spot stage left, roughly eye-level with the room's disco ball, as the nine-piece band begins its first set.

*My heart is overtaken*
*My soul is overwhelmed*
*The worst of me succeeded by the best of You*

The people around us sing and sway, arms raised, eyes closed behind their thick-framed glasses. Flecks of light ricochet from the disco ball across the scene, including Andrae's bulging-wide eyes, which are saying what I'm thinking: *This is church?* Yes, it is. A megachurch based in Sydney, Australia, Hillsong now has congregations in London, New York, Paris, and half a dozen other cities, plus a burgeoning music ministry whose songs have become staples in thousands more churches around the world. (Its most famous song, "Shout to the Lord," was even featured on *American Idol* in 2010.) Its worship style: vocal, exuberant, the antithesis of the butt-in-pew Methodist or Presbyterian service. Its mission: to be relevant.

"So good! *So good!*"

An arm's length away, a twentysomething woman wearing a vintage-looking peasant-style dress, clanging bangles, and carefully messy, high-piled hipster-meets-Marie-Antoinette-style hair, is feeling it. Everything that's said onstage, everything that's sung, evokes her stage whisper.

"So good! *So good!*"

Andrae rolls his eyes, edges closer to me, and says sotto voce: "I don't know that I can sing any of this honestly." Honestly or not, he winks at me and starts belting it out:

*I love my life to shine Your light
'Cause there's none beside You, God.*

As the song ends, Andrae turns to me again, eyebrow raised: "I'm just not sure that's enough for me." He shrugs.

To our left, our new friend is exultant: "So good! *So good!*"

I give Andrae a look. He looks upward and exclaims: *"So good!"* Then he bursts out laughing.

During the "say hello to someone you don't know!" part of the service, a short woman with a mass of tight curls gives Andrae a handshake and a stare. "You look familiar!" she says, absorbing his shaved head, olive complexion, and Cheshire-catty smile. This happens all the time. "I was on TV," he says. *Project Runway*. Season two. Repeatedly crafting wildly creative if polarizing designs, he finished sixth—the judges axed him for a topiary-inspired, moss-covered frock—and was best known for crying on camera.

Really, he was destined to be on the margins of fame. As we walk a few blocks west to Union Square for a postchurch brunch, he tells me about growing up in Los Angeles, the long-awaited son of a couple who had been in the Jesus Movement. His namesake is the famed gospel singer Andraé Crouch, who's also his godfather. "My parents couldn't have a baby. He prayed for me—well, for my mom," Andrae says. "And she got pregnant." He was born in 1973.

His parents' upbringings were strict. His grandmother rejected his mom, the daughter of a Filipino Assemblies of God minister, "for playing music that had a beat to it," Andrae says. (Today his mother is still a worship leader in a church in south-central Los Angeles.) His childhood wasn't quite as strict, although there was enough hellfire and brimstone preached that, at the age of nine, he "went through a period where I got saved every night before I went to bed! Every night, I'd pray, 'Please forgive me for all my sins, because if you come back tonight, I want to go to heaven.' It was because of all those rapture movies. Later, I decided I wanted to do a movie about the rapture where the Christians are all gone, and the world works beautifully—no traffic jams, because every car with a fish on the back is off the road."

This is classic Andrae—mischievous, deeply felt, veering in wild and often unexpected directions. For example, a verbatim nugget from my interview with him: "There's some magical age of account-ability when you have to choose Jesus, and before that age, you're not responsible. You know, I wish I knew how to ride a skateboard. I wish I understood vaginas."

The development and subsequent erosion of Andrae's faith was a little more linear. When he was thirteen, his parents divorced. He, his mom, and his sister left their Pentecostal congregation, which belonged to the Foursquare Church—"no youth group, nothing for kids, lots of exclusion because I seemed gay, I guess"—for a Presbyte-rian one, which he attended throughout high school.

"I really loved the Lord then. I was still gung-ho. Why is that?" Andrae stops. His speech typically gushes, slowing only so that he can ask himself a question. "It did seem like there was somebody on the other line when I prayed," he finally says. "High school was a very, very lonely time for me. In retrospect, I totally realize what happened: It was because of my sexuality. Just about the time all the other kids were pairing off, I found myself without a group of friends. So church was a refuge. I did have church friends. In that way, it provided an extra society."

This is true in another sense: Church was where he met his first boyfriend, a seventeen-years-older guy named Brad who worked with the youth. Andrae insists that nothing sexual happened until after high school, but in those early years, he and Brad, who had previously dated only women, became close friends. Their nine-year romantic relationship, Andrae says, helped him reconcile his belief in God with his sexuality. "I grew up in L.A., which compartmentalizes things geographically," he continues. "I guess that's what was going on in my life and in my brain. I was segmenting my sexuality and my faith. I believed in Jesus. I believed there was a God. Then I came to the conclusion that this can't be a sin because it comes from so much love. If God is love, and that really is true, then this must be good."

I'm still processing Andrae's pure, almost childlike declaration when he suddenly tells me he has recently become a Lady Gaga fan. "I always had kind of a Yoko Ono respect for her," he says. "I got that. I saw her pictures, the aesthetics. I just wasn't sure about the music. At the beginning, it was *soooooo* tedious to me." Then, inexplicably, Andrae put all her albums on his online playlist, and during a particularly sleep-deprived season, he listened to them over and over: "I basically brainwashed myself into becoming one of her Little Monsters."

With respect filling his voice, he elaborates. "It's like this church we just went to, and it's something that the Catholic Church has figured out. You use a lot of the same aesthetics, the same baroqueness, to proselytize, and you combine them with a message that is simple and very, very affecting. She taps into that same vein. It's not that different from a religious experience."

Not that different, but different enough—even though he grew into love with Lady Gaga, he grew out of love with Christianity: The expectations weren't the same, nor could they be.

The falling-out didn't happen all at once. When he moved to New York City to study art history and fashion, he stuck with the

Presbyterians for a while. "It still mattered enough to me. And I wanted to prove to them"—he never gets more specific than "them"—"that my sexuality was the only difference. Nothing else had changed. I still went to church and I still tried to be a good person and I still believed in God and Jesus and the entire Apostles' Creed."

But churchgoing is different than faith, and churchgoing to prove something to someone else is different than churchgoing to feed your soul. Ultimately Andrae began to pay less attention to the former and more to the latter. "I crave complexity, but that makes it really hard to be a Christian because so many Christian traditions do not embrace complexity," he says.

He and Brad ended up attending Episcopal churches, which (mostly) sated Andrae's intellectual cravings. "I was in academic environments all the time. I was studying art history and fashion and doing a bunch of analytical writing. I still felt God was real. But I began to believe that I didn't know if the planner of the universe was thinking very specifically about me. In those years, I didn't feel ignored—I thought God regarded me, but I didn't feel the love of God."

Andrae asks me to imagine myself at Versailles, at its most glorious point. "If you're the forty-fifth courtier at Versailles, you're definitely aware of the king of France, and there's evidence of him all around you," Andrae says. "But does he miss you if you're sick that day? Maybe not. I kind of felt like that. I was in the presence of the Sun King, but I was way down the hall."

There's a small set of Bible verses that are often used to reassure believers of God's plan. One that gets heavy use around life's major milestones—birthdays, graduations—is Jeremiah 29:11: "'For I know the plans I have for you,' declares the Lord, 'plans to prosper you and not to harm you, plans to give you a hope and a future.'" Another popular one is Psalm 139, where King David writes, "O Lord, you have searched me, and you know me. You know when I sit and when I rise; you perceive my thoughts from afar. You discern my going out and my lying down; you are familiar with all my ways. Before a word is on my tongue you know it completely, O Lord."

For a while during my adolescence, I clung to these verses. Then I paused. In the first example, God was talking to the Israelites who survived the Babylonian exile, not to Jeff Chu, a pimply-faced gay teen in Miami. In the second, King David, shepherd boy-turned-sovereign, is talking, which makes it a little grand for me to claim the same mantle. So my confidence in the power of those words faded.

"It *was* a gradual erosion," Andrae agrees. "Was there a moment? No, no. I think it had to erode, because I was still going to church, to those more intellectual churches, which ask core questions and don't sit there and just give answers. What I loved about the Episcopal Church is that I'd run into people and say, 'Well, what about God?' And they would say, 'I don't know. I really don't know. But I also don't think it matters.' That was my answer for many, many years. I don't know if Jesus was the son of God. I don't know if he even existed. But should I love my neighbor as myself? Yes. Unequivocally. That is a good idea."

At times, Andrae's faith feels less his own and more the product of his circumstances, and he confesses that his boyfriends have hugely influenced his beliefs. His current boyfriend, Jamie Benson, "has no room for a Christian spiritual path. His conviction is that God is you—it's all within you. Which makes sense to me now. Whether you believe God is within you and a part of you or it's just gravity, the idea of a faceless God makes a lot of sense to me. I do remember listening to Christopher Hitchens on the Bill Maher show. He really made me go, 'Oh my God, I think he's right! There's no God!'

"Nothing good follows the statement 'Well, I'm a Christian,'" Andrae says finally. "It's a preface to some hard-core asshole statement. I'd say I'm a nontheist. Atheist implies there is no God. Nontheist suggests something softer and less personal—there may be some incredible force. I just can't believe anything else anymore. I suffered so much, Jeff."

I ask him how exactly he has suffered. He begins to talk vaguely about discrimination, but then he stops.

"Why do I feel I've suffered so much? I have no proof of it! I'm like, I get hangnails!"

He cackles at himself and promises to think about why he's so convinced of this suffering.

Later, in an email, he elaborates a little, in a general meander: "Why do so many good people experience intense hardship, when they've done nothing to deserve it? My only answer to this was that if there is a conscious god of creation, he is remarkably cruel or simply indifferent. I'm basically more comfortable thinking that god might exist in some form, but it doesn't intervene, and it doesn't take sides. This belief got me through both Bush administrations."

One February day, I clicked on a link on a friend's tweet. It led to a video posted by a Maine college student named Michael Dean Gray titled, "We're Not Straight." It's a well-made, eight-minute-long student film in the vein of a public service announcement, mixing Gray's own story with the voices of dozens of other gay people, arguing that homosexuality is nature, not nurture. Impressed, I emailed him, and then, in June, I make the drive up to Maine to meet him.

I find Michael at the Gay Pride Festival in Bangor, Maine. It's a damp, dank day, and he has set up a forlorn little table in the town square. Nobody else from his college, the New England School of Communications, has showed up. "I feel like I should be here to represent," he says. "One of my favorite quotes is 'Be the change you want to see in the world.' It's visibility. It's showing people we exist."

Michael, who is twenty-three, still lives at home in the small town of Charleston, about an hour's drive away. His curfew is 10 p.m. I ask whether his parents, who homeschooled him all through junior high and high school, know he's here. "They would make my life hell if they knew," he says. "Sometimes they still ask where I've been or where I'm going. But they've gotten a little better about not asking."

I spend the afternoon hanging out with him, observing as guys flirt with him and he smirks puckishly back. Just before I go to sleep that evening, I get a totally unexpected text from Michael: He didn't make his curfew after all, and he's staying the night at the Howard Johnson. Could I pick him up there the next morning?

A few minutes before 7 a.m., I pull into the parking lot of the Bangor HoJo, where Michael is pacing anxiously. He hops in and we head toward Charleston. "People come to Bangor and say, 'What a cute little town!' Well, that's my big city," Michael says during the forty-mile drive. "Charleston is my hometown, and the two worlds don't really mix."

As much as he'd like to live in Bangor, economics dictate that he live at home for now. It's infantilizing to be twenty-three and have a curfew, but it's also freeing to be twenty-three and not have to pay rent. Anyway, he tells me he has broken his curfew multiple times, and been kicked out twice for doing things his parents see as "gay-related." I ask him how he feels about the costs of living at home. "When I have to mow the lawn, I pick a tree to aim for, instead of looking down," he says as he gazes out the car window. "If I don't, I'm swerving all over the place. If I keep my eyes on one tree, I'll go straight there. That's what I try to do in my life: I try to decide what I want to do and I do it."

The operative word there is *try*. What actually happens is that Michael ends up aiming at two different trees, depending on where he is. "I have to be a different person with everyone," he says. In Charleston, life revolves around home and church: "I wish my parents understood. I don't want to disappoint them." In Bangor, it's classmates and gay friends: "I wish my gay friends understood—some of them call me the Bible Thumper. They know I grew up Pentecostal, but we don't really talk about it."

I ask Michael to find me a decent radio station, and he raises an eyebrow. Pretty much the entire radio dial is Christian and country. He chooses Solution FM—contemporary Christian music. "No Christian rock," he says. "My dad thinks Christian rock isn't really Christian."

I'm speeding along when suddenly Michael says, "Wait! Okay, that's my house." He flicks his hand to the left. "Drive past it about fifty yards, do a U-turn, and then drive past it and pull over the side of the road." I follow his instructions and then stop. He opens the car door, gets out, wriggles out of his canvas jacket—which still has a rainbow ribbon pinned to it from yesterday—and tosses it onto the seat. "I'll be right back."

After about ten minutes, I glimpse Michael emerging from his house. At the same time, an aging sedan passes me in the other direction and pulls into his driveway. It's his dad, returning from his night shift at the Super 8 motel. I watch in my rearview mirror as Mr. Gray lowers his window to chat with Michael. Then Michael gets into the car, which turns around and onto the road, back in the direction from which it came.

I text Michael: ARE YOU OK?

He texts back: STAY.

I text him back. OK. BUT ARE YOU OK?

He texts back: STAY.

Fifteen minutes later, he calls me.

"Hey," he says.

"Hey," I say back. "You okay?"

"Yeah, just drive to the Countryside Restaurant."

We'd passed the restaurant on the way to his house, and I remembered it because there aren't a whole lot of other landmarks around. On my way, I pass Michael's dad's car, and when I get to the restaurant, Michael looks sheepish. His dad had asked him where he was going, and rather than explain why he was going to get into a car with another guy, he said that he was walking into town for breakfast. By himself. So Mr. Gray offered him a ride.

As we sit down for breakfast, he looks nervous, glancing around constantly. But eventually, he settles, and we begin talking about his faith, as opposed to the faith his parents would like him to have. "It's easy to believe something when everyone around you believes it," he says. "I doubt when what I believe gets challenged."

He starts into a straight-from-Sunday-school argument about creationism: If it's true, then everything in Christianity must be, but if it's not, "then everything Christianity is founded on is untrue." When I observe that there are plenty of faithful Christians who don't buy that God went on a six-day creative binge six thousand years ago, he says nothing. So I ask another question: "Do you believe Jesus really loves you?"

He plays with the food on his plate. "It's not so much a question of whether or not he loves me," he says. "It's more that he has not proactively loved me yet." Of course, the whole crucifixion-for-the-sake-of-your-soul thing could be interpreted as a gesture of proactive love, but Michael doesn't take it personally. "He can say he loves me all he wants. But he hasn't shown love to me. . . . I'm tired of people who say things and don't show them. Obviously I don't expect Jesus to come out of the clouds and strike me with lightning, and if I go to heaven, not hell, then great," he says, increasingly agitated. "But he's been very impersonal. That's not what I believe inside—it's what I've experienced. He has not shown me personally that he loves me."

We both play with our food.

"It's just like with my dad. I know he loves me. I just never see it. He always got angry at me and my brother for stupid things," Michael continues after a minute or so. "He always makes me very defensive. He's a good father. He provides for me and all that stuff, but sometimes it seems like he's trying to buy my obedience. I know he loves me, but I want him to show it."

As if on cue, Mr. Gray walks up to the table, gives me a sharp look, and turns to Michael with a sharper one.

"I'm Jeff!" I say, sticking out my hand. He shakes it without a word. Then he turns to Michael.

"I thought you might need a ride to church," he says in a stern dad voice.

"I'm good," Michael replies, staring at the table. "See you there."

Charleston Pentecostal Church looks like an overgrown tract home. In centuries past, church architects built up—the idea being that grand spires and steeples focused observers skyward, buttresses flying toward heaven. But American churches nowadays seem to prefer to hug as much ground as possible. Fortunately, as the Charleston Pentecostal Church website notes, "the church is far more than a building. The church is people."

So let's look at the people. Michael is the youngest person in his Sunday school class by at least a decade. We take our seats about ten minutes before class starts, but curiously, as the other students stream in, not one greets us.

This morning, the teacher, a robust, loud man who might make a half-decent game show host and is totally unnecessarily using a microphone to talk to a room of maybe thirty people, is proclaiming God's reliability. "God does not have PMS days!" he says. The women titter. "He does not have emotional highs and emotional lows. He's the same, all the time. He's like the anchor, and we're pulling on the rope. As long as you hang on to that anchor, you'll be safe. He is the anchor, and he'll take you through!"

After that pep rally for Jesus, we head to the sanctuary for the morning service. Michael and I climb into the near-empty balcony. He points out the head pastor on the stage, and recalls when they met to discuss Michael's homosexuality. "He's honest and he's real," he says. "He made it clear that he's not for homosexuality. But he did say that he watched my video and it was a good-quality video!"

The service is a mini-version of the televangelistic worship you see on TV, complete with big-haired backup singers swaying for the Lord. But the graphics on the big screen where we follow the lyrics are completely unnerving: During the second song in the opening medley, "There's Wonderful Power in the Blood," each slide is ani-mated with a background of blood seeping in and out of the picture.

The third song, an old favorite of mine called "In Christ Alone," is a crowd-pleaser. As the worship team launches into the song, the congregation applauds, and mid-song, there's cheering. The sanctu-ary's main floor is packed, and as they sing, people begin moving into the aisles and the wide space between the front row and the altar. Arms stretch toward the ceiling. Chins point up. Eyes shut.

The last verse always gets me.

*No guilt in life, no fear in death*
*This is the power of Christ in me.*
*From life's first cry to final breath,*
*Jesus commands my destiny.*

*No guilt, no fear.* What does that even feel like? I don't think I or John or Andrae or Michael could truly say we know. Any glimmer of guiltlessness, any sign of fearlessness, has been outside the walls of the church, not within it.

Michael, who is standing to my left, shuffles his feet a little, as if he's at the junior high dance, but he hasn't sung a word. Then, just after the song ends and before the sermon starts, we slip out.

It's a quiet ride back to Bangor. Michael has said all he has to say and we let Solution FM—worship songs and Sunday praise—fill the silence. After I drop him off for the second day of Bangor Pride, I keep driving south, and slowly the static takes over. Soon, I can't understand anything, except an occasional "God!" or "Jesus!" that breaks through the audio fuzz. Then I just switch it off.

# JOSH COOK

*"My Christianity became a vague spiritual notion."*

Syracuse, New York

Syracuse University student Josh Cook's spiritual journey has been altered and re-altered by his obsession with one word: *why*. Cook, the son of an Irish Catholic mother and a father who veered from Catholic to evangelical, was once a fervent believer himself, but no longer believes in a supernatural, otherworldly God. Active in the Occupy movement and environmental causes, he traces his growing awareness of his homosexuality as well as his journey to atheism and secular humanism.

---

When my parents divorced, I was twelve. My dad dealt with the divorce by going to church much more frequently, and my sister and I tagged along with him. When the adults were at Bible study during the week, we could hang out there. That was my introduction into actively engaged religion—religion that was more than just cultural.

In high school, I was reading a lot of stuff, most of it Christian or something relatively close to Christianity, such as American transcendentalism, which had Christian images to it. I would only read theology books that said that Jesus was literally the Son of God, born to a virgin, raised from the dead. As a kid, I just accepted that. Reality was that there's a heaven, an earth, and a hell, and I took them to be facts just like water is $H_2O$ and freezes at thirty-two degrees Fahrenheit.

I didn't come out of the closet for a while. I was fourteen, I think. One day, I was on the phone with the girl who everybody assumed was my girlfriend. She was madly in love with me—I know that sounds terrible. Anyway, I explain to her,

"Look, I'm gay. I know I'm gay. I've known since I was eleven and had a word for it—and I knew I was different well before that. I just didn't have a word to put on it. And this isn't going to happen." She's crying and I'm trying to comfort her. She says, "You should tell your mom. She's worried about you." I say, "I can't. I don't know what she'll do."

Meanwhile, my mom has picked up the other line. She heard, "You should tell your mom"; of course she's going to listen!

She sits me down and says, "I heard what you said."

We cry and she says, "Do you want to go to a doctor?"

I say, "Fuck no! I don't want to go to a fucking doctor! I don't want some stranger interrogating me."

She says, "I just want you to know I love you. I'm proud of you. I just want you to be happy and have a good life."

I say, "Okay, whatever."

I go up to my room and just sit there in shock. She calls Dad and he has a complete breakdown. He says he was a failure as a father—which is complete nonsense, because he's a great dad.

Whenever I was visiting Dad—almost every weekend—we'd go to church. The questions were "What does the Bible say about this? What does the church say about this?" Sometimes he would yell at me: "You know this is wrong!" And I'd be like, "Dad, I haven't done anything. I'm gay. I can't change that. Trust me, I've tried. People threaten to beat me up at school. Why would I choose that?"

Gradually, he realized that I couldn't just flip the switch. His pastor and his church wanted to send me to some conversion-therapy place or pray over me. Dad said no. His parental intuition kicked in and told him it would probably traumatize me. He finally left that church because they kept bothering him and pestering him about it.

Some evangelical books pull out Scripture passages—many of them out of context—along the lines of "I have a plan to give you a future, to pour out blessings more than you can imagine." There was a lot of powerful psychology there. I was a young gay kid, struggling with my place in the world, not sure about what most of my family thought about me. I was navigating an often hostile school environment. And there was all the other stuff that life throws at you, besides. Of course it was awesome.

When I was seventeen, I joined an independent church that claims to affirm all people regardless of sexual orientation. Over the course of about a year, I gradually came to realize it was something of a personality cult. The pastor was really twisting these people's arms. I left that church with a deep feeling of distrust for people who benefit by using other people's faith. That taught me a painful lesson: that no matter how sincere you were, you couldn't count on other people. It dawned on me that faith by itself wasn't really a virtue.

The most intense spiritual experience I had was at a Catholic church. At one point, the priest lifts up the Eucharist and displays the body of Christ for the adoration of the congregation. At that moment, I had this feeling that there was some kind of energy radiating out of the Eucharist. The energy was just intense. It was warm and loving and sacrificial—the whole story of Jesus dying, the metaphor of body and blood being broken for you. I fell right down on the floor crying. It was the sense of complete forgiveness and complete love, this cosmic sacrifice and universal drama of suffering and redemption.

When my more intellectual side starting asking questions about where this came from, sometimes it was painful to say to myself that it's possible that the image I have of God might not be correct. You don't want to question things like that, especially if they're lending some kind of comfort. But for integrity's sake, I had to. I've always been really encouraged, both by my parents and my teachers, to always do my homework, so to speak. Plus, I was the nerd in high school and I always felt driven to understand things. So I didn't ever want to commit to anything without being sure about it.

My Christianity pretty much became a vague spiritual notion and an admiration of one particular historical figure, and I realized it was a fairly narrow view, given that there's a whole world of other cultures that evolved across humanity. I did love how poetic their expressions of the human condition were. But I had lost any interest in the supernatural.

Naturally, there was a lot of interplay between my sexuality and my spirituality—both are essential and defining aspects of who I am. I happen to have been dealing with these things at a time when the world's religions collectively have been wrestling publicly with the place and meaning of the LGBTQ community in relation to their congregations and theological understandings. But while it's true that the experience of coming out deeply impacted the evolution of my spiritual life, I don't want that to overshadow the fact that other things were just as, if not more, important. For example, despite having had intense Christian beliefs and experiences, I couldn't sustain an exclusivist, fundamentalist notion of salvation. I knew many Muslims and Buddhists who were wiser, kinder, gentler people than I was! Was I supposed to wait until some hypothetical afterlife to know which of us was "right"? If faith doesn't transform how we are in the world here and now, what good is it?

If healthy faith is telling us anything, it's "be responsible to each other and the world. Take care of each other and the world." That quintessential, ethical message is the most important thing I have distilled from my experiences. I deeply value religious writing, religious experience, and religious culture. They can be manipulated—people will manipulate anything— but they can also be a source of great good.

I'm grateful now that I am gay. I'd never have said that when I was in high school. But now I see that it helped sensitize me

to abuses and injustice. It has prevented me from simply walking through life with the privilege of never being a target for
someone's fear or hatred. Experiencing the systemic homophobia of our culture firsthand, and being able to empathize with
others who've known the suffering of oppression and hatred,
has made me more critical of institutions, especially ones that
give their participants a prepackaged worldview. In that faith is
about growing beyond one's self to embrace something larger, I
am grateful for the experiences I've had since coming out—be
they good or terrible.

I consider myself to be deeply secular and I don't interpret
secularity to mean antispiritual. I interpret the word *secular*
from the original Latin, which means "of this world." I consider myself to be very much in love with religious values—
reverence, for example, or gratitude; they're wonderful expressions of humanity. I don't know about heaven or hell. I don't
think they exist. I don't have reason to be concerned with any
other world, but I have every reason to be concerned about
this one. There are people right now who are starving to death,
who are enslaved, who are in chains. Huge swaths of our ocean
are dying off because of our wastefulness and greed. And I
think those things are forever more important than arguing
about God.

My grandmother is the only person on earth I'm not out to.
I think she knows, but is in total denial. Picture in your head
the stereotypical grandmother who bakes pies and cookies and
is short and fat and lives out in the country in a gingerbread
house: That's basically my grandmother. She's a saint. But she's
also very old-fashioned, conservative, Catholic. Am I going to
agree with her backward views? Not at all.

But I definitely hold a lot more bitterness for people who go
out and force people to conform to their idea. As a gay man,
I've had religiously based hatred spewed at me on more than
one occasion. I think most people just haven't been given the

resources to explore. Maybe they don't have the intellectual curiosity to dig deep. Instead they just go with the flow. They see something they like about the church culture and they adapt themselves to it, which is just what people do.

If there is one thing I miss, it's praying. It's kind of strange. I have no intellectual reason to pray anymore, but I've often gone and meditated, not in any particularly religious way, but just to sit in silence. As a Christian, I was so accustomed to praying. I do miss that.

# YES, JESUS HATES YOU

## Westboro Baptist Church

*Topeka, Kansas*

The term *Christian* means radically different things to different people. There are social justice Christians, moral crusader Christians, Christians who believe in "Jesus-as-good-man-but-no-more," and those who hold to a "Jesus-is-the-only-way" Christianity. But gradually over the last few decades, the word *Christian* has become associated with condemnation. Nearly all former Christians I interviewed cited judgmental behavior as one of the push factors that sent them running from the church. And no institution has been more associated with being extremist and anti-gay than Westboro Baptist Church.

No congregation in the world spends as much time preaching against homosexuality as this small Topeka band of believers. No church is more disliked by homosexuals, their allies, and even other Christians who would never ordinarily align with the gay rights movement. At a protest against New York State's legalization of gay marriage, I witnessed Maggie Gallagher, a pugnacious, Roman Catholic leader of the anti-gay-marriage lobby, scream at a group of Westboro members: "You blaspheme the name of Christ!"

Gallagher's fury had not a little to do with the semantic choices that Westboro has made—and which have made it famous. Nobody else today uses, with total impunity, the "f" word that has become integral to Westboro's unbelievably widespread brand:

GOD HATES FAGS.

FAGS GO TO HELL.

FAG LOVER OBAMA.

But every time I saw a photograph of church members picketing with these signs and every time I read an article about Westboro— and there have been many in recent years—so many questions arose. Why do they hate gay people so much? Why do they believe homosexuality to be worse than other sin? How did a church with just forty members manage to gain such outsize influence, provoking the media, politicians, and even the U.S. Supreme Court to help them spread their message of hellfire and damnation? Why do they look like they're having so much fun?

So, early in the summer of my pilgrimage, I packed my bags for Topeka.

I was scared. Some nights before my departure, I had nightmares, and many mornings, I'd wake with my jaw tight and teeth clenched. Friends tried to convince me that it was morally wrong to give the church any more ink than it has already received, and one pastor, upon learning that I'd be visiting Westboro, rejected my interview request, saying there was no way he'd be quoted in the same book.

Loved ones repeatedly asked if I was going alone; I was not. I asked a multimedia journalist and friend named Tim Meinch and his photographer fiancée, Dana Halferty—both strong Christians with a good knowledge of Scripture—to come along as photo and video assistants (read: human security blankets). My boyfriend, having already given up on persuading me not to go, had visions of me getting bashed in some Kansas parking lot, so he asked me to stay in a hotel far from the church and with interior hallways. (Priceline defied him on the first count, but obliged him on the second.)

My own biggest fear wasn't my safety; I figured that Westboro was too media-savvy to hurt me physically. Rather, I was haunted by a more appalling thought: What if I found that they were not in fact crazy? Worse, what if I decided that they were right?

On a good Sunday in Brooklyn, I slip into a pew at around 11:03 a.m., just as my pastor has opened the service with the standard litany. But on my Sunday in Topeka, I go to church four times—or rather, I go to four churches. Every Sabbath day, before their own noon service, Westboro's members protest outside other Topeka churches as worshippers arrive.

Tim, Dana, and I had asked if we might shadow church members on the picket line, so we are assigned to Team B, led by Jonathan Phelps, an affable lawyer who is the third-eldest of Westboro founder and pastor Fred Phelps's eleven children. This morning's itinerary features an Evangelical Lutheran church, a Methodist congregation, and finally a Catholic parish. "It's going to be a good morning," Jon tells us as we gather outside his house. "Sometimes it's just Methodist, Methodist, Methodist. This is a good mix!"

Outside Our Savior's Lutheran Church, the ten-person team sorts through the signs they've brought along. "You can take a FAG PRIEST one if you want to," Jon says cheerily to one of his sons, before explaining to me that the signs "are almost universally applicable. GOD HATES FAGS works everywhere." He points to one that reads U.S. ARMY and has stick figures simulating anal sex. "We've had U.S. ARMY ones since 1991 or 1992, just after we started doing this," he says. "We know the military is dominated by homosexuals."

For Our Savior's, Jon chooses a sign that says LUTHERAN FAG CHURCH. (In 2009, the Evangelical Lutheran Church in America had approved the ordination of gays and lesbians.) Another team member has picked a poster that reads, YOU'RE GOING TO HELL. Frankly, I feel as if I might already be there. It's a stick-your-head-in-the-icebox kind of day; the weather forecast said the mercury would rise to 105, and with the humidity, the breezeless air would feel like 118.

When we move on to the Methodist church, I spend a few minutes with one of the youngest picketers, a towheaded, slightly pigeon-toed, unsmiling six-year-old boy named Ben. Ben tells me that his favorite thing in the world to do is to jump on the trampoline in his backyard. It's barely summer, yet he's already worried about starting public school in the fall—all Westboro members send their kids to public school, in part because they consider their children, well known to everyone as Westboro youngsters, to be walking picket signs. He has heard that his school does not have a trampoline. Also, he says, "home school is more funner." Tucked under Ben's chin is a child-size sign that says, FAGS DOOM NATIONS.

Because of the heat, Jon decides we'll move on to St. Matthew, a nearby Catholic parish, earlier than planned. When we get there, a few cars are just pulling in for ten-thirty mass, and the picketers choose from a range of Catholic-specific signs: DYKE NUNS, POPE IN HELL, FALSE PROPHET, which features a menacing photo of Pope Benedict XVI. Jon's sister Abigail, who is wearing a tattered American flag around her waist and dragging it on the ground, holds four signs at once, including one that says, DESTRUCTION IS IMMINENT. She's belting out a Westboro version of the Vanessa Williams song "Save the Best for Last"—retitled "God Saved His Best Wrath for Last." "God's day of wrath is coming soon," Abigail sings. "The day the sun won't light the moon. God saw the lust that filled your lives. We told you truth—don't act surprised."

A few feet away, Jon's wife, Paulette, stands with a sign that reads HAIL MARY, with two stick figures, one bent over in front of the other. "You know what a Christian is?" she yells to a parishioner who's locking up her car. "You're supposed to *follow Christ!*"

I ask Paulette's niece, Sara, whether she thinks these messages—written, sung, shouted—will actually get through. She shakes her head: "If the Lord hasn't given you the heart to hear, you just won't understand."

The reason they preach anyway is that you never know who has that heart and who doesn't. Spreading their gospel is their duty and their gesture of kindness to a hell-bound world. They cite Leviticus 19:17, which instructs the faithful—in the words of the King James Version favored at Westboro—to "not hate thy brother in thine heart," but "rebuke thy neighbor, and not suffer sin upon him." In other words, if you don't point out your neighbor's sin, you not only fail to show that person love but also share in his guilt.

"A day doesn't go by that I'm not constantly searching out preaching opportunities. Every day, we say to the people of this earth, 'The Lord is soon returning and will destroy the earth with fire,'" Jon says. "People say to us, 'What ever happened to 'love thy neighbor'? That's exactly what we're doing. We have words that cut to the heart. If you truly know what the Lord said, then you know we are loving our neighbor."

Westboro meets on the ground floor of a brick building that doubles as the longtime home of Fred and Marge Phelps, who have lived in Topeka since 1955. The décor of the sanctuary, just off the Phelpses' kitchen, is 1960s suburban ecclesiastical—standard-issue pews, wood-veneer paneling, and shockingly mauve carpet. Many of its accouterments would be familiar to most churchgoers. At the front of the sanctuary, there's a small, boxlike electric organ, and a small elderly woman who plays it. And there's a traditional wooden communion table not so different from those in thousands of churches around the world, featuring Jesus's familiar words from the Last Supper: "This do in remembrance of me."

There are two remarkable things about the space. The first is the overwhelming smell; an olfactory mixologist might describe it as sour, almost chemical, with overtones of formaldehyde and must. The other is the set of posters that flanks the pulpit. One says GOD HATES FAGS. Another has a photo of the president of the United States and the words FAG LOVER OBAMA. A third, on the back wall, reads TULIP—an acronym for the five points of traditional Calvinism.*

The sanctuary aptly reflects the church's dogma: While Westboro's attention-grabbing teachings are the unconventional ones—the Obama poster, for example, reflects their belief that he's the Antichrist—the church shares many other beliefs with scores of conservative Christians. Westboro, an independent church that doesn't belong to a denomination, shares some views with strict Presbyterians, including the idea that God handpicks which people will go to heaven and which will go to hell. And a host of people across the theological spectrum, from Catholic to mainline Protestant to all manner of evangelical, would agree with the basis for Westboro member Steve Drain's call for homosexual repentance, if not quite his delivery: "Quit being homosexual!" he says. "If you're not doing it, you're not homosexual. It's not an immutable characteristic, like being black or a woman. It's a behavior. So just stop the behavior."

Westboro fixates on sexual morality, and it's strict on these issues: There should be no premarital or extramarital sex. Remarriage after divorce is adulterous; Ben's father, one of the church's recent converts, was forced to leave his second wife before being admitted as a member, because his first wife was still living. But in promoting such morality—by which I mean calling out other people's immorality—Westboro members often deploy extremely profane, totally unchurchy language. For instance, at a picket in Manhattan on the first day of legal gay marriage in New York, Margie Phelps, who a few months earlier had delivered an erudite and ultimately winning argument before the U.S. Supreme Court, maniacally screamed, "I

---

* *T* is for "total depravity," meaning a human is, without God, sinful and unable to choose holiness. *U* is for "unconditional election," meaning that God and God alone selects whom to save from damnation. *L* represents "limited atonement"; Jesus didn't die for everyone's sins—only for those of the saved. *I* means "irresistible grace"; if God chooses you, you will believe. And *P* stands for "perseverance of the saints": Those whom God has called will never lose their faith, and anyone who does fall away from belief never truly believed to begin with.

don't even know what's growing inside your crusty assholes!" at gay men who were in line to wed at the city clerk's Marriage Bureau.

Westboro's Sunday service, on the other hand, uses more of the ecclesiastical vernacular of centuries past—lots of "thee" and "thou." The service is quick and simple: hymn, prayer, sermon, and hymn. The music is equally throwback; the closing hymn, "On the Mountain's Top Appearing," is from 1802. Fred Phelps, who preaches every Sunday, invokes more than a dozen different passages of Scripture, Old Testament and New, in his rambling discourse about the nature of God's love. Later that afternoon, when I stop by the home of Phelps's son Tim, he explains that the worship service reflects their understanding of what the Bible says church should be. There is no Sunday school, for instance, because "there is no biblical support for Sunday school. The body of Christ is supposed to meet at one time."

The traditional music, the ye-olde prayer language, the "for the Bible tells me so" worship style—all are manifestations of Westboro's strong nostalgia. The church believes that society has never been more wicked or more ignorant of what God requires of us and who He is. Homosexuality is technically no worse than any other sin; they just focus on it because our tolerance of it shows how bad things have gotten. Nor do they believe that they are morally superior. "I am not worth a crap," Jon Phelps says to me at one point. "I am not even a worm."

Few things irk Westboro's members more than the widespread belief, even beyond the church, that Christ was a sweet, all-loving man. God does not actually love everyone, they say, only those whom He chose for heaven. "God foreordained some people to go to heaven and some to go to hell. But people can't stand that they got put in the wrong category. That's a buzzkill!" says Steve Drain, who came to Topeka in 2001 to make a film debunking Westboro's beliefs and ended up converting and moving his family up from Florida. "But Jesus did not die for everyone."

This kind of thinking isn't unique in the American church. Mark Driscoll, a prominent pastor who leads Seattle's Mars Hill

Church, which regularly draws more ten thousand worshippers, gave a sermon in the fall of 2011 in which he said: "Some of you, God hates you. . . . He doesn't think you're cute. . . . He doesn't care if you compare yourself to someone worse than you. He hates them, too. God hates—right now, personally, objectively hates some of you."

It's almost an echo of Tim Phelps, who tells me: "We've got to get off this notion that Christ was a kissy-poo preacher. He was a hellfire-and-brimstone preacher."

Finally it was time to meet Fred Phelps, and boy did things not go well.

Dana, Tim, and I arrive in Phelps's book-lined office, upstairs from the church sanctuary, just before noon. The wall behind his desk reflects the complexity of his history: Phelps was an Eagle Scout and to the right of his merit badges is a plaque from the local chapter of the National Association for the Advancement of Colored People. Before Westboro launched its quest against homosexuality, Phelps, a lawyer, was respected for his ardent advocacy of racial equality. And to the left is one of the church's original protest posters. Compared with today's invective, the 1991 version is surprisingly gentle: WATCH YOUR KIDS, it reads. GAYS IN RESTROOMS! Said restrooms were in Gage Park, a few blocks from the church, and the picketing began after a few teenage Phelps boys were propositioned by cruising gays.

Slouched in an office chair behind his desk, his skin sallow, Phelps looks all of his eighty-two years. His frosty eyes, peeking out from the brim of his white cowboy hat, are several shades paler than the blue of his Kansas Jayhawks jacket, which seems to protect him from his own chill.

It's a struggle to draw out details of his personal history. When I try to get him to talk about how he was called to the ministry, he shoots back: "Is that a real good question you got there?" He eventually admits that he has always been a rabble-rouser. In 1951, he proudly notes, *Time* featured him preaching at John Muir College in Pasadena, California. Phelps, then twenty-one and "a tall (6 ft. 3 in.), craggy-faced engineering student from Meridian, Miss., . . . [would] walk up to groups of boys & girls munching their lunchtime sandwiches in the quadrangle, ask 'May I say a few words' and launch into a talk," the *Time* article says. "Over and over he denounced the 'sins committed on campus by students and teachers.' "

"That was the best issue *Time* ever put out," he says. His father didn't think so. "My daddy told me, 'Bubba, you seem to know how to get everyone mad—and we don't like it. I recommend that you take a shortcut. Just haul off and kick them in the shins,' " he says with a satisfied smile. "He didn't really want me to do it—or maybe he did! Well, I haven't made all the people mad all the time, but I've come close."

Finally, after a few more strained minutes of back and forth, he goes for a little kick at our shins: "You guys planning on staying much longer?"

"I'll take as much time as you have," I say.

"It's three minutes after twelve," he says, glancing up at a clock. He suggests we be out of his office at five after twelve—"fifteen, if you insist."

I just keep asking questions. In the end, it was my grandfather, along with some stuff I learned in Christian school, that saved me.

Phelps seems to approve of a question I ask about Jonathan Edwards, the eighteenth-century theologian who traveled colonial America stoking Christian revival. Nobody preaches truth anymore, Phelps tells me, because "there are no good preachers left." ("Present company excluded" was quickly understood.) "We need about fifty Jonathan Edwardses let loose!" he continues. "And I don't know any!" He cites Edwards's most famous piece of oratory, "Sinners in the Hands of an Angry God," as "an ideal sermon."*

---

* In this piece of preaching, which cemented Edwards's reputation as a fire-and-brimstone preacher, the word *fire* appears seventeen times, while *brimstone* shows up just twice. Perhaps it should be called a "wrath-and-hell" sermon; those words show up fifty-one and fifty-two times, respectively.

When I ask Phelps what biblical figures have inspired him, he cites the long line of prophets and faithful servants of God from the eleventh chapter of the Book of Hebrews.

"The faith hall of fame!" I reply, using the nickname for that passage of Scripture.

Phelps seems surprised that I have any idea what he is talking about.

A little later, I make a reference to Scripture that catches him off guard. For a moment, he looks confused. "You know something of the Bible?"

"I hope so," I say. "My grandfather was a Baptist preacher."

He narrows his eyes. "How old was he when he died?" Among some Westboro members, living to what the Bible calls "a ripe old age" signifies God's blessing, while an early death can be an indication of divine disfavor.

"Ninety-one," I say, whispering a silent prayer of gratitude that Grandpa hung on as long as he did.

"I think we might be able to have a little bit of friendship," Phelps responds, a touch of softness entering his voice.

But just a little bit—Phelps no longer holds much hope for me or for the rest of the world, given that we haven't joined Westboro. He has stopped praying that America would be saved. He likens the moral situation today to ancient Israel in the days of the Prophet Jeremiah. "Three times the Lord told Jeremiah, 'Don't pray for these people anymore. I'm not listening,'" he says. "The message now is that it's too late."

Perhaps he's right and this is society's twilight, but the evidence seems stronger that Phelps himself is close to his own end of days. He still mounts the pulpit and preaches every Sunday, though his voice doesn't thunder as it used to. You can still see the fight in his cold blue eyes, and though he rarely goes picketing anymore, he revels in the loathing that the church's activities generate among the rest of society. "Blessed are ye when men shall hate you. When they do that, leap for joy," he says to me, paraphrasing Jesus's words as recorded in the Gospel of Luke. "When they do that, I dance a little jig."

"Then you must do a lot of dancing," I reply.

He turns to Steve and says with a half smile, "That was a good one."

When I ask what will happen to the church when he dies, he glares at me and says sharply: "I'm not expecting to die."

I ask him what else I might read to better understand the teaching that he believes is sound. He gazes around his book-lined library and thinks for a long moment. *"Precious Remedies,* with *The Doctrines of Grace,"* he says, citing two works by the seventeenth-century Puritan writer Thomas Brooks. "That wouldn't be bad." He names John Bunyan's *The Pilgrim's Progress* ("heartwarming") and Jerome Zanchius's *Absolute Predestination* ("what I quote out of more than anything else"). And finally, he points at two massive, leather-bound volumes on a table to his left: Joseph Caryl's exposition of the Book of Job. "That's a good book," he says. "Bless the cow that gave his life for that book." (Later, when I study his recommended-reading list, I realize that every text that he mentions is from the seventeenth century.)

Just as we are leaving—we made it nearly to one o'clock—he has another thought. He pulls out a newspaper article that accuses him of misinterpreting Scripture. "Thou shalt not lie with mankind as with womankind: it *is* abomination!" he thunders, quoting Leviticus 18:22. "They say I twist the Scripture to provide me with preaching material to persecute poor little homos? You don't need any expositions at all. Those are pure Bible words. And I'm twisting it? Whoever wrote that article is dumb!"

He rambles on for a few more moments, unspooling a mini-sermon on God's judgment, leaping from Leviticus to 2 Chronicles and on to Jeremiah and then the Gospel of Luke.

Finally, I thank him for his time and ask if I can take a photo with him before we go. He nods, and I step around his desk and position myself behind his chair. For a moment, he can't see exactly what I'm doing or where I am, and he startles, turning his head left and then quickly right.

"Don't worry," I say. "I'm right here."

Shortly after the first pickets in Gage Park, Phelps had an epiphany that *gay* was not the right word at all. He decided that *fags* would be more appropriate, and explained it as the short form of an antiquated word for kindling. Appropriate, Westboro's argument goes, because such sin is sending the whole world into the flames of hell.

The members of Westboro use the word *fag* constantly and casually. When I asked Jael Phelps, one of Fred Phelps's twenty-three grandchildren, whether she's a fan of *Glee*, she said she used to be something of a Gleek "until those two fags started kissing! Then I couldn't watch it anymore." And during a chat with Jael's cousin Rebekah Phelps-Roper, Rebekah confesses merrily that she didn't always understand the signs she would hold during pickets. "We started picketing when I was three," she says. "I remember I would usually hold a sign that said No FAGS and it had a happy face in the middle. I always thought it meant No HAPPY FAGS. I guess it wasn't until I was fifteen or sixteen that I really knew."

*Fag* isn't the only pejorative term they regularly deploy. *Whore* is another favorite, slapped on everyone from former first lady Betty Ford (because she was a divorcée when she married Gerald Ford) to Billy Graham ("lying whore," for not preaching the gospel as they see it) to Elizabeth Taylor ("world-famous filthy Jew whore"). Paulette Phelps, Jon's wife, even describes her own sister to me as a whore, because she is not a Westboro member.

This kind of talk is especially jarring because every member of the church we meet, except for Fred, is warm and welcoming. They're good, easy conversationalists, chatting about everything from the Harry Potter books to photography to the movies. And they can be charmingly self-deprecating. One evening, we go over to Steve Drain's house for pizza. "Do you want anything to drink?" he asks, opening the fridge to do a quick inventory. "We have Coke,

Diet Coke, iced tea, juice, water. But we don't serve Kool-Aid. It makes people a little nervous!"

Steve explains the language choices as pragmatic: They're just trying to speak to people in the current vernacular. "How all this lands on a person's heart is God's business," he says. But this multi-part defense of the use of *fag* is like me telling my mother that it is okay to say "fuck" instead of "sex," because it has a long and rich history (which it does), lots of people say it, and the responsibility for interpretation is ultimately God's. That's not only disingenuous but also dishonest. They know precisely how that word will be received—as a marker of their hate. They also know that it will provoke strong, equally colorful responses, which help them amplify their message that the world revels in its sin. Steve still remembers one from a picket in Missoula, Montana, that said, "Love thy neighbor in the ass." "Really? Seriously?" he says, incredulous. "They get as filthy as they can." Adds his wife, Luci, a cheery mom of four who makes the best iced tea I've ever had: "It's just a sick scene, the youth of this nation."

It's impossible to understand Westboro according to the logic of the outside world. In some ways, this is little different from any religion—in fact, it's an inherent quality of faith, which requires belief in things unseen and unprovable. When others try to reason with Westboro's members, a common response is that God has not opened their eyes, so they just can't accept the truth. "Sometimes you look at people going by, and you think, Why are we the only ones who see this?" says Rebekah Phelps-Roper. "Well, who am I to question my Creator? This is the Lord's will, and it is perfect."

Jon Phelps says that he often hears from counterprotesters that Westboro is a cult, that it's weird that the church is largely from one family. "Who got on the ark?" he asks. "Everyone that got on the ark was related to Noah."

Drawing a firm line between "us" and "them," the sheep and the goats, the chosen and the un-, allows church members to rationalize the shunning of those who have left the congregation. Not that they are entirely able to eliminate the pain of seeing their children, brothers, sisters, cousins depart.

Rebekah recalls when one of her older brothers left. She had just had a cross-country meet. "He picked me up from the bus. The next morning, we were going white-water rafting in Colorado, but he was not there," she says. "I saw some of my brothers and sisters crying, but I've seen other people leave and I did my crying then. My mom explained it to me then: They were not of us. If they were, they would have stayed. It's the perfect will of God."

Jon still occasionally thinks about the two of his four children who have rebelled. "I wish it was otherwise. It's a little bit discouraging that they didn't take advantage. We gave them as much tools and gospel teaching as we could. But it's sad in the sense that they weren't granted the grace," he says. Normally garrulous, he falls silent. "People who are constrained to do something are not happy people," he continues. "They were given the chance."

Jon's eldest brother, Fred Jr., has watched two of his four children leave the church, too, but they still take care of their apostate daughter Sharon's young daughter. "The baby's a cutie!" Fred Jr. says. Adds his wife, Betty: "Any grandparent would like to see their grandchild have a nice life and be exposed to the truth. But we cannot control their hearts. That is God's business, and if their hearts turn, it's not because of us."

Many of us are bedtime theologians. For good or ill, that's one of the few times I'm alone with my thoughts. And in those too-quiet moments at day's end, when sleep has not yet rescued me, sometimes epiphanies come. Often, I get panicky. Always, I have questions—and there is no better and no worse time for those big What-ifs.

I asked most of the Westboro members we met to tell me the stories of how they came to believe. When did they know?

SAM PHELPS: One night, I was lying in bed, and I was overcome with fear—a fear of hell. I knew the only way to not go to hell was Jesus Christ. . . . It's not a question of whether the Lord lives or whether his blood is effectual to save me. The only question is, was it shed for me? I hope that it was, but no man can have that certainty. At some level, absolutely that fear is still there.

VICKY PHELPS: I was in my room and getting ready for bed. It hit me like a ton of bricks that this was real. It's not just words that people say. If I'm not a part of the church, I will go to hell. For eternity. That's a long time. I thought, I don't want to be in pain for eternity. It's a scary thought. I told my parents I didn't want to go to hell. And I kept hoping that Christ wouldn't come before I got baptized. I kept hoping it wasn't too late.

TIM PHELPS: It was cold, and I was lying in what we called the dryer room. They were these big old Speed Queens—industrial size—and you could open them when they were running and the warm air would come out. It just hit me like a ton of bricks: I was going to hell. I was doomed. And I still walk in the fear of the Lord every day.

I can't count how many times I've thought similar things. How many nights have I spent, sweaty and panicked and drained of tears, because I thought I would go to hell—for being gay, for being me? Other sins I had repented of, but this one didn't go away. It was different—fixed. How many nights did I spend, in sleepless anguish, praying that God would take these feelings from me? How often did I imagine what hell might be like, wondering, If he didn't make me straight, what the fire and brimstone would feel like?

Before I went to Westboro, I expected that its members would take every opportunity to remind me, not only because I'm gay but also because they now believe that they are the only true Christians left on earth. But in my four days in Kansas, nobody ever asks me about my sexuality. Nobody says a word about my salvation, except for Jon, who at one point generically and somewhat blandly says, "We have to tell you you're going to hell."

The closest we come to discussing my faith and my fate is as we're leaving Fred Phelps's office. Steve Drain is walking us back to his house. "You're searching for something, aren't you?" he says gently. I am, of course—this journey is about finding God, but it's also about finding a church—but I don't respond. He glances at me. "Well, I really hope you find what you're looking for."

Steve says this so sweetly that, for as many seconds as it takes for the words to form in my mind, I think, What if they're right? Maybe they're right. Damn! But just as quickly, I know this in my heart: Their god is not my god, and their faith is not my faith, and there can be no middle ground. My logic is unacceptable to them— nothing more than the devil's lies—just as their logic makes no sense to me. My heart and my head cannot accept a god so cruel as theirs, so cavalier that he would create people just to destroy them. And I cannot believe in a fear-based faith. I don't want to be scared into belief. I don't want to be frightened into submission.

The wonderful film *You Can Count on Me* chronicles a period in the relationship between a sister and a brother, played by Laura Linney and Mark Ruffalo, as they grapple with, sibling stuff. It uses no huge set pieces, no big action scenes. Instead, it finds its power in small, intimate moments, which collectively offer one of the truest depictions of real life in recent cinema. Linney plays Sammy, the churchy, stable sibling; Ruffalo is Terry, the peripatetic one. At one point, Sammy asks her pastor, Ron, to sit down with them to talk.

In a rare moment of clarity, Terry answers a question that Ron has posed about whether his life is important and—by extension—about the nature of his faith. "I don't know: A lot of what you're saying has a real appeal to me, Ron," Terry says. "A lot of the stuff they told us when we were kids . . . But I don't want to believe something or not believe it because I might feel bad. I want to believe it because I think it's true."

He could have been speaking for me.

On our last morning in Topeka, I wake too early. As quietly as I can, given the squeaky Holiday Inn sofa bed, I pull the Gideon Bible out of the nightstand to play that game where you open the Bible and see where God sends you.

Daniel 6.

This is the story of the Prophet Daniel being thrown into the lions' den by his enemies and surviving, miraculously unscathed. My eyes settle on verses twenty-six and twenty-seven, where it says: "For He *is* the living God, and steadfast forever; His kingdom *is the one* which shall not be destroyed, and His dominion *shall endure* to the end. He delivers and rescues, and He works signs and wonders in heaven and on earth, who has delivered Daniel from the power of the lions."

"He delivers and rescues." These words are encouraging. But here's the thing about Scripture. You can play that game of biblical roulette. You can tell yourself that this is your word from the Lord and imagine yourself as a Daniel. You can believe that God is on your side. But your adversary can do the same thing. I know Fred Phelps feels like a Daniel, too, clinging to his God at a time when others tell him and his people that they are wrong.

Before I put the Bible away, I turn to Proverbs 12. When I was a young boy, my grandmother taught me that since there were thirty-one chapters to Proverbs, I could read a different one each day of the month.

Each couplet in Proverbs 12 contrasts good with evil: A good man does this, while a wicked man does that. I fixate on verse eighteen: "There is one who speaks rashly like the piercing of a sword, but the tongue of the wise heals."

One of the few biblical expositors respected by Westboro is John Gill, who lived and died in the eighteenth century. He explains this verse by noting that words that heal are "comfortable, cheerful, and refreshing words to the injured and abused; especially the tongue of a wise minister of the Gospel is health, or healing, to wounded souls."

But if Topeka teaches me anything, it is that many words—*healing, health, wisdom, love*—mean such different things to different people. It's almost as if people are speaking entirely different languages. And it's almost as if people are preaching totally different faiths.

# THE POWER AND THE STORY

The Scandal of the *Harding University Queer Press*

*Searcy, Arkansas*

Partway through a summer internship in Washington, D.C., Sarah Everett called home. She had something important to tell her dad.

Everett, a lesbian who was then twenty-three and a rising junior at Harding University in Searcy, Arkansas, grew up in Oklahoma in a religiously and politically conservative family. At family gatherings, Everett says, relatives "would make these snarky comments about how stupid Democrats are and how awful liberals are. Some of the things they were saying were so hateful and un-Christian." Especially after Barack Obama was elected president, "it just came up all the time. I don't feel like we talked about politics that much before. Now, pretty much everything that's wrong in the world is embodied in Barack Obama. It's socialism and Obamacare and the gays."

While studying abroad in Italy and then in D.C.—where she worked at Peace Corps headquarters—Everett began to realize that she was not in synch with the conventional wisdom of her childhood. She remembers one kitchen table debate with her parents about gay marriage. "I had always avoided that issue because I knew I wouldn't be able to argue it very well," she said. "They act like this would destroy society—Rome was destroyed because of the gays, in case you didn't know. Their position is that it's not biblical. I argued that our laws aren't based on the Bible."

That statement was tantamount to heresy in the Everett family. Based on this and other little comments she'd made, her father already kind of knew what she would eventually confess. Yet when the time came, she couldn't get the words out. "I just don't think I can tell you things sometimes," she said.

He paused. "Sarah, are you pregnant?"

She laughed. "No, Dad," she replied with a sigh. "I'm a liberal."

"As long as you're not burning your bras in public!" he replied.

A few months later, it was time for Sarah to tell her parents about another L-word. It was almost bedtime one night shortly before Christmas, and the Everetts had clicked the TV off after back-to-back episodes of *Diners, Drive-Ins and Dives*.

"I have to tell you something," Sarah said.

She handed them a note that said she was gay. (It also said she might marry a man or be single forever. "I wanted to ease them into this," she explains to me.) They read it. Then they reread it. And then they read it again.

"I wanted to die," recalls Sarah, who was sitting on the couch across from them, furiously live-tweeting the ordeal.

Finally, her dad said, "I think we were afraid of this." He continued by saying that if she ever brought her girlfriend home, "We will love her and treat her with respect, but we can't condone that."

Her mom added: "I think of this just like I would if you had told me you were pregnant, or doing drugs, or living with your boyfriend."

Sarah tweeted that line, because it was the first thing all day that had made her laugh.


The Harding University campus is a shiny emerald oasis amid the greige strip malls and dull concrete of the small Arkansas city of Searcy. Once a women's college, Harding is largely built of red brick, and the heart of campus is a grassy quadrangle shaded by tall oak trees and fringed by azalea bushes heaving, when I visit, with fuchsia and white blossoms. Here and there, you'll find freestanding white wooden swings, and there's a campus saying that goes "three swings and a ring"—if a couple swings together three times, they're destined for engagement.

Harding is the educational crown jewel of the Churches of Christ, a denomination so conservative that, for modesty's sake, men and women are forbidden from swimming together (the church's inelegant term for this is "mixed bathing"). Tobacco use is frowned upon. Drinking and dancing are prohibited. So are musical instruments in church, an attempt to bring twenty-first-century worship closer to how the church believes it was done in the first century. While the 1.1-million-member Churches of Christ is an adamantly nondenominational denomination—it is entirely congregationally governed, with no central hierarchy, no headquarters, no bishops or presbyteries, no constitution apart from the Bible—Harding is occasionally referred to as its Vatican.

Harding—which, with just over seven thousand students, is the largest private university in Arkansas—maintains its cultural bubble, or at least the pretense of it, proudly. Think of those old cartoons: the angel on one shoulder, encouraging the right thing, and a demon on the other, extolling temptation; Harding students have a third, perhaps a little bison, the school's mascot, reminding them of the university's strict code of conduct. It's nearly impossible to sin significantly without everyone finding out. Most spectacularly, a student body president was allegedly caught a couple of years ago having sex in the Harding-undergrad equivalent of the Oval Office, not only proving that he might have a bright future in American politics but also incurring a semester-long suspension from the school.

At times the regime seems almost Saudi. In a recent incident, a young man broke the rule that forbids unchaperoned, unmarried students of different genders from staying overnight in the same house or apartment. He felt so guilty that he confessed to university officials. He and the female student whom he was dating and who stayed in a different bedroom were both suspended, even though, by all accounts, nothing untoward happened that night.

Attempts to liberalize have been met with anger from Church of Christ traditionalists. A few years ago, the university slightly re-laxed a policy that prohibited male students from growing their hair long, which prompted a tirade in chapel from a famously fiery-and-brimstoney preacher named Jimmy Allen. "In 1 Corinthians 11, Paul said to men: 'Doth not even nature itself teach you that if a man have long hair, it is a shame—SHAME!—to him,'" Allen roared. "I've seen a few fellas around here that I was tempted to kiss. I'd get up kinda close to them to see what was under the hair and back out. Even on a holy kiss." Allen's talk produced a historic level of collective eye-rolling, which, incidentally, has not been banned; one student took the "Shame! SHAME!" clip and turned it into her ring-tone, while another remixed the talk into a dance track.

"I realize as much as anyone that our code of conduct is not consis-tent with the world's view," the university's president, David Burks, says. "It's not commonplace, but it has been our standard since our beginning, whether it's drinking or homosexual activity or hetero-sexual activity outside marriage." Monte Cox, who is dean of Hard-ing's College of Bible and Ministry, puts it differently when I stop by his office: "As far as mainstream American culture is concerned, we look like idiots." Then his face broadens into a proud grin.

On the Harding hierarchy of sin, homosexuality occupies a high and special place. In this, it's no different from much of Christian America, though in conventional Protestant thinking, no hierarchy of sin exists; all sins are supposed to be equally repugnant to God.* Here, as at Westboro Baptist Church and in many conservative Christian institutions across the country, homosexuality is viewed as

---

* The Roman Catholic Church does rank sin. Mortal sins, such as murdering someone, are graver than venial sins, such as telling a white lie ("the dog ate my homework"). And even within the category of mortal sin, some are considered worse than others; abortion, for instance, merits automatic excommunication according to Canon Law.

a particularly disturbing outside-world problem. It happens almost exclusively beyond the university's gates and outside of its ethos, and to say *happens*, as opposed to *exists*, is important, because homosexuality is seen as thought and act—lust and fornication—not a valid identity. Nor is it a choice that good Christians make—and the thinking at Harding is that homosexuality is definitely a choice. That there exists a special ministry at Harding called Integrity, designed to help students battle same-sex desires, testifies to homosexuality's special place on the spectrum of sin; no ministry exists to help those who are struggling with, say, greed or malice or other forms of lust. "Same-sex attraction is a difficult disposition to have in this environment," says Scott Adair, a professor in the Bible department. "The students I know about . . . well, it would be at a great cost if they were to be more open about it."

Religiously inspired bubbles are a commonplace of life in Christian America, created both to unify the group within it and to distinguish—and protect—that group from the rest of the world. But Sarah and a small, mostly gay group of her friends knew that the picture of homogeneity at Harding was false. Not everyone in the community agrees with the university's stated values. And not everyone is straight. To stir dialogue and to reach those at Harding who are still closeted, they decided to publish a zine called *HU Queer Press*, chronicling their experiences as gay and lesbian Harding students. This move rocked the campus, horrified the administration, and drew national media attention. But did it succeed in creating any kind of constructive conversation, or in making other gay Harding students feel less alone?

The zine was born in the weeks after Sarah told her parents that she was gay. After Christmas, she drove up to Chicago to visit Greg Lyons and Kevin Cherry, two Harding alums who had followed her coming-out on Twitter. One afternoon, the three wandered into Quimby's, a bookstore that stocks hundreds and hundreds of zines on all manner of minutiae, from surgical birth control ("Ask Me About My Tubal Ligation") to the musings of a transvestite metal-head ("Blue Floral Gusset") to art from the 1976 edition of *Joy of Cooking* ("Foie Gras #3"). There, they had their epiphany: *We should totally write a zine about the gay experience at Harding!*

"The goals were twofold," says Greg, who is straight and became the zine's editor. "First, to expose people on campus to stories of people they likely knew or were acquainted with, but were actually completely unaware of, and in doing so, begin dialogue and discussion that was just not being had. In my experience, dialogue about queer morality and experience at Harding is limited to, 'Well, gay is evil.' The second goal was to show other queer students at Harding that there are people like you here, and you don't need to feel alone."

"Our stories are their stories," says Zach Seagle, a gay alumnus who joined the zine's staff. "It's a shared struggle. When I was in the closet at Harding, I kept thinking, Shit, I'm the only one. I felt dirty. And I knew I wasn't going to heaven. It wasn't until I figured out that I wasn't crazy that I started to come out. We weren't trying to create controversy. We just wanted to create some dialogue, to the point that Harding can't just turn its back on this."

The zine's staff, which through word of mouth eventually grew to six, made all decisions by consensus. They never met in person and still have not; everything was done by email and during weekly teleconferences. The zine would be posted on the Harding network, but the group also recruited about a dozen friends to help with distribution of five hundred copies that were printed at a local Staples. Ahead of that, they emailed a few bloggers in the Harding community who they thought might be empathetic. They also tipped off local media. "We were worried that if the administration were to ID any of the authors who were still on campus, they'd probably seek to expel them," Greg says. "We thought a little bit of media attention would maybe mean they would not feel as free to do that."

Within hours of the zine's release, the administration responded. "I was offended by what was in the website," President Burks says. "I made the decision to withdraw the website." This played right into the *Queer Press*'s plan. "If something is blocked at Harding, it will go all over campus," Zach says. "That's just human nature."

Within the week, bloggers at the *New Yorker*, the *Huffington Post*, and *Jezebel* had sniffed out the controversy. The *New Yorker*, in a blog post titled "War at Harding," noted that the zine came out on the same day that the U.S. Supreme Court affirmed Westboro Baptist Church's right to picket military funerals. It praised the zine staff, saying that "instead of fleeing, they are taking a stand for their right to be treated as humans in the society to which they already belong. Moreover, they are questioning the right of the Church of Christ and Harding to interpret the Bible the way they do."

Such external commentary infuriated the administration. Cox, the Bible college dean, says the zine embarrassed Harding and its foundational faith. He was particularly hurt because he had been close to one of the zine staff—though he never identified which one by name. "For him to launch a smear campaign to garner national attention, that hurts," Cox says. "And if he is truly committed to the way of Jesus, well, national smear campaigns are not part of the way of Jesus."

But there was no smear campaign—the allegation gives the students far more credit than they deserve. "We didn't plan for any high-profile articles," Greg recalls. "We didn't even have a spokesperson!" What's more, when they saw the *New Yorker* post, the to-the-barricades spin on their mission dismayed and even shocked them. Though they'd considered what benefits media coverage might have on campus, they'd naïvely never worked through how the outside world might perceive and write about the zine and Harding.

In the end, it was the emails from other gay students—a few at Harding, but many more at other conservative Christian colleges— that redeemed this experience. "A lot of them were scared. A lot of them hadn't come out to any of their friends or family," says Becca Burley, another member of the zine team. "It was all both sad and happy: I was sad that there were so many people who felt so alone, but happy that we did this. They are the ones that make me not regret it all."

Harding tries to create a culture of enforced holiness. Mandatory chapel takes place each morning at Harding, at nine, though each student is allowed ten skips per semester. (A black market—five dollars for a skip early in the term, perhaps ten dollars later—thrives because the women taking attendance don't usually recognize the students; they just make sure a body fills the seat.) When I visit in the spring of Sarah's senior year, I go with her up to the balcony of the six-thousand-seat auditorium, where the disinterested kids sit. I notice during the hymns that nobody in our section of the auditorium is singing.

All students at Harding must take a Bible course every semester. After chapel, I go with Sarah to one called Christian Home. The class's textbook, *Family: A Matter of Relationships*, by onetime Harding professor Allan Isom, offers advice on life and living. One section provides tips to be read "before purchasing a mobile home or a house." Another delineates the differences between the male and female subcultures: "The male's subculture clusters around the following two areas: 1) sporting events 2) automobiles. The subculture of women centers around the following two areas: 1) home décor 2) shopping." Obviously, Isom writes, there are significant differences between men and women: "Men see parts becoming a whole while women continue to search for more parts. Men are focusing in achieving in life, while women are interested in quality of life." He also spends pages and pages on a woman's "wifely responsibilities," cautioning that she "should remain at home and accept only jobs which do not significantly interfere with her motherly and wifely responsibilities." On the day I visit, the professor is lecturing about how to buy a car. This university education costs somewhere north of twenty-four thousand dollars per year.

Jimmy Shaw, a pastor and former Harding lecturer who mentors some of the university's more liberal students, places the Church of Christ firmly at the nexus of conservative Christianity and Southern sociopolitical mores. But he explains that it only became so identifiably right-wing during the Cold War. Before that, "the Church of Christ was named in the list of recognized 'peace churches': the Mennonites, the Brethren, Quakers. Pacifism and noninvolvement in the military was almost a universal conviction prior to World War II, but since then, our culture has been much more typically evangelical," he says. "Right now, the political climate here is right-leaning, reactionary, and quite frankly scared. It seems like hardheartedness. It seems like hatred and phobia. But fragility is the key elephant in the room."

Much of what the university teaches is meant to strengthen a Christian ethos that's seen as being under attack. Though there are constant references to faith's solidity, the prevailing mood suggests the opposite of confidence, and the stance seems to be more often "anti"—anti-society, anti-liberal, anti-godlessness—than pro-anything. "Harding does not prepare people for the real world. It prepares people for Southern white suburbia," says Sarah. "We create our own culture so we don't have to be offended." That day, she was wearing dangling heart-shaped earrings printed with rainbow stripes—to her a small and defiant sign of her homosexuality and to almost everyone else on campus just dangling heart-shaped earrings printed with rainbow stripes.

According to Kim Baker-Abrams, an assistant professor in Harding's Department of Social Work, the university's culture-wars-obsessed mentality has hurt its ability to educate its students. One casualty: that do-unto-others sense that it's important "to have common ground and be decent to each other," even if you disagree on major issues. "Everybody here is struggling with their place in the world—what you believe and what you don't," she says, "but they can't do it openly."

Baker-Abrams is the type of teacher you never forget—the one who opens your eyes to new things, who gently asks whether there might not be a different way to think. She's a quiet renegade. In her lightly honeyed and occasionally giggly voice, she finds ways to push her sometimes resistant students to grapple, to equivocate, not to remain complacent in the status quo.

Each year, she gives her Human Diversity class one of the more unusual assignments on campus: Write a paper imagining how your life would be different if you were of the opposite sexual orientation. It's an exercise in empathy. "Most of them have only thought about this issue from a theological point of view that amounts to 'If I'm gay, I'm going straight to hell!'" she says. This may seem acceptable for those who intend never to leave that bubble, but Baker-Abrams sees this position as not only thoroughly unrealistic in the modern world but also unprofessional for those pursuing careers in social work.

She gave me a stack of the "A" papers to read. In the most powerful ones, the students adopt the voices of gay men and women. "Today was a better day," one begins. "I was only called 'fag' once." A particularly comprehensive paper, after noting family resistance, homophobia, and harassment, added: "It is estimated that I will make more money than heterosexuals. The average income of lesbians is $80,000 annually." Then there was this keen observation: "I certainly would not be writing this paper if I were openly homosexual, because I would not be allowed as a student at Harding University."

One student told Baker-Abrams he shouldn't have to write the paper because he shouldn't have to imagine himself sinning. (He didn't get an A.) "He wanted to write about what his life would be like if he were a midget," she says with a laugh. "Well, I'm not interested in what his life would be like if he were a midget. I want to know what it would be like if he were gay." The student told Baker-Abrams that she had an agenda. "Yeah, I do," she admitted. "I want you to think outside your box."

In chapel the day after *HU Queer Press* was published, Dr. Burks explained what the administration had decided to do about the zine, but he refused even to say its name. The staff of the zine was outraged, believing Dr. Burks to be so homophobic that he would not even acknowledge the existence of queers at Harding. In truth, Dr. Burks tells me, he was raised at a time when the word *queer* was as derogatory as the n-word. "It's a word I never use," he says. "The word is offensive."

But he never explained that clearly to the students, and the students never got that there might be a semiotic generation gap. Indeed, those who worked on the zine seem so convinced they'll encounter hostility on campus that sometimes they don't even know to look for friendship. None of them knew, for instance, that they had a potential ally in the incoming student body president, Bruce McMullen. "I don't know why the school makes such a big deal of this gay thing. Where I come from, nobody raises an eyebrow," says McMullen, a South African who was recruited to Harding to play golf and wasn't even a Christian when he arrived on campus. (He has since been baptized, but doesn't consider himself a Church of Christ member.) "I don't want to say people here are narrow-minded or blinded, because that sounds rude, but I would love to see Harding kids struggle with this a lot more than they do," he says. "The fact that they're not says they're just going with tradition and heritage and Mommy and Daddy. But they need to decide for themselves. Fear of God is good, but I think people here have fear of the wrong things and for the wrong reasons."

The *Queer Press* staff was also unprepared for the criticism they received from secular sources. Bloggers would praise the zine but add, "Why would you go to a school that doesn't accept you for who you are?" or "Why not just leave?" These questions reflect a different type of thoughtlessness. For one thing, Harding students are just like millions of others everywhere who depend financially on Mom and Dad. "It's not easy when you're seventeen to say to your parents,

'Screw you!'" Sarah says. "Especially if it means you won't have money to go to college." Then there's the fact that, again like millions of others everywhere, these students are in a season of fragility and flux. They're still wrestling with their identities, their faith, and their homosexuality, which many had not even acknowledged before college. As one puts it to me, "It's not like someone woke up one morning and said, I'm gay but I'm going to go there and make my life suck."

Kevin Cherry, who had acknowledged his orientation during high school, chose Harding in part "because I hoped that there would be someone who would help me get a 'handle' on my struggle with homosexuality," he says. During freshman year, he underwent what he describes as counseling "to make my homosexual desires go away and to make me identify as a straight man." Through the process he realized "there wasn't a magical spirit of God at Harding to make me straight. I was a little disappointed."

A few weeks after the zine's publication, the Harding administration announced two special evening chapels focused on homosexuality. The theme of the first chapel is supposed to be what the Bible says about homosexuality, but really, it's what conservative evangelicals say the Bible says about homosexuality. The faculty members on the evening's panel start in Genesis, with a slightly more artful explication of that old canard, "it was Adam and Eve, not Adam and Steve." From there, they wind through Scripture to Jesus. I'm sitting with two *Queer Press* staffers, and we're all interested in what Scott Adair, the Bible prof assigned to handle this one, will say, since Jesus never mentioned homosexuality. Adair gamely acknowledges this fact, then quickly moves on to a presentation of some things Jesus said about marriage and sexual purity. Absolutely nothing unexpected or interesting happens during this first chapel.

The next night is different. This chapel also has a theme: "What would you say to the homosexual on the bus?" The weird framing was inspired by an incident a couple of summers ago, when the then-student body president sat next to a gay man on a bus from New York to Washington, D.C. This was apparently enough of a landmark event that he told a lot of people about it, because he wasn't sure what to say.

Three unusual things happen during this chapel—and the fact that they're unusual says so much about Harding. The first comes courtesy of psychology professor Ken Cameron: He challenges the conventional wisdom at Harding that gay people choose to be gay. "At what point did they make a choice?" he asks. "If you make this choice, you're likely to be bullied and harassed by a lot of people. It doesn't sound like it's a choice most people would make. . . . Let's not be so cavalier about the idea of choice." Sarah whispers to me: "This is *huge*!"

The second remarkable moment is when Scott Adair reads part of an email he received from one of his students, who has disclosed that he is gay: "If you are the average Harding guy, and your friend comes out to you, you probably won't be thinking of all the great Bible verses you have. You'll probably be experiencing an odd mix of feeling and thoughts that include deep pain for that brother, deep confusion, some thoughts on how this revelation will affect your relationship—perhaps even a few shameful flashbacks into all the times you used the terms *faggot* and *gay* derogatorily in everyday con-versation. Students need to be able to put themselves in the position of being a long-term, unconditional friend to one whose attempts to follow God make them feel worthless and inherently broken. Stu-dents need to learn how to have their hearts broken by the pain experienced by these individuals, to learn what it's like to keep a ter-rible secret alongside that friend, to learn to compassionately flinch when part of that friend's identity (for homosexuality, whether you are actively practicing or celibate, is always a prominent aspect of your identity) is jokingly compared to the actions of murderers, child molesters, and rapists. It is only when the average white, Southern Christian heterosexual wills to lower himself and be counted among his despised and stigmatized brother that the foundation for real conversation can be established."

To have something read aloud about the experience of being a hidden gay man in such a gay-unfriendly setting is rare in most churches and religious institutions, let alone in a Harding chapel. To have homosexuality discussed in a way that sets aside the question of the gay person's (potential) sin and instead addresses the question of the allegedly Christian community's (potential) sin is perhaps unprecedented here. Do these students even have the capacity to process what was just read? Is the silence in the auditorium guilt, or sadness, or discomfort, or all of the above?

Finally, Suzanne Casey, who works in Harding's counseling center, piles on by questioning how Harding ostracizes homosexuals. "The world assumes all Christians hate gay people," she says. "We have somehow sent this message to the world . . . because we have made it a dividing line of fellowship. Shame on us for sending that message!" She continues: "The followers of Christ must be a safe place for all who seek refuge here. The church ought to be the safest place there is."


President Burks did not attend the chapels. He also has no interest in making this campus the "safest place" for all gay students. For those students who are "struggling" with homosexuality, "we have provided what I think is a safe place," he tells me, pointing to Integrity, the campus-affiliated group "for students with *unwanted* same-sex attractions."

The word *unwanted* is paramount. Burks acknowledges that Integrity "doesn't meet the needs of everybody" and quickly disabuses me of the notion that Harding is a community for all. "Our responsibility is to help the student body as a whole. Can I say to those students that our doors are open, that we want you to come here if you want to pursue [homosexuality]?" he says. "The answer would be, no. This is not where they should be. If you find yourself completely out of line with what the institution stands for, it's better if you leave if necessary."

This message has not been made clear to the faculty. The morning after the second chapel, I drive to downtown Searcy, to the Underground, a typical college-town coffeehouse complete with tattered sofas, mismatched tables and chairs, and questionable hygienic standards, to meet music professor Cliff Ganus. The Ganuses are the Kennedys of Harding. Professor Ganus's grandfather Clifton Ganus Sr. served as Harding's board chairman from 1940 to 1954. His father, Clifton Ganus Jr., was the university's president from 1965 to 1987 and is now Harding's chancellor. The family name is on both the athletic center and the building that houses the political science and foreign languages departments.

For a time after the zine came out, Ganus's Facebook status read: "Don't block it. We must have a dialogue." The zine "was offensive, but you've got to be able to allow even the profanity and even the anger," he says. I wasn't expecting a scion of Harding—a graduate, son of a president, father of four Harding grads—to speak so supportively, and I tell him so. Gay people "are such a convenient target," he replies after a few moments of thought. "We all look for validation in our lives, and we all put ourselves against each other—white folks versus black folks, straight folks versus gay folks. We think it's a continuum, but it isn't. It's a sphere. And we are all over the place."

Ganus is downbeat about the prospects of dialogue at Harding—more so than nearly all the students. While the chapels were introduced to the community as a dialogue, "that wasn't a dialogue. It was a monologue. And I'm afraid that what happened the last two nights will be, 'Well, we've done it,'" he says. "I've not seen any deliberate steps forward at the administration level."

"Why do you think?" I ask, my mind going to moral questions.

"We're a business. We depend on our supporters for financing," he says. "To many of those of us who are straight, the idea of having sex with another guy is strange, and once you offend your constituency, well, where is your funding coming from? You have to understand that there is a monolithic culture that's going to be very difficult to open to dialogue."

Then Ganus tells me about an unusual meeting he attended earlier in the spring in this very coffeehouse. Harding students and a handful of faculty gathered with representatives from the gay-straight alliance at Hendrix College, a historically Methodist school in nearby Conway. The Hendrix students wanted to offer their support and their stories to their Harding counterparts. That this meeting had to take place off-campus was significant, but so was the fact that, in addition to Ganus, Monte Cox, the Bible college dean, and Scott Adair, the Bible professor, showed up. It was an eminently civil gathering—unlike the zine, it was the type of gentle interaction that Ganus believes Harding can both handle and will need. "There are some eloquent gay people who need to find a way of expressing things in a nonconfrontational way," he says. "They need to say: This is who I am. This is how I got here. But who is going to out himself?"

Later, I go to meet Adair. He expresses similar concerns and seems particularly affected by the emails he received from a gay student, who identified himself in his message only as "one of the guys in your 1pm Christ and Culture class." Adair tells me, "While I'm theologically opposed to having the church affirm same-sex genital expression"—honestly I'd never heard it referred to that way, but okay—"I do believe we need to provide a safer and more caring environment where students don't have to hide. It will be really hard, but it would be really right."

The challenge and the responsibility, Adair believes, is ultimately a matter of education—which means it's a job for him and his colleagues. He reflects on the chapels and shakes his head. "Those chapels went well for heterosexual students. It affirmed their convictions, but they don't even know the basic Bible teachings behind those convictions," he says. "They need to feel pain for those who are crying out, and I don't think they do."

Late one evening at Midnight Oil, a coffeehouse that sits on the very edge of campus, a group of Harding students muse on their feelings about Harding. "We wouldn't be who we are without this place," one says. After one of them pulls up the Jimmy Allen "Shame! SHAME!" sermon on iTunes U and fast-forwards to the bit about long hair, another adds: "I really love it, in a sick, twisted sort of way." Says a third: "There are things about Harding that I really love, and just because there are some things I don't like doesn't mean it hasn't been a major part of my life. There are teachers I love. There are classes I have loved. This is home."

One could easily replace the word *Harding* with "the church," and yet in all my conversations with the *Queer Press*ers, I hear much more love for the university than for the faith on which it's allegedly built. Of the zine staff I spend time with, only Sarah still unequivocally identifies as a Christian. Two others claim to be atheists; a third says, "It's still too painful" to think about faith; and a fourth cryptically identifies himself as a "Christian atheist."

This bothers me, less because they no longer believe in the god of their childhoods—I'm not sure I believe in that god, either—than because they didn't lose their faith so much as have it taken from them. In a denomination that believes in free will, they were stripped of it. They were taught that homosexuality was their key choice, a sinful and eternity-changing choice that put God off-limits to them.

The most remarkable thing is that, despite how Harding has insistently preached this anti-gospel to them, they've been so forgiving of it. They've ended up more easily accepting this institution, which teaches a vision of the world that's all blacks, whites, and dogma, than they have the faith that undergirds it, a faith that, to me, is so much more diverse, able to deal with complexity, and open to addressing the grays of life.

During chapel one morning, Sarah and I have a long and whispered conversation about her struggle to believe and the spiritual whiplash she's suffering because of what she calls her "mood swings of faith." At one point, while reading Sam Harris, the atheist author of *The End of Faith* and *Letter to a Christian Nation*, she was convinced of "how crazy it is to talk to someone you can't see." But inexplicably, her spiritual mood would always surprise her, swinging back toward belief. "When I see someone hurting, I ask God to be with them," she says. "I don't know if that will happen, but I hope it will. I've always known God was there."

Somehow she has managed to separate various strands of religion and faith. For instance, she says, "I don't know if I believe that the reasoning for the common Bible story is what I always thought it was. Like I'm not sure about the whole idea of the Trinity—that just confuses me. But I don't think you have to have it all worked out to have faith. I mean, I don't think you can.

"My faith gives me a reason to love and to serve," Sarah continues. "It's easier for me to say there's something inside me that helps me be a better person, control my anger, be more patient. I just need to find a place that's not like this. I need a group of people who love and respect you no matter what, and who are willing to have dialogue even when you disagree."

Her father has been an unexpected source of wisdom as she has sought to figure out her place in the family of faith. "Every time I complain about the church to my dad, he says, 'The church is not perfect. The church is not God,'" she says with a smile and a sense of serenity that has been otherwise absent from her words. "I know there is someone there. If there weren't, I don't think I could get through this. I don't think everything would be all right."

I've thought that same thing a thousand times: Call us fools, but our faith, our belief in something mysterious and invisible, which very well could be the figment of our hopeful imaginations, is real enough to help us through.

Suddenly, the auditorium swells with several thousand glorious voices, rising up in a stirring a cappella rendition of "The Solid Rock":

"On Christ the solid rock I stand," they sing, "all other ground is sinking sand." It's a beautiful old hymn, belted out with such seeming certitude. And I can't help but wonder how it is that so many people who purport to represent that solid rock actually become the sinking sand, their dogmatism and lovelessness completely swallowing other people's faith.

**@jeffchu** Jeff Chu

Conundrum: How do I find a totally closeted gay Christian to profile?

VIA WEB      FAVORITE      REPLY      DELETE

**@Gaybygrace** Chuck Watson

**@jeffchu** I'm a very strong completely closeted gay christian, only a couple close friends know. I am planning on coming out this year

VIA WEB

---

from: _____@hotmail.com
to: jeff@byjeffchu.com
subject: Hi, "Chuck" from Twitter
Fri, Jul 22, 2011 at 7:55 PM

Hi, thanks for your twitter message, you can reply to this email. My real name is Gideon

—Gideon Eads

*The Lord bless you and keep you*
*The Lord make His face to shine upon you*
*and be gracious to you.*
*The Lord lift up His countenance upon you*
*and give you peace*
Numbers 6:24–26

---

from: jeff@byjeffchu.com
to: _____@hotmail.com
subject: Re: Hi, "Chuck" from Twitter
Fri, Jul 22, 2011 at 8:07 PM

Hi Gideon! Nice to "meet" you.

Where do you live? What kind of church do you attend? Let's start with some of the basics, and then we can go from there.

Here's a brief excerpt from my proposal, so you get a sense of what I am doing with my project.

Look forward to talking with you more.

Best,

Jeff

---

from: _____@hotmail.com
to: jeff@byjeffchu.com
subject: Re: Hi, "Chuck" from Twitter
Fri, Jul 22, 2011 at 9:09 PM

Nice to meet you too! I read through your proposal, and I am excited for the journey you are on!

I was born and raised "in" Kingman, Arizona. My family purchased a large chunk of property about 10 miles north of the town long before I was born, so I grew up kind of in the desert country. I guess I'm a half-and-half boy, part country and part city.

My family has been very strong Christians ever since I can remember. I have had the same mother and father my whole life, they never had a divorce or anything. I have an older brother and a younger sister, who also continue to be amazing people for the Lord. Aside from the minor struggles all families have, I pretty much have a "perfect" family.

I also was raised my entire life in a First Southern Baptist Church, which I am still attending. I rarely ever missed a day of Church, and I was put in a teaching position right out of Youth Group.

I am now 24. I have been in the closet my whole life, which is about how long I've known I was gay, or "different" as I would describe it before I had actual attractions for other boys.

I think that's all the basics I can think of. LOL. Let me know if I forgot anything. God bless

—Gideon Eads

---

from: jeff@byjeffchu.com
to: _____@hotmail.com
subject: Re: Hi, "Chuck" from Twitter
Fri, Jul 22, 2011 at 10:43 PM

Gideon,

Thanks for your email. In your tweet, you suggested you're planning to come out to people soon, right? What is your thinking on that?

Best,
Jeff

---

from: _____@hotmail.com
to: jeff@byjeffchu.com
subject: Re: Hi, "Chuck" from Twitter
Fri, Jul 22, 2011 at 9:09 PM

Yes, I never wanted to "come out" until before I finally settled my faith and my sexuality as being able to co-exist. That was about 2 or 3 years ago, over a long period of time, through praying, reading, and research.

I feel I can't fellowship or really know people through this shell of pretending to be straight. I want to be open to God bringing anyone into my life, whether it's a gay friend who needs support and encouragement, or who can support and encourage me, or a companion/

partner type.

What has held me back from doing this sooner was my fear of rejection. I am surrounded by a sea of people who think being gay is the lowest thing someone can be. They seem to love the straight me so much, will they love the gay me?

Coming out has been something I have prayed over for a very long time, and I feel God is leading me to make the move here soon, probably within the next few months. I'm waiting on Him for the "right time." I only know that every time I consider it in prayer or revise my coming-out letter, the fear of everything I had before begins to melt away, a little more each time, replaced with a little more courage. I want to be honest with everyone with who I am, even if that means total rejection from the ones I love most.

—Gideon Eads

# STRUGGLING

"Thou didst attempt wrong ways to be rid of thy burden, whereas thou shouldst have stayed till thy Prince had taken it off."

—PART I, THE FOURTH STAGE, *THE PILGRIM'S PROGRESS*

# EXIT STRATEGY, PART I

## Exodus International's Reorientation Ministry

---

*Orlando, Florida; Irvine, California*

"Coming out" is an overly reductive term, as if at one moment you're in the closet and then the next, you're not. For most of us, that's not how it happens. The process of revelation is more like an Advent calendar, where you open door after door, behind each of which is a different element of identity. For me, the public opening up about my sexuality began in the spring of 2005, when I was working on an independent research project at Princeton University. My grant funded an investigation of the history of complaint in America, but the focus of my research in those months was really me. I needed that time to open some of my own Advent-calendar doors to myself.

When I began telling people that maybe I wasn't straight—and it really was that oblique, not a rainbow-flag-wearing "I'm here, I'm queer" declaration—I first told two of my best friends (one a Christian, one not). I knew Beth and T would be accepting, so they were safe starters, good practice for the tougher ones.

The first of those "tougher ones" was a wonderful and devout couple, Clay and Anne, who served as unofficial campus chaplains to evangelical students at Princeton. One night, I went over to their home and my news came washing out on gushers of tears. I'm not even sure what I said, but it got the point across: I more than liked guys. Clay and Anne embraced me. They cried with me. They prayed with me. They prayed for me. I especially remember Anne's soft and otherworldly voice—that voice that, I used to joke with my friends, was a holy hotline to God—calling for divine protection and comfort.

After the amen, Anne suggested that I look into a ministry called Exodus, the world's largest organization for those who are "struggling with same-sex attraction." I nodded, but that nod was a lie, and even in that season of overwhelming confusion and uncertainty, when I was confident of almost nothing, I knew it was a lie. I knew what I knew about Exodus. I knew I had fought and fought, and I wasn't going to fight anymore. No way was I going to be part of an organization that would tell me, as another chaplain had, that I was "undisciplined" and "sexually unruly." (That sounded a lot more fun to me than anything resembling my reality.) It wanted to change me—its tagline, after all, was "Change is possible." But I knew that, short of a lightning strike from God Almighty, that transformation wouldn't happen.

The hugely controversial organization Exodus International is less a single ministry than an umbrella. The Orlando, Florida–based not-for-profit organizes one national conference each year and a few regional ones, while its grassroots work is handled by its 120 affiliate ministries. Some of these are connected to churches: large, influential ones including Boston's Park Street Church, the Victory World Church in Atlanta, and Mariners Church in Southern California have Exodus affiliates. Others are independent outfits focused on sexuality and healing.

Applying to be part of its network is a two-year process. It has requirements including oversight from a governing board; regular attendance at major Exodus conferences; the payment of a membership fee of $250 a year; and the somewhat less auditable demand that directors abstain from homosexual activity. Meet all these, and you can be listed on its website. Other than that, Exodus doesn't keep a tight grip on its affiliates, which vary in size and approach.

If you're pro-Exodus, chances are you believe that homosexual behavior—and perhaps homosexual desire—is a choice that can be controlled and perhaps even conquered.* The Mosaic imagery associated with the word *exodus* may evoke thoughts of divine aid, of a journey to the spiritual Promised Land. You likely also see "gay" not as a legitimate, immutable identity but as a lifestyle.

If you're anti-Exodus, you probably believe gay people were born that way.† You also likely think the work of organizations like Exodus is, at best, a flat-earth-style joke and, at worst, a harmful lie that helps perpetuate the idea that change is possible.

Neither of these positions seems to satisfy longtime Exodus president Alan Chambers. "That we are focused on changing someone's sexual orientation is probably the number one misconception about Exodus these days," Chambers says when I reach him by phone at his Orlando office. "We are not a ministry that's converting people to heterosexuality. The opposite of homosexuality is not heterosexuality. It's holiness." Chambers makes his argument from a curious position, since he is often identified publicly as a former homosexual. (He shies from that language himself, though he does attempt to clarify for me: "I don't struggle with wanting to be in relationship with a man. I don't have any draw whatsoever toward gay life. There's not one iota of a temptation for a gay relationship or a sexual relationship for a man.")

---

* Thirty-six percent of Americans polled by the Pew Forum on Religious Life in 2012 said homosexuality can be changed. Fifty-two percent of white evangelicals and 58 percent of black Protestants polled agreed. Interestingly, only 31 percent of Catholics agreed.

† Since 1977, the Gallup Organization has regularly asked the same question in its polling: In your view, is being gay or lesbian something a person is born with or due to factors such as upbringing and environment? In 1977, 13 percent responded "born with" and 56 percent said "upbringing/environment." In 2011, the numbers had shifted to 40 percent "born with" and 42 percent "upbringing/environment."

Chambers traces his homosexual desires back to "gender insecurity" in childhood—being called a sissy numerous times by his dad, being teased endlessly by his peers in school, being sexually abused by an older boy. In his book, *Leaving Homosexuality*, he chronicles how he "decided to participate in gay life"—an oddly stilted way of referring to his lifestyle, which consisted largely of drinking and pursuing sex, a combo he calls "the hunt": "Going to the bars was my feeding ground, and men were my prey."

After his sister-in-law invited him to attend Discovery Church in Orlando, he was set on a path out of homosexuality. In 1996, he met his wife, Leslie, with whom he now has two children. "Where I once viewed my love of design, decorating, and music as 'gay,' she thinks [these] are fine attributes for her man," he writes. "I had allowed the enemy, through the world, to tell me I was something I wasn't simply because I wasn't stereotypically male."

"My temptations are different today than they used to be," he tells me. "Do I notice what is attractive? Of course. Beauty is beauty. To see an attractive man is to see an attractive man in the same way as I used to see an attractive man, but the temptation to sexualize that isn't there for me anymore."

He is insulted by those who assert that he is fooling himself, that he's hiding in a reconstructed closet made of heterosexual marriage. "To say I should accept who I really am and come out and leave my wife and family is like telling me to rip out the core of who I am and"—and this is the important part—"who I want to be."

Chambers constantly and subtly makes value judgments about homosexuality's inferiority. He says, "The life I am living—and this is my experience with my closest of friends, who have struggled with same-sex attractions and who are married—is a more authentic relationship that is more the core of who they are than the life that they tried to make work when they were pursuing homosexuality." Or this: "I lived a portion of my life trying to pursue homosexuality, trying to pursue gay life, trying to make that work . . . [but] I was more than that attraction. What I have found in my relationship with my wife is a pure attraction, a pure desire, a more satisfying emotional, physical, spiritual, relational connection than I found when I was pursuing gay life."

So it seems that Chambers got super unlucky with the guys he met—who hasn't been there? But he also bases his sweeping assessment of homosexual "lifestyles" on a falsely narrow sample: his own limited dabbling in what one might call gay-bar life, because it's certainly not fair to call it gay life. This is his story and it is his right to tell it as he sees it, but to hold up that one experience as some kind of widely applicable norm is misguided.

Chambers does acknowledge that the change that has been possible in his own life—a fulfilling heterosexual marriage and a near-total reduction in homosexual temptation—is by no means guaranteed or even likely for everyone who joins an Exodus group. "This is my experience. I believe it is an experience that others can have," he says. "But I don't think it's the majority or the norm. People who have a relationship with Christ believe that in Christ all things are possible, but more often than not, the struggles that we have or the proclivities we are faced with don't automatically go away."

"The issue of converting people or curing people, that was never a part of the language or the landscape of Exodus," Chambers insists. The most he will allow is that "there was a period of time where the tagline 'Change Is Possible' wasn't explained as well as we've tried to explain it in the last five years. I think that probably there was some ambiguity and probably some purposeful ambiguity in a way that isn't there today. We try to be very clear what we believe change is and what it looks like."

These misconceptions have a simple source: Exodus itself. Shortly after I spoke with Chambers, I went to the Exodus website, where I found links to articles about the successes of "reorientation therapy" and to Web pages with titles like "Healing Homosexuality: Case Stories of Reparative Therapy." (The latter is maintained by the much-vilified National Association for Research & Therapy of Homosexuality, aka NARTH, perhaps the world's leading proponent of reorientation therapy.)* Despite what Alan Chambers says, other people who were involved with the organization long before he was told me that Exodus did preach conversion to heterosexuality. And Exodus has in the past helped to fund studies to show the possibility of change; the most recent, whose results were published in 2009 by professors at two Christian institutions, Stanton Jones of Wheaton College and Mark Yarhouse of Regent University, found that 23 percent of Exodus participants in the study sample reported a change of sexual orientation and 30 percent reported "a reduction in homosexual orientation and behavioral chastity."

More and more Christians who have been active on this issue have been shifting their positions. Most recently, Warren Throckmorton, a psychologist and professor at Grove City College, which the Princeton Review named the second-least gay-friendly university in America (Wheaton College in Illinois was number one), repudiated his former support for reorientation therapy and cut his ties with NARTH.

One of the earliest to switch sides was Michael Bussee, an Exodus cofounder. We meet for breakfast one warm morning near his home in Riverside, California.

When he was twenty-one and married, with one young daughter, Bussee became a volunteer for a suicide hotline run by Melodyland Christian Center in Anaheim, a conservative, charismatic church "where Jesus was scheduled to do healings on Thursdays," he says. There he was introduced to "the first gay person I've ever met. Jim Kaspar was a former homosexual, a white man with an afro," Bussee recalls. "He was very, very effeminate. I actually don't know how he considered himself a former homosexual. We became very good

---

* In the months after my interview, the Exodus website was rejiggered and many of these links disappeared.

friends, and we decided to put together training for volunteers on how to respond to gay callers."

This was a fateful decision: Even though the pair had zero training, they were suddenly deemed experts in how to reach gay people and convert them not only to the Christian faith but also to heterosexuality. Jim had come out of the gay community, but Michael had never even been to a gay bar. In 1974, they launched a Tuesday evening Bible study for men struggling with homosexuality, and the ministry was dubbed the Ex-Gay Intervention Team (EXIT). It quickly became a full-fledged program with one-on-one counseling, small-group sessions, and prayer meetings. Not too long after that, Pat Robertson invited someone from the ministry to appear on his show *The 700 Club*, which the church took to be a sure sign of divine blessing.

Melodyland began hearing from other, similar ministries, including Outpost in Minneapolis, Love In Action in the San Francisco Bay Area, and EAGLE (Ex-Active Gay Liberated Eternally) in El Paso, Texas. In September 1976, the leaders of these ministries gathered for a conference in Anaheim, where they decided to form a loose coalition. "Someone came up with the name Exodus, and we had this grandiose vision that we were going to lead hundreds of thousands of people out of the gay lifestyle. I felt called," Bussee says. "There was a feeling of liberation, because we were working on our issues."

The exhilaration gave way, over subsequent months, to exhaustion and exasperation, especially in the Tuesday evening group. Many of the participants were seeing no decline in their same-sex attractions. Some were dropping out. Bussee says that one member, who had seemed to the leaders to be a success story, went crazy; he went home from church one Tuesday, took a razor blade to his penis, and poured Drano on the wounds.

A further, more personal complication for Bussee: He was in love with Gary Cooper, a ministry volunteer who was also ex-gay and married with kids. En route to lead a seminar on ex-gay ministry in Indianapolis in 1979, they confessed their love for each other. "We knew we would need to go home and come out to our wives and our families," Bussee recalls. Upon his return, Bussee told his wife, Ann, that he was in love with someone else. She already knew. "Is it Gary?" she asked. Gary told his wife that same night.

In the world of Exodus, the official line was that both Michael and Gary had relapsed. "It was a lie," Michael says, because they were never truly ex-gay in the first place. But he was in no position to argue his point publicly. In 1982, the couple had a commitment ceremony ("My mom said it was worse than my dad dying of leukemia," Michael says, "and that she wanted to drive her car off a cliff"), staying together until Gary died of AIDS in 1992.

"People try to present [Exodus] as a hate group, but they're really not," Bussee says. "They're based in homophobia, but they don't preach hate." This is a distinction that isn't made often enough. Fear isn't always hate-based and hate isn't always fear-based. Homophobia isn't the same as anti-gay sentiment; they can accompany one another, but they don't always. "Most of them are loving, gracious people with strong faith. Their understanding of the Bible is that homosexuality is a symptom of the brokenness that resulted from the Fall. They have had to refine their message. Originally, it truly was that the change process would take place. Experience has taught them that is not true. Now they say the opposite of homosexuality isn't heterosexuality. It's holiness."

While he continues to criticize the work of Exodus, he can turn tender when he thinks back to the genesis days. "We meant well," he says softly. "We really did. And I think they still do."

There are two key truths in Michael's assessment of Exodus. First, the organization has changed with the times—to a degree. Second, it will always be difficult to have a real dialogue when there's a fundamental disagreement with what homosexuality is. Does it rise to the level of immutable identity—or at least an aspect of identity? Or is it just a bad habit, a behavior that can be mitigated or conquered? Is it an expression of what God has made—and therefore an element of human diversity that Christ calls us to embrace? Or is it a manifestation of the world's brokenness—the very thing that Christ came to heal?

In 2011, Justin Lee, the founder of an online community called the Gay Christian Network (GCN), attended the annual Exodus International conference. For years, he had avoided it, believing Exodus to be an organization that demeaned people like him—those with the conviction that the Christian faith and homosexuality are not mutually exclusive. He found an atmosphere that was more welcoming and less judgmental than he expected.

Over the years, he maintained a respectful, if distant and occasional, conversation with Alan Chambers, and in late 2011, Alan asked if Justin might allow him to attend the Gay Christian Network's upcoming conference, which was being held not far from Alan's Orlando home.

Justin knew that many of the conference attendees had gone through Exodus ministries; some were still bitter about it. At the same time, he has cultivated GCN as a community where Christians of all convictions can come for conversation, even if they disagree. After considerable debate and discussion, he and Alan agreed to a compromise: a panel discussion that would not be listed on the official conference program. Justin would moderate, and he would also invite Wendy Gritter, Jeremy Marks, and John Smid, three former Exodus leaders who now oppose the work of ex-gay ministries.

In his opening statement, Justin spoke of his own ambivalence. "One part of me is like, I want to look at the world through Alan's perspective. . . . I respect that you're trying to do what you think is right, even though I disagree with you," he said. "There's another part of me that's like, I'm really angry. I'm *really* angry about a lot of things that have happened in Exodus and other ex-gay ministries and I kind of want to have a big fight with Alan onstage. And I feel torn." He acknowledged that many people were nervous about the session, but said, "We're going to try to do this as lovingly as we can and as honestly as we can."

Throughout the two-and-a-half-hour conversation, the other panelists pushed Chambers on various points of Exodus practice and policy: allowing "misleading" language, tolerating misrepresentation of the possibility of change, using the tagline "Change is possible," equating the word *gay* with promiscuity, and helping convince parents and families of gay people that orientation is changeable.

Chambers surprised the crowd by acknowledging that "the majority of people I have met—and I would say the majority meaning ninety-nine-point-nine percent of them—have not experienced a change in their orientation or gotten to a place where they could say they could never be tempted or are not tempted in some way or experience some level of same-sex attraction." In other words, reorientation hasn't happened.

The entire conversation, even during the spells of disagreement, was polite and cordial. Not so the subsequent discussion online, especially on a website called exgaywatch.com, which is devoted to opposing Exodus's every move. One of their commenters called Chambers a "rainbow colored lisping gay duck."

The angry online responses make clear that many of Exodus's so-called survivors won't be content with coexistence or toleration. They want Exodus not only to shut down but also to repent, and that repentance has to look and feel like a full embrace of gay and lesbian Christians.

The philosopher-priest Henri Nouwen, in his searingly honest journal *The Road to Daybreak*, writes of the transformative year before he joined a L'Arche community of disabled people in Ontario. Nouwen, a celibate homosexual, was a needy, affection-hungry man. Whenever he perceived rejection, he could be petulant. He demanded of one friend: "Why didn't you call me? Why didn't you write me? Why didn't you visit me?"

One day, Nouwen had a long meeting with his spiritual director, Pere Thomas, about this yearning, and in his journal entry for that

day—Thursday, October 17, 1985—he wrote some stunningly contemporary commentary:

> [F]or many of us in this highly psychologied culture, af-
> fection has become the central concern. We have come to
> judge ourselves in terms of the affection that is given or re-
> fused to us. The media—television, radio, magazines, and
> advertisements—have strongly reinforced the idea that human
> affection is what we really need. Being loved, liked, appreci-
> ated, praised, acknowledged, recognized, etc.—these are the
> most desired prize of life. The lack of these forms of affection
> can throw us into an abyss of loneliness and depression, and
> even lead us to suicide.

The next day, Nouwen added some more insights, noting that
"much church discussion today focuses on the morality of human
behavior: premarital sex, divorce, homosexuality, birth control,
abortion, and so on. Many people here become disillusioned with
the church because of these issues." But, he continues, this focus on
morality diverts attention from "the life of the heart," a term he uses
for one's relationship with God.

"The heart is much wider and deeper than our affections," he
writes. "It is before and beyond the distinctions between sorrow and
joy, anger and lust, fear and love. It is the place where all is one in
God, the place where we truly belong."

The power in these passages rests in how Nouwen identifies a
weak spot in himself—one that many of us can find in ourselves,
too—and gently diagnoses a problem of locus and focus. His words
crystallize for me the distraction of ego, of the need for validation on
the human plane, and how that can avert our gaze from the divine.

So while the anger among those who have suffered because of
organizations such as Exodus makes sense, to channel it as they do—
through online tirades, vehement criticisms of anyone who doesn't
adequately condemn the ex-gay movement, and haughty statements

identifying the alleged foolishness of anyone who sees even vague merits in anything that comes out of Alan Chambers's mouth—helps nothing, heals nothing, and draws nobody closer to God.

As Nouwen so eloquently writes, "God's unlimited love allows us to be deeply involved with the suffering of the world without being swallowed up by it." In that spirit, I went to Seattle, to understand better what it is that compels those who run Exodus at the grass roots.

# EXIT STRATEGY, PART II

## A Visit to an Exodus Group

*Kirkland, Washington*

Pilgrimage is tiring. By the time I depart for Seattle, I'm several months into the journey. My body is weary. My soul is almost physically heavy. My spirit feels at once honored to have been entrusted with so many stories, and burdened with the responsibility of accounting for each person and each family's insecurities, theological hang-ups, and biases. But as the plane descends on Seattle, I feel an inexplicable lightness. The sun—the sun!—sparkles on Puget Sound, and the land below looks comfortingly like an afghan, the grays of the cityscape knit together by the greens of the trees.

From the airport, I drive out to Kirkland, just east of Seattle, a town best known as Costco's birthplace. A ministry called Tower of Light is based in a Baptist church in Kirkland, though the church's pastor asked that it not be named; while it supports the ministry, it didn't want this work to overshadow everything else it does.

Tower of Light is led by Jeff Simunds, a fifty-year-old Micro-soft retiree and full-time volunteer who has long "struggled with same-sex attraction." Jeff runs two groups, one on Tuesday evenings that's exclusively for men with same-sex attraction and another on Wednesday with a curriculum, called Living Waters, that's targeted more broadly at men and women suffering from what the church calls "sexual brokenness."

The rigorously structured men's small group typically draws five to seven guys. The session opens with a couple of worship songs and prayer. Next, they talk about the previous week's reading—usually a chapter from a two-volume series called *Taking Back Ground*. Finally, they go around the room and do what Jeff calls an "accountability check-in," with each member updating the group on how things are going and anything specific that he might be struggling with.

Jeff sees this as a recovery group, not a support group or a circle of friends. To him this distinction is crucial—and it's the basis for the strict rules that attendees must agree to. They may not ask questions of each other. They may not offer advice. "If that happens, people might push someone to probe deeper than he wants to go, and he might shut down completely," Jeff explains as we sit in his office, one wall of which is painted bright orange, in rebuttal against the usually gray Seattle skies. "If he says something and four people start giving advice, he might shut down completely." They are urged to focus on their own circumstances when they share—"I" and "me" statements, not "we" or "you" or "us" statements. "In a recovery group, you are here to work on your own issues, not other people and their issues," Jeff says. "Also, crosstalk can start developing emotional ties. They can get too interested in each other's stories."

If it's all about "I" and "me," why not just one-on-one counseling? "If you tell your counselor, 'I can't believe I did this, but I've had sex with forty guys,' and he accepts you, that's one level of shame that you're dealing with," he says. "You tell six guys in a group who owe you nothing and they accept you, that helps deal with more of your shame. It's about being known." (And yet not too known.)

Profanity is discouraged. "I ask they keep any verbiage regarding sex or body parts to what they would find in a biology book," Jeff says. "It keeps things more professional. If someone says, 'One of the things I struggle with is I think I have a small penis,' that's easier for guys to hear than, 'I have a really small dick.'"

Members may not exchange phone numbers or email addresses, nor may they meet outside of group. "These guys need to develop friendships with guys who are heterosexual, not same-sex-attracted guys," he says. "These boundaries encourage them to go out to their churches, join a men's group, and get friendships out there, not with other guys who are similarly broken." And while this may seem like a given, the group is only for those who genuinely "struggle" with unwanted same-sex attraction. "One person who had been on the fence about homosexuality announced to the group, 'I've made up my mind! I'm pursuing guys!' But he wanted to continue coming to group," Jeff says. "I had to ask him not to come. It's difficult for guys who are trying not to go out and have sex with guys to have someone there who's happily going out and pursuing them."

The group is modeled on one that Jeff attended in the mid-1990s at a now-defunct Seattle-area Exodus affiliate called Metanoia. He landed there after a circuitous, soul-wrenching journey. Raised in what he calls "very much a Christian bubble," which included not just church but also Christian school, Jeff says all his crushes growing up "were for girls." Guys, he says, were "more of a curiosity, not a strong attraction."

When he was in his early twenties, he says, a guy in his Bible study "seduced me. We were involved for a few months, and then I cut it off. But at that point, my attractions were more reinforced toward guys. My world was completely rocked. I was like, 'What have we done?' I was horrified. Horrified!" While he insists he abstained from anything physical after that, porn became his outlet after the emergence of the Internet in the early 1990s. "I had two major bouts with it, bookending a decade," he says, "and I had a boatload of shame about it." His most porn-free period was the five years he spent backpacking around the world after his retirement from Microsoft, because he didn't have much Internet access. But once he was home, it became a habit again, and at one point "I contemplated suicide. Better to do that than sin ten thousand times. But then I wasn't sure I could go to heaven if I did that. So I'd pray every night, 'God, take me home tonight!' Heart attacks run in my family, so it would just have been a minor miracle. It wasn't asking for much. But then I'd wake up every morning."

Finally, Jeff found Metanoia and made a deal with God. "I said, 'I will dedicate a year to working on this,'" he recalls. He did no other work or travel. He went to counseling weekly, read, prayed, and delved into the whys, hows, and whats of his struggle. He quit masturbating—which, he says, "was hell on earth for the first three months." He also joined a Metanoia recovery group. "The first time, I was petrified. Completely utterly petrified," he says. "I can still picture it. I remember walking into the room, being scared to death. I had to talk about some of the really shameful stuff, and I remember sobbing. But it was so encouraging to hear other people's stories, to hear other people wanting to follow Jesus. To know that I wasn't alone."

Group became the one place where Jeff felt wholly himself. "A couple of months into it, I noticed that I'd drive away and I'd get this heartache. It was a physical pain in my chest. I was like, 'Why am I getting this?'" he says. Was it the heart attack he had long prayed for? That seemed like perverse timing. "Then it dawned on me that I was leaving this place where I was completely utterly known—I was me!—and going back into this fake, plastic world."

At Metanoia, Jeff made a connection that would prove transformative: He traced the roots of his homosexual desire to what he unfortunately calls his "father wound." "I grew up really distant from my dad," he says. "I grew up hating my dad, actually. In group, I wrote a list of everything I hated my dad for, and I spent months working through it. I would spend time on each painful memory. I would go back and get in touch with that hurt and pain I felt as a kid. And then I would invite Jesus to be with me—he was there, and he saw it all—and I'd give him my bitterness and hatred for my dad for that one specific thing. I'd forgive my dad for that."

The result of Jeff's "father wound" was a skewed view of masculinity. As he puts it, "When we don't know we're men, we try to acquire manhood. Love of baseball and football. Ripped body parts. But then I went to Scripture and said, 'God, what do you say about what it means to be a man?' I'd go through each item—I probably had a hundred things—and say, 'I just repent of using playing baseball to define me as a man. Help me to know the core of who I am that's relevant.'"

After Metanoia wound down its Seattle-area operations in 2002, Jeff's church asked him to lead a small group for people struggling with homosexuality. At first he resisted. But he thought back to his own shame and how Metanoia helped him work through it. He also realized that "most people aren't going to spend a year of their lives focused on this twenty-four hours a day." They'd need help. And that glimmer grew into Tower of Light.

In our first few hours together and especially while he is telling his own story, Jeff repeatedly uses the phrase "in the gay lifestyle." I point out that there are all kinds of homosexuals leading all kinds of lifestyles. He demurs, but only briefly.

So, I ask, what does "the gay lifestyle" mean to him, if he has never lived it? "Homosexual is more the orientation, gay is more the lifestyle," he replies. "I wouldn't call someone with same-sex attraction 'gay.' That means highly effeminate, hitting all the bars and being on the scene. Of course, women in general tend to be far more monogamous. They tend to get a partner and emotionally enmesh. Men tend to have more of that cannibalistic drive, looking for more partners and being more out in the party scene than the women."

By his definition, I am either not gay or maybe mostly lesbian.

"I believe same-sex attraction is brokenness in our lives," Jeff says. "And I believe God wants to bring healing for our brokenness. What does healing look like? Sometimes life is like a forest fire and a whole hill is burning out of control. Over time, as you work on the issues that drive those attractions, the frequency and intensity can start to die down. Over time, who knows? Maybe that raging fire becomes a medium fire. If that happens, praise God. That's awesome! For some guys, it becomes a low fire. If that happens, praise God. That's awesome! Or it becomes embers. If that happens, praise God. That's awesome! For a few guys, it totally goes out, but for most guys, it doesn't. That's okay, because the attractions aren't sin anyway. It's what you do with them."

Jeff refers to the teachings of controversial Connecticut psycho-therapist Joseph Nicolosi, who believes that everyone is heterosexual. "It's just that some of us have a condition of same-sex attraction, of brokenness," Jeff says. "God has made all of us to be heterosexual, and some of us are just broken in this way."

His sweepingly emphatic diagnosis comes to mind when I meet with Jeff's supervisor, Lupe Maple, who oversees all the church's counseling and recovery ministries, including Tower of Light. She knows that Tower of Light is out of step with what much of the rest of the world believes about human sexuality. "It's an anything-goes kind of culture right now," she says. "Any restriction on impulsivity is frowned upon. People who are twenty-five and virgins are weird!"

Lupe was never a twenty-five-year-old virgin: Her life journey has been beyond turbulent, from her confused gender identity and teenage promiscuity with both men and women to drug addiction, an abortion, a pregnancy that ended with her giving up a baby for adoption, and her eventual healing and marriage. Like Jeff, she has found her salvation and mission in Jesus. "I'm an expert in being forgiven," she says with a laugh. "And I do believe Jesus is the way. I believe what the Bible says."

But what strikes me is that where Jeff sees black and white, Lupe lives among the grays. Her path has given her not only an appreciation for God's mercy but also a belief in God's ability to handle the complexity of human experience. "It's really hard for Christians to think in grays," she says. "Black and white makes God small and manageable. It squeezes the mystery out of God. It makes him easy to follow. But Christian maturity is partly about living in the tension of not knowing, and it's okay not to be sure."

When I ask Lupe whether she believes that people can seek godly answers honestly and yet end up in different places, her eyes brim.

"I'm tearing up because you're getting to the crux of the mystery of God, and I guess I can't answer that question. It's messy. I can't say that if someone ends up in a different place, they're not honestly wrestling," she replies as she wipes her eyes. "All I can say is that God knows the heart."


Like every other man I meet at Tower of Light, a fifty-year-old husband and father of four whom I'll call "Tommy" begins his story by talking about his experience of "father wound." When Tommy was young, his dad, who "suffered from mental illness and was abusive toward my mother," converted to Mormonism. "I think whatever irritated my mother was what he wanted to do, because he was really agnostic."

Tommy, who says he is drawn to both women and men, remembers feeling attracted to other guys as soon as he hit puberty, and he fooled around with a neighbor kid. "But I couldn't bring myself to even think I was gay. I just liked sex a lot, and I didn't care if it was boys," he says. Nobody would have suspected anyway, because he was a guy's guy. He didn't date a lot, but he played basketball and football. Motocross racing became his passion.

Tommy, whose mom had taken him to Methodist and Presbyterian churches, found God for himself at nineteen and eventually went to work for a missions organization in Texas, where he met his wife. "To some degree, I was physically attracted, but I don't think I was driven by that the way some men are. I really wanted to be married. I wanted to have kids," he says. After they married, things seemed to be fine. The sex was good; they had two children.

To earn extra money to support his growing family, Tommy took a part-time job about an hour and a half away, in Dallas. "One time, coming back from work, I stopped at a rest stop to use the bathroom. And this man came on to me. I didn't do anything that time, but it awoke a sleeping giant in me," he says. "It just became a regular pattern, a weekly thing. I would stop and see if someone was there. For months, it was just looking. Then for months, it was just touching and then thinking, 'Oh no! Don't do that again!' Then it went in circles: Falling. Repenting. Guilt. Moving on. Falling."

Tommy says he was exclusively interested in older, father-figure types, and after he moved his family to Seattle and he and his wife had two more children, his search for anonymous sex expanded to other places—parks, restrooms, wherever. His guilt grew, too. "I knew if I kept on this path, I would not make it. My faith was not going to make it. My marriage wasn't going to make it. My family wasn't going to make it," he says. "I absolutely loved my wife. Our marriage wasn't perfect, but I absolutely loved her."

Finally, in late 2000, he decided it was time for a life reboot. He started going to a support group for men: "I told the guys I'd been struggling with same-sex issues for the past ten years, and it was overwhelming." The admission was liberating and propelled him on a cleanup course. As part of that, though he had only had intercourse with a man once—"and it was protected," he says—he decided to get checked for sexually transmitted diseases. The HIV test came back positive.

"In my mind, I was a dead man. Did I infect my wife? Were my kids infected? That night I went home, and I felt like I was experiencing insanity—no sleep, guilt, remorse. I called my pastor, and I shared everything with him. The next night I decided to go ahead and tell my wife everything after the kids went to bed. I said to her, 'Obviously, if you want to leave me, I give you full freedom to do that. And if you want me to leave, I fully understand that.' She was in shock. She asked lots and lots of questions. And then I went to sleep."

The next morning, when he woke up, his wife was sitting on the bed with a guitar, singing worship songs. She looked at him and said, "I don't know what the future holds, but we're going to do it together." (One of the first things she did was to be checked for HIV herself. The test came back negative.)

Tommy continued to attend a group for men with same-sex attractions and got medical advice about his HIV. One day he went to a clinic to have his immune system checked. The results, he says, prompted the nurse to tell him to get retested for HIV, because she was surprised by how strong his counts were. "It was negative. And a month later, it was still negative. And six months later, it was still negative," he says.

There could be scientific explanations for what happened. The original test could have been a false positive, which, with the least reliable HIV test, occurs in 1.5 percent of cases. There could have been a mix-up with the samples, although the clinic contacted the others who were tested around the same time and all retested negative. But Tommy insists it was something else: "I believe God can heal, and I believe he did heal. I do believe I was positive and now I am not. But even if it was something else, I don't think it makes or breaks it. This has been wonderful. It has helped me to create different habits and to get healthy in other ways."

Today, he says, his same-sex attractions are almost irrelevant. "It used to define me, and now it's just not an issue for the most part, especially when I'm abiding in the Word. Life has moved on. But all this has shown me I am just as able to be a victim of sin, a proponent of sin, and a perpetrator of sin as anyone else," says Tommy, who now works as a prison guard. "Every guy that comes through the prison door, it helps me not to have the same disdain that I might have once had. None of this is because of who I am. It's all God."

Only one person I meet at Tower of Light has ever fully engaged in what Jeff Simunds would call "the gay lifestyle," and that person happens to be a no-nonsense, middle-aged woman whom I'll call "Pam."

Pam grew up in southern Idaho. She moved to Seattle just after college to pursue an engineering career, and at her new church she met the woman who would become her girlfriend. That relationship was the most wonderful thing that could have happened, and it was the most terrible thing that could have happened. "We were both in the same church!" Pam says. "I was living the dual lifestyle. I felt like I had a divided heart. I did feel that it wasn't right, but I remember very clearly, saying to God: 'I am going to do this.'"

The relationship lasted for five years, and as Pam explains it, the end came suddenly and supernaturally. She had become close friends with a man in her office, "a very godly man—I call him my spiritual dad. He helped me walk out of this relationship. We were at work one day, and he just knelt in his office and prayed. He cried out to God on my behalf. Nobody had ever done that for me," she says, her voice swelling with emotion as if this had just happened last week, not twenty years ago. "Within two weeks, she had found a new job and a new lover and left the state. It was such an answer to prayer."

Convinced that God was nudging her in a new direction, Pam started going to Metanoia—the same Exodus affiliate where Jeff Simunds went—in the fall of 1993. "If Jesus can raise the dead, make a blind man see, make the lame walk, he could certainly rearrange this," she says, as casually as if the components of sexuality were living room furniture that simply needed to be shifted to make the room right. "There, I found some of the roots of why I was attracted to women, and I invited Jesus to come in and heal them."

She lists some examples.

Her family of eight—alcoholic, nonpracticing Mormon, truck driver father; Catholic mother; six kids—meant "too many kids and not enough Mom."

"My father wanted a boy. I was their second girl. He treated me like a boy." (This included sometimes not allowing her to bathe.)

"My mom didn't treat me like a daughter. She was twenty-one when she had me, and she would call me Sis."

A history of abuse at the hands of men, including not only emotional torment from her father but also sexual molestation from a male babysitter.

This seems to be the female version of "father wound," compounded by the way Pam was treated during her season of attempted rearrangement: Twice, she says, she was kicked out of churches.

The first was an Evangelical Free Church congregation. "Some really neat people in that church tried to help me," she says. The senior pastor was not one of them. He told her that she would never change her lesbianism, nor would she serve in that church. Her response: "Apparently, my God is bigger than your God."

The second was a church of the Conservative Baptist Association. Oddly, she says, "they wanted me in counseling to accept my homosexuality." Not that they wanted her to act on it—they wanted her just to acknowledge it. "I said that I didn't want to accept it, but they wanted me to be more confrontational about it. There was gossip, and I started being ostracized."

For years after that, Pam's prayer was constant: *Change me, God, change me.* She was wrestling with all the emotional scar tissue of her childhood, with her identity as a woman, with what femininity meant to her. Slowly, she realized her prayer was changing, her expectations shifting. "I came to a point where I said, 'God, regardless of whether my feelings change or not, I will follow you,'" she says. "And when I told God this, I felt change. It was like I was going through puberty in my thirties. I remember going to a Christian conference, and at the end of the day, the Lord says, 'How was your day?' And I thought, I was checking out the men! There is that hymn 'Turn Your Eyes Upon Jesus,' and in the first verse, it talks about 'the light of his glory and his grace.' I saw this become true in my life. I don't have those attractions at all anymore. God has healed me."

Today Pam helps teach the Living Waters course at Tower of Light. Despite the diversity of the people who come through the program, she sees one major commonality. "We're all sexual beings. This is a healing and discipleship ministry that deals mainly with sexual brokenness—of all kinds," she says. "Everybody walks a different path, but do I believe God can heal? I do. Some people will believe this, and some people won't. That's okay. This is my story."

It's dark, cold, and drizzly by the time I get to my last interview in Seattle, with a young man named Bryan. As amazed as I've been by the stories I've been hearing, they've also felt distant. As a journalist, you get used to forging conversation with people of totally different backgrounds, but it always feels a little like coming home when you find things in common with your interviewee. I hear echoes of my story in his—Bryan, too, is a son of Chinese immigrants, did the fancy-college thing, achieved parent-pleasing professional success. Also, he's the first person I meet in Seattle who confesses that he has never been attracted to girls.

Bryan has participated in both kinds of groups offered by Tower of Light. "I learned a lot, but I wouldn't say I came out of it a free man walking out of the homosexual situation," he says. But he did buy into the "father wound" theory of homosexual origins: "My dad was frequently absent from home, because he was working on overseas ventures. I didn't really have a male role model." (At times, I had a somewhat distant relationship with my incredibly hardworking dad, too, but by this cause-and-effect formulation, homosexuality should be much more prevalent in societies where fathers are traditionally less involved—and there's no evidence that is the case.)

He's humble about his Calvinist leanings. "I think I buy into it because it's what was taught to me when I was most impressionable. It basically says that God is in control, that He made me who I am, that He knew me from the get-go, that He ordained the circumstances in which I find myself," he says. "I love the idea that God is fully sovereign." I, too, understand the appeal of believing in that kind of God, because what's better than someone who has a grand plan when you feel so out of control of your own circumstances?

"I feel romantic feelings and lustful feelings for men," Bryan confesses, though he says he has never had sex. "I've acted on my feelings in fantasizing and masturbating with Internet porn." A guilty look floods his face. "I'd do it, knowing I was abusing God's grace." When he was in college, he became close with another Christian guy who was wrestling with these issues of theology and sexuality. "We really enjoyed hanging out with each other. It felt good to be desired," he says. "But I just couldn't reconcile it with what I believed, and I told him I wasn't ready to declare anything." He looks a little wistful, a little sad. "We met sophomore year. He's an Episcopalian. It still is hard for me. Now that he has decided it's okay, we fundamentally disagree on something that's so core to our beings."

Maybe it's a generational thing, or maybe it's an experiential one, but when I ask him what he thinks of the phrase "in the gay lifestyle," he looks puzzled. "For me, it actually encompasses numerous lifestyles. It's the clubbing guys, but it also includes monogamous same-sex relationships between people who would marry if they could. It's anyone who is okay with gay sexuality and is comfortable enough to live in it."

Toward the end of our conversation, I ask Bryan what he wants. He sits up a little straighter in his chair and goes into Good Chinese Christian Boy mode, which I know well.

"At the highest level, I want to live a life that pleases God. I want to finish this life and be called 'good and faithful servant,'" he says. Then he relaxes a little and for the first time, I hear a softness, a new candor, in his voice. "That's the good Christian mental goal—the one I know is right. At the heart level, I honestly just want to be happy. And I know that's not necessarily guaranteed for the Christian life. It's not. But I still want it. To me, that means feeling free and being able to enjoy my sexuality, whatever it is or becomes. It means not having to struggle as I currently do."

*Are you lonely?* I ask.

He thinks for at least thirty seconds before responding. "I really appreciate that question," he says. "I feel like I really want a significant other. At this time, the only gender I think I'd be satisfied with is a guy, and because I won't let myself pursue that right now, I do feel somewhat lonely. I have amazing friends whom I care about and who care about me, so I struggle with whether I should really say I'm lonely. But I desire more in terms of relationship. How about that?"

He looks at me eagerly, and admittedly I take off my journalist's hat and say, as gently as I can, *I wonder if you overthink things, Bryan.*

He looks a little stricken.

"Yeah, I overanalyze," he says with a sad smile.

*So what would you say to someone who says to you, "Bryan, you're just not being honest about who you are?"*

"I guess I'd appeal to my own doctrine, my theology: The core of my being is deeper than the symptoms of whom I am attracted to. The core of my identity is that I'm a sinner redeemed by Christ. I know my most important identity is Child of God. But I would like to be able to resolve this because I appreciate having an identity. I'd like to be able to say, 'This is my sexuality,' just like I say I am Christian, an engineer, and a Chinese-American. It does feel innate. This isn't something I can just switch off. So I have to preach the Gospel to myself: God sees me as so much more than my sexuality," he says, sounding a little uncertain of whether he's buying his own message. "Right now, I wouldn't call myself gay. But then I wouldn't call myself straight. I'm basically undeclared!"

I laugh so that I won't cry, because, not long ago, I said almost exactly the same thing (minus the part about being an engineer— never would have happened). The guilt, the loneliness and longing, the theological somersaults? That was me.

---

On my flight home after meeting with Bryan, I try to find a word to describe what he is seeking from God. I'm reminded of an anecdote Lupe shared: "Let's say there's a woman and she's a prostitute. At night, she falls into bed exhausted. As she goes to sleep, she cries, 'God, help me!' She wants to be helped. But then she gets up the next morning, she prays, she gets ready for work, and she goes to turn tricks. At the end of the day, she says again, 'God, help me!' What is that? Is that a woman who loves God and is crying out? Is that a woman who God is not going to reach out to until she stops sinning?"

In a soft maternal voice she answered her own question. "After years of listening to people's stories, I tend to think God knows she's trapped. He *loves* her," she said. "He's glad to hear from her. *Whenever*."

Lupe then questioned the premise of her question. *So which woman is it—the desperate one who is truly seeking God's aid, or the forsaken one who needs to turn to face God before He'll face her?* Maybe it's not one or the other. Maybe it's both. Maybe God will meet a prostitute—or a gay man or anyone—wherever he or she is, just as Jesus met the adulterous Samaritan woman at the well *before* she stopped sinning.

Is there even a word to describe that magnanimity? Do we have a way to conceive of that expansive love, that gesture of meeting? For Lupe, the lesson is that we're called to cast our minds. "We need to think outside of ourselves," she concluded. "There's always a danger of pigeonholing; humans are masters at it. But we can't let patterns get set in our heads or ask questions just to verify them."

But isn't this precisely what Exodus and Tower of Light, Jeff Simunds and Alan Chambers do, with their oversimplified notions of the "gay lifestyle" and the "father wound"? When they equate "gay" with flamboyant, hard-drinking, promiscuous go-go boys on a big-city pride-parade float, what happens to dull folks like me? When they explain the origins of our homosexuality, I'm offended for all our fathers, who apparently are to blame. When Jeff explains how he deals with his own flare-ups of same-sex attraction—he spends more time with his straight male buddies—I have to allow that this may work for him, but I also wonder what's wrong with my straight male friends. Hanging out with them has never made me straighter.

At one point, I asked Jeff, if a struggling Christian such as Bryan ultimately decides that he is okay with a full relationship with another guy, does that make him less of a Christian? "I don't want to offend somebody by saying something I don't intend," he says. "But you're calling sin holiness. You're calling black white. I have an issue with that. If you say you can follow God and yet engage in a gay lifestyle, I cannot in good conscience give them full assurance of salvation."

It's not my place to tell the men and women who believe they have benefited from Exodus-related ministries that their experiences have been invalid. I've met enough of them and heard enough of their stories, not just in Seattle but across the country, to know that such ministries have given some people what they wanted. One grateful former group member told me that his Exodus group had been a necessary spiritual springboard, a safe place to share with others. "It really did help me focus on my faith," he said. "Also, nobody ever pressured me to turn heterosexual or even suggested that was a possibility."

But it's also not Jeff's place to disqualify the rest of us from salvation. When I asked him whether a self-proclaimed follower of Christ could engage "in the gay lifestyle" and be a true Christian, he may have answered candidly. But I wish he'd said that it wasn't up to him to say.

By the way, I eventually did think of the word to describe what Bryan sought and what Lupe described. It's *grace*.

# JOHN SMID

*"Things I've taught have been wounding."*

Memphis, Tennessee

In June 2005, Memphis-based Love In Action, a founding member of the Exodus network, shot into the public eye after Tennessee teen Zach Stark posted on his Myspace page that his parents were sending him to the "fundamentalist program for gays. They tell me that there is something psychologically wrong with me, and they 'raised me wrong.'" Stark's post prompted worldwide media coverage and a Tennessee Department of Children's Services investigation of Love In Action. (It found no evidence of abuse.)

John Smid—who divorced his first wife, came out, then "left" homosexuality and remarried after becoming a conservative Christian—was executive director of Love In Action. In addition to Refuge, the boot camp–like program Stark attended, the ministry also ran a residential program for people trying to "leave the gay lifestyle." Today Smid runs a ministry called Grace Rivers. He still lives in Memphis with his wife.

———————

Love In Action was never an outreach. We prided ourselves on the fact that we did not proselytize. We were not trying to go into the gay community and call them to repentance. It was always a response to people calling us for help. I really wanted to help people reconcile their lives, and I only knew how to do that from one angle. It's the only one I'd ever known, and I believed the Scriptures were clear. When I heard people try to make a case for reconciling homosexuality and Christianity, my thinking was, They're twisting Scripture to satisfy their own lustful desires. They're unwilling to submit themselves to Christ. We're communicating the truth and they don't like it.

In 1995, I had a pretty strong awakening of the reality that my same-sex attractions had not in any way diminished. But for the most part, nobody in the Exodus network really talked about that. Everyone wanted so desperately to believe they could be transformed from a homosexual to a heterosexual orientation, and there were people who would talk about their lives as though that had occurred. When I heard those testimonies, I felt hopeless. I thought, I'm the only one.

Ten years later, in 2005, something began to change in me. I started to see a tremendous need within the gay community to have a safe place where they could explore their faith. But I kept this hidden.

In the early part of that year, Love In Action bought an old church campus. I kept looking at it, thinking, God, what do you want to do with this? It seemed like God was blessing us. We had a surge of people contacting us, and everything seemed to be going well.

What people didn't know was that we were going through some struggles internally. One staff member was acting, in his personal life, in a way that was very divisive for us. I felt strongly convicted to walk alongside this man. He was a friend! But other staff members just wanted to eliminate him. If he produced some sign of repentance, they said, we would embrace him. If not, he should be put outside.

On June 6, 2005, the first day we had anyone in that new building, the protest occurred. It was huge. There were colorful flags and bullhorns, and media on all sides. With the exposé on the harm of Love In Action and the "dangers" of our programming, we felt very exposed. It became really traumatic. That day, the protest is going on up front, in this conservative older neighborhood of Memphis, and I am driving out of the driveway, through all the protesters. Then I heard one of them saying, "God loves you." This was shocking to me.

The internal staff problems continued, so in 2008, I resigned. I didn't have the answers for how to heal the divisions on our board and on our staff. The only thing I could think of was to leave. I was still very convicted about ex-gaydom and everything that goes along with that, but it was time to clean my slate. I just did not want to focus on homosexuality anymore.

But underneath, I was still dealing with the issue, and God began to open me up to seeing things in the gay community that I'd never seen before. I began to build a friendship with the man who initiated the protest, Morgan Fox. We started meeting and I found him to be an amazing man—humble and honest and forthright. Over the next several years, we developed a friendship.

A friend also introduced me to Todd Ferrell, the president of the Evangelical Network (TEN).* I found him to be a strong Christian and a humble man. Todd invited me to a TEN conference. I was shocked at the spirit there—at the joyfulness, the obvious love for their faith, their relationships with Jesus. They wanted so much for people in their communities to know Jesus, which was surprising to me because I thought all they did was talk about gay theology all day long. I thought they were there to find gay partners. But it wasn't like that. I was humbled.

On the heels of that, I came home to Memphis. I found out there was a meeting at the Gay and Lesbian Community Center here, where people could explore their faith in relationship to their homosexuality. I contacted Martha, the lady who led those meetings. I'd known of her for maybe ten to twelve years, but I had just judged her to be a lesbian who was off her rocker and seducing the gay community with false doctrine.

---

* The Evangelical Network is a loose association of gay-affirming Pentecostal churches across America.

I started to share some of my journey and then she stopped me and said, "John, you realize I had to muster all of the grace I had within me to sit in the same room with you, because of what you stand for. Don't take it personally, because I don't know you as a person. But what you represent has been hard for me." I looked at her, and I said, "Martha, I understand. And I appreciate your honesty."

We related well, especially on how the church is such a toxic place for the gay community. It's very painful. The legalism. The rejection. The theological arguments. We talked a lot about that. That was the common ground we worked from.

After that meeting, I really began to ponder all of the issues surrounding homosexuality and Scripture and culture. The idea of two men having sex with each other is something that, in many men's minds, is so repugnant. So it's easy for them to embrace an interpretation of Scripture that says all homosexuality is wrong. But is it possible that we've been sold a bill of goods based on that personal bias?

I can't deny now that I see it: Scripture really is not clear in favor or against same-sex relationships. It is very clear about immoral relationships—selfish, idolatrous, inappropriate, serially unfaithful relationships—being harmful and not healthy. But when it comes to loving relationships, I just don't see it.

Recently, I've been finding amazing opportunities to offer amends to a number of people in the gay community for things I've taught or said or inferred that have been shame-producing and wounding. I've come to understand how my involvement in the ex-gay movement was not helpful—and in some cases, really harmful. One guy said, "John, I thought that by [my] paying Love In Action, Jesus was going to remove my homosexuality."

That didn't happen. Someone came in with an open heart and with the desire that their conflicts be resolved, and then they come out the other side and that hasn't happened.

I've been married now for twenty-two years to my wife, but I have not had any diminishment in my same-sex attraction. I have a good marriage. My wife and I have a great love and mutual respect for each other. But there are certain complications because of what we experience in terms of a mixed-orientation marriage. People don't want to admit that their marriage isn't everything it should be. They fear that if they explore this, it will nullify their marriage, but it doesn't. My wife is really walking alongside me. And I am so grateful for that.

# FREEDOM TO MARRY

## Jake and Elizabeth Buechner

---

*A city in the northern United States*

Jake Buechner's story begins like those of thousands of other gay American guys.* He grew up in a pretty happy, tight-knit family that was Christian but not overly churchy. He knew from his earliest dodgeball-playing, playground-roughhousing days in suburban Texas that other boys simultaneously intimidated him and attracted him. A couple of times in junior high, when he attended an all-boys' school, he fooled around with friends, but it wasn't like they ever talked about it.

Then, "all the way through high school and college," he says, "there was nothing. Nothing. No sexual interaction. Just fantasies!" During high school, he did have a girlfriend for a little while. "Once, she kissed me, and it was gross to me."

---

* "Jake" and "Elizabeth" asked for pseudonyms, so I asked them to choose. "Jake" alludes to Jacob of the Old Testament, who wrestled with God, and "Buechner" is for the writer Frederick Buechner, whose account of that wrestling match became an important image for Jake during his struggle. "Elizabeth" chose to be pseudo-named after the mother of John the Baptist. "I relate to women who wait a long time for something to come to fruition," she told me. "Elizabeth was patient as she waited on the Lord, was thankful to Him when He granted her desire, and then was able to see beyond both the hardship and joy of her own situation to the coming of Christ."

As his Christian faith intensified during college, Jake couldn't—or, let's be honest, wouldn't—articulate that he desired men, not women. He tried to make it work with a postcollege girlfriend; it seemed the right thing to do, and on paper, she seemed the perfect woman for him. But eventually they broke up. He moved to Asia, where he had his first homosexual physical encounter since childhood, a too-weird-for-fiction episode. One night, he hailed a cab with an unusually flirtatious driver. "He basically invited himself into my house. One thing led to another, and he was on top of me," Jake recalls. "We almost had sex. But then I said, 'This is wrong.'" So Jake deployed the ultimate buzzkill card, getting his Bible out and flipping furiously through Scripture to try to explain to the cabbie why what they were doing was bad. The cabbie, a Muslim, replied: "Yeah, it's wrong, but then you just take a shower." Jake shakes his head at the memory of the incident: "It scared the hell out of me. And the poor guy—he must have been like, 'What is going on here?'"

Jake's confusion intensified his loneliness, which grew into depression of the soul-rending, sky-blackening, cry-yourself-to-sleep-every-night sort. "I had this hunger that wasn't going to be fulfilled, but I couldn't tell anyone. I was too ashamed. I naïvely hoped I would autocorrect," he says. "But I was ignoring my sexuality, which is this central thing for us. It's so core to who we are as humans."

The problem was compounded by his strong desire to pursue a career in Christian ministry. After a couple of years working in Asia, he moved back to the United States to attend seminary, and slowly, he began to believe that his sexuality was something to be managed, not changed. He joined an Exodus group and sought counseling.

Partway through seminary, "I fell in love—or maybe it was an extreme crush. I don't know what you'd call it, but whatever. I found myself obsessing about him," Jake says. "I idolized him like he was the most amazing person I'd ever met." The guy was straight, which, depending on your perspective, was the best possible or worst possible thing. "We were hanging out a lot and we were going to be roommates," Jake says. "But I decided I couldn't do it."

He questioned his ability to have even a platonic friendship with anyone. "I thought, What is my life going to be like? Am I always going to have to be distant from everyone, putting up fences and guarding my heart?" he says. "I won't be able to have normal relationships with straight men. I won't be able to have normal relationships with gay men. I won't be able to have normal relationships with straight women, so I'm left with lesbians? I feared this lonely, lifelong existence."

During this time, Jake had slowly begun opening up about his sexual orientation—first to close friends, then family. Sharing what he had learned about himself, as well as his feeling that he did not expect anything to change, lessened his isolation. "I felt better understood, better known," he says. Many people would try to empathize, saying, "This must be difficult," or even, "I'm sorry." A couple of his male friends said: "Does it bother you when I hug you?" He thinks they just didn't know what to say and were trying to be helpful, but they never needed to say anything at all—he just wanted them to listen and to keep being his friends. Even now, "the telling is still going on. When I get close to someone, I want to tell them."

Then, a couple of summers ago, after telling a woman named Elizabeth, Jake went and did something unexpected. He married her.

Humans are expert box builders. It's what we do to make sense of the world. In *The Black Swan*, economist Nassim Nicholas Taleb writes about our tendency to look for patterns—in his words, "the drive to 'focus' on what makes sense to us"—and our seeming inability to recognize an anomaly. He identifies a syndrome called "the triplet of opacity," three conditions that afflict the human mind whenever it reviews the past. First, "everyone thinks he knows what is going on in a world that is more complicated (or random) than they realize." Second, "we can assess matters only after the fact, as if they were in a rearview mirror (history seems clearer and more organized in history books than in empirical reality)." And finally, we suffer from a "curse of learning," in which we overvalue "factual information and the handicap of authoritative and learned people, particularly when they create categories—when they 'Platonify.'" Our "desire to cut reality into crisp shapes" happens every day even for the most nonconformist among us, the alleged mavericks and the supposed renegades. Nonconformity only exists after you've defined the model(s) everyone else is conforming to.

Countless times during this journey, gay people have said to me (and I've said to myself), sometimes wistfully, sometimes defiantly, always adamantly: "We just want to be seen as normal." *Normal*, of course, can be interpreted and embodied in myriad ways, but for thousands of people who are at least partly inspired by that desire and a conservative picture of what marriage ought to be, it has meant a "mixed-orientation" relationship.

I was on that path for years, too, even toying with the notion of buying my last long-term girlfriend an engagement ring. I had the wedding all sketched out in my head, from the liturgy (Book of Common Prayer, slightly tweaked) to the hymns ("Be Thou My Vision") to the Chinese-banquet reception. [Insert gay-groomzilla comment here.] But in my relationship, as in the vast majority of mixed-orientation cases, my girlfriend didn't know about my homosexuality. (And how could she, since I hadn't accepted it myself?) Far rarer is the kind of full-disclosure, mixed-orientation relationship that Jake and Elizabeth have, which to the rest of us seems so uncomfortable and so *wrong*.

Jake and Elizabeth are an adorable couple. He has a muppet's wide grin, bright Caribbean-blue eyes, a mop of curly dirty-blond hair, and a laugh ten times too big for his small, wiry body. She is more reserved, porcelain-doll pretty and petite, with expressive eyes that look a little weary. They could be characters out of *Toy Story* living in a cozy, one-bedroom apartment on the second floor of a stolid, early-twentieth-century walk-up building full of couples like them—young, professional, ambitious twenty- and thirtysomethings who eat at the fancy nouveau-barbecue joint around the corner and shop at the farmers' market.

Elizabeth is an architect. She favors spare and minimalist designs—she rolls her eyes at the overwrought flourishes of postmodernism—and her speech is likewise understated; whereas Jake tends to spill and blurt his thoughts, punctuating them with loud guffaws, she employs a slow and occasionally wry reveal. Jake, an assistant pastor at a church a couple of miles from their home, bikes to work at a congregation of the Presbyterian Church in America (PCA), an evangelical denomination that, among other strictures, does not ordain women or allow them to be deacons.

It's all so confounding: Why did she marry him? How does their relationship make any sense? The longer I spent with Jake and Elizabeth, the more I realized that, to me, it doesn't and it can't—not when I try to fit them into the boxes I've already created to make sense of my world.

"Every woman fantasizes about the ideal husband," Elizabeth tells me one afternoon as we sit in their tidy living room. "I had my list of fifteen things." She wanted, among other things, a guy with strong faith. She wanted to spend much of her life abroad. And she hoped to work with her husband in some kind of Christian ministry. What she definitely did not want: "To live in the suburbs with a high-paying job. And in my mind, Jake fit all of those." She pauses and half-smiles. "I forgot to put 'heterosexual' on the list."

Elizabeth describes her upbringing as nominally Christian—her family went to church occasionally, but regularly—and she characterizes her teens and early twenties as a season of prolific, if unhealthy, dating. It wasn't until college that she began focusing more on her faith, and it wasn't until after college that she "committed to the idea of marrying someone who seeks to follow Christ as I do." The new standard meant a severely reduced eligible-guy pool, which meant she stayed home a lot more.

In 2004, Elizabeth met Jake at a Christian conference. She thought he was cute, but given that they lived in different time zones and he was planning to move to the other side of an ocean, it seemed as if nothing would happen. A couple of years later, she, too, moved to Asia and she of course thought of him. But on the day she arrived, he sent out a mass email announcing that he was moving in a month.

They had dinner together once before he left. They ended up going on a long walk along the water, and came to a pier where there was a restaurant with sweeping views of the city. "It was very romantic. We had appetizers and watched the sunset," she says. "If it weren't for the fact that he was trying to make clear that we were just friends, it would have felt like a date. But it was very Dutch treat."

At a lunch at Jake's house shortly before his move, she suddenly had the feeling that something was wrong. She went into the bathroom to think and pray. "I felt at that moment that he was struggling with homosexuality and that I had to pray for him," she says. "Then I thought, Maybe it's for the best that he's leaving because I definitely do not want to get involved with a gay guy. I wasn't sure he was gay. I had doubts. But I also thought, There's no harm in praying!"

She wasn't the only one who thought so. In the months after Jake left Asia, unbeknownst to him or to Elizabeth, a couple of their mutual friends also began praying that they would get together. Anyway, the idea of a heterosexual relationship—not specifically with Elizabeth, but more generally—had on rare occasions popped up in conversations between Jake and a few of his closest friends. Once, he told a friend, "I should never marry. It would be horrible for my life." His friend replied: "She'd be really lucky. You'd be a great husband." Jake's reply, then as now, seems totally sane for a gay man: "I thought that was just crazy."

At this point, Jake was continuing his preparation for a life and career as a pastor, and he had been spending a lot of time with "Liam," a pastor who had become something of a mentor. They talked extensively about faith, about loneliness and companionship, about sexuality, and as Jake remembers those conversations, he refers to theological principles that are core not only to the PCA's brand of Christianity but also to much of American evangelicalism. "We are all fallen creation. We're all going to desire things that are out of accord with how things are supposed to be. I wasn't expecting to be able to leave my sexual orientation behind, and I think I began to feel resolved in who I was. But I had a lot of questions about whether being single, with these homosexual attractions, was going to work for me in ministry in the long term. Could I be faithful in this call to celibacy?" he says. "I did have a desire to share a life with someone. I was running once in the woods, and it was snowing, and it was so beautiful, and I desired to share it with someone—someone more than just a running partner."

One day, Liam surprised Jake: "I'm not sure," he said, "but I think you should get married." As Jake mulled that, he started having flashbacks to his last relationship with a woman. He recalled instances where even the slightest prospect of physical intimacy made him recoil, which was depressing for him and insulting to her: "I was afraid of feeling trapped, like I was bound to have an intimate relationship with this *lady*"—weird word to describe a girlfriend! "She might feel it and I wouldn't," he says. "I'd be so starving for intimacy that I'd destroy her life and my life. That's the scenario that played out in my mind."

Less than a week after Liam shared his hunch, Jake got an email from another friend. It said, "We're a little timid about saying this, but the more we've gotten to know Elizabeth, the more we think you could be great together." They had a number of reasons, some of them just weird, such as "Our kids love both of you!" But others were slightly less bizarre: Jake and Elizabeth have similar aspirations in life. Both are deeply faithful. Both are passionate about evangelism and hope to spend a significant part of their lives abroad.

"So I started thinking about her and praying for her," Jake says. A grin spreads across his face. "But it also popped into my mind: I don't think I want to kiss her."

———

Jake and Elizabeth begin each day with breakfast together at their small wooden dining table. They pray together and they read a psalm. On the first morning of my visit, they were on Psalm 60, which begins: "You have rejected us, God, and burst upon us; you have been angry—now restore us! You have shaken the land and torn it open, mend its fractures, for it is quaking. You have shown your people desperate times."

The verses come to mind later on as Elizabeth recounts how their romantic relationship began. "Some people think I was desperate," she says evenly. "And then there's the idea that I'm a martyr. I did not do this to be a martyr. Truthfully, if God was going to bring us into some sort of relationship—well, it was going to take an act of God. I wasn't going to initiate."

Jake took care of that. He began to email Elizabeth more frequently. He posted on her Facebook page—something he never did on anyone else's, "according to my lurking," she says. She had an opportunity to respond when he was suddenly hospitalized with a suspected heart ailment; she sent a loaf of banana bread that she stressed and fretted over. "I put a lot of heart into it," she says. Jake interjects: "And a lot of saturated fat. I'd just had a fake heart attack!" (Pericarditis, actually.) She smiles and shoots back: "I said a lot of heart, not a lot of thought."

Jake then asked for her mailing address, which ignited a storm of speculation in her mind.

This is what she got:

*Dear Elizabeth,*

*I hope this finds you (snaps to the postal service!) and finds you well. As I think about how clearly the Lord has worked in your life ever since I've known you and been receiving your prayer letters, I have all confidence that He is taking good care of you. I also have great encouragement at seeing you find your rest and hope in Him. It has been a delight for me to see you joyfully follow our Father. I'm amazed at how you honestly and lovingly embrace what life brings you in its colorful variety: your family, your profession, your village, your last roommate, your adopted country, the church, friends.*

*I'm writing to humbly ask your permission to get to know you better. As we've spent very little time together (how oddly your arrival to _____ and my departure coincided), I feel like we don't know each other that well. But the time I've enjoyed with you and what I do know of you very much impresses me and makes me want to get to know you more.*

*I ask you this with excitement and a bit of trepidation. Trepidation—because I know my own fallenness and shutter [sic] at the thought of it hurting you as we would grow closer. I also know that we live in different countries right now and that even though emails, chats, Skype, + occasional visits help bridge distance, a long-distance relationship can be hard. I ask also with excitement because I know our God delights in working beautiful wonders.*

*So you know, S____ + C_____ know I am writing this letter and even encouraged me to do so. I won't tell anyone else at _____ to honor your privacy and our ministries there.*

*Eagerly awaiting your response and gratefully,*

*Jake*

Elizabeth emailed him back right away. Her reply: "Yes, definitely!" Even as they began emailing back and forth every day and then Skyping, that question of his sexuality still niggled at her. Was that the mysterious thing—the fallenness that could hurt her—that he referred to in his letter? No way she was going to bring it up. "If he's gay, he wouldn't want to date me," she rationalized.

Finally, after two months of long-distance dating, they were both back in the States and made plans to spend ten days together. They knew that they had to talk about this thing, whatever it was. "I'd really hoped it was something else—a difficult relationship he had with his pastor or something else not important that he had just built up in his mind," Elizabeth says. "I wasn't sure how I would deal."

One Sunday after church, they went for a walk. "I was scared to death," she remembers. "Then he just said he was attracted to men—that was the language that he used. He didn't talk about past experiences." Jake interrupts: "I think I said that my strongest sexual attractions were for men, and I had not been sexually pure. I said I was technically a virgin but not in my heart." Elizabeth doesn't look at him as she continues: "When he told me that, it was the last thing I wanted to hear, but I was somewhat prepared. It was easier for me that he was so up front."

She says "easier," but as she describes the rest of their ten-day date, nothing about it seems easy, including the fact that she cried every night. "My greatest fear was getting married to a homosexual. Whenever I've read stories about that, it has resonated with me. I was crying out of fear that I was making the wrong decision, but I was also crying for Jake and the struggles he had gone through. And if this relationship was to continue, I was crying for what was lost: I knew he might not feel completely in love with me in a way that someone with heterosexual attraction might feel," she says. "If your husband is attracted to a man, you don't have what he's looking for—and I did not want to be faced with that at some point." She smiles a little. "The Lord let me in on this for a reason. I couldn't just walk away. But it changed the way I looked at Jake."

After they got engaged, Jake and Elizabeth met a sweet elderly couple in North Carolina who had married decades before, after an extremely short engagement. "Remember how giddy you are!" the old lovebirds told them. But how do you hang on to the memory of something that never happened? "We both felt sad," Elizabeth says. "There was definitely a sense of loss."

In his masterful book *The Art of Loving*, the social theorist and psychologist Erich Fromm muses on the nature of love, which he defines as "primarily giving, not receiving. Giving is the highest expression of potency. . . . Giving is more joyous than receiving, not because it is a deprivation, but because in the act of giving lies the expression of my aliveness. . . . In thus giving of his life, he enriches the other person, he enhances the other's sense of aliveness by enhancing his own sense of aliveness. In giving he cannot help bringing something to life in the other person, and this which is brought to life reflects back to him . . . and they both share in the joy of what they have brought to life."

Later, Fromm turns to the Book of Jonah, in which God tells Jonah to serve as a prophet in the Assyrian city of Nineveh. Jonah's response would seem to bring into question whether he has the backbone for jobs much less difficult than prophet: He flees.

When Jonah boards a ship to wherever is not Nineveh, God, being the type of deity not much inclined to giving in, churns the waters into a fierce storm. His would-be prophet throws himself overboard to save the others on the boat and gets swallowed alive by a whale. From this, Fromm extracts a moral that I had never before seen: "God explains to Jonah that the essence of love is to labor for something and to make something grow, that love and labor are inseparable. One loves that for which one labors, and one labors for that which one loves."

Fromm's argument and the careful way in which he contrasts fleeting, romantic love with lasting, laborious love resonated with Jake and Elizabeth. "The point," Jake says, "was, Don't waste your life trying to capture that romantic love."

Instead, they spent the year or so of their courtship doing the hard work of getting to know each other more intimately, poking, prodding, fighting together through thickets of insecurity and frustration and complication.

There was the time in the coffee shop when Elizabeth asked Jake about his history with porn. It was as awkward as you would imagine, even if her motives were noble. "I wanted to be able to understand the role this has played in your life," Elizabeth says to Jake, "and to bear it with you." Jake turns to me and says: "I've heard straight men say their wives did not want to know about their struggles with lust. My response has always been 'Well, that really sucks!' My sexuality is such a big part of my life. To not be able to share that with my wife would seem like living a lie. Especially with my homosexuality, if I wasn't able to share, would she even really be marrying me. So it was kind of a relief that she wanted to know."

There was the time after church when Elizabeth asked him about another guy in the congregation with whom Jake was developing a friendship. "My gaydar went off!" she says. "I asked him about it because I sensed something." "I did feel an attraction," he says. "I didn't want her to have to worry about that, and I appreciated that she helped remind me what my relationship with that guy was supposed to be about. It really helps me to talk about things. It's a reality check."

There was the time Jake and Elizabeth, both then living in Asia, went to Texas to meet his family for the first time. By then, he was thinking hard about whether he wanted to marry her. He was particularly nervous, not because he worried that his family wouldn't like her but because his family is less conservative than he is, "and I thought they might find this unethical." He went for a long run with his father and asked him, "Is this weird? Could this work?" Dad was reflective but supportive: "What is it that keeps a marriage going? What is the substance?"

Later on, Jake took Elizabeth for a walk, and inexplicably, everything clicked. "I felt like we could do it, but there wasn't really a 'should,'" he says to me, seeming a little stunned at the memory. "We were taking a walk, and it really crystallized for me." Then he turns to his wife. "I want to be a part of your life. I want to love you. I don't know why. Why do I want tea or coffee?" He turns back to me: "I was impressed by her. I wanted to be there with her. I wanted to minister to her. I wanted to love her. I wanted to fight off everything that was against her."

For Elizabeth, that walk presaged their path forward: "On that walk, Jake expressed that he wanted to be with me in particular," she says. "Not his ideal of me, but me. Not just the void, but me. I don't think he had ever done that before."

The wedding took place seven months later—just about a year after they started dating.

Thomas Barrett,* Jake's boss and one of his closest confidants, performed the ceremony. He had had concerns throughout the budding relationship, but as he spent more time with Elizabeth, he grew surer that this marriage had as good a chance of success as any. As Barrett explains it to me, "A lot of people get married who shouldn't get married. They do it for all kinds of crazy reasons. My conversations with Elizabeth involved questions about why she wanted to do this, knowing that she was going to struggle."

"Whenever anyone gets married, we sacrifice," Elizabeth says. "My real question was, Is this going to be the best decision or the worst decision of my entire life? And then I realized that the answer to that question is, It's not one or the other. It's a mixed bag: There's blessing and there's struggle, but that's not something to be scared of."

In my days with Jake and Elizabeth, they never seem less than open and honest and candid. They encourage me to ask anything I want, but, prude that I am, I can never bring myself to ask about sex. And so it is a great, if somewhat awkward, relief when Jake suddenly blurts out, "Let's talk about sex!"

"Okay!" I reply.

"It's been really good!" he says.

"Okay!" I say.

"One of my fears was that our sex would not match my fantasies.

---

* Not his real name. He chose "Thomas" because it's been a favorite name of his going all the way back to Jesus' doubting disciple and "Barrett" in honor of the late New Testament scholar C. K. Barrett, who was as much a historian as a theologian.

A lot of that is probably just the nature of fantasy, which gives me an intense, immediate sense of feeling whole, yet it's really paper-thin. What we have is a lot better, but it's definitely different. What a woman does—what my wife does—is different. But it satisfies me," he says. "You know, it's been very different from what I expected. It's less intense but it has felt very good. It's not like pizza or french fries—it's more an acquired taste that I've come to like even better." He pauses. "It's like olives."

Elizabeth looks bewildered, which is probably how I look moments later when Jake compares his gay fantasies to dime-store novels and sex with his wife to "real literature."

Bizarre metaphors aside, the fact that their sex life has been, by both accounts, not just functional but enjoyable and real—and who can fact-check that?—raises the question of whether Jake has experienced any kind of reorientation. His answer is no.

"The temptations have been greatly diminished since we got married," he says, "but if you showed me pictures of men and pictures of women, I'd still be drawn to the men. I haven't acquired a taste for all women—I have for Elizabeth."

Elizabeth is realistic about what this means. "I can't fill the void that Jake has filled in the past through homosexual fantasies and his attraction to men," she says. "If in the future, he does struggle with pornography or attraction, I have to remember and keep it all in perspective: It's not because I'm not good enough. It's not about me."

Jake says at this point, as he does in several other instances throughout our time together, that he doesn't really think much about homosexuality these days, nor do they talk about it, except when people like me ask. While he's still attracted to men, the urge to act on those attractions—by watching porn, say, or masturbating—has declined. "I don't know why the pull to it has been less strong since we got married," he says. Occasionally, he has wondered about the roots of those attractions. "Talking to other people who are homosexual, there are lots of similar stories: feeling distance from Dad, not being able to relate to other boys, not being able to relate to the jock, being intimidated," he says. "But was being distant a cause, or is it that you're gay and so you have that distance? I don't know. How can we know?"

Anyway, there are other things to think about: Jake and Elizabeth are now trying for their first child.

On our last morning together, Jake says something that surprises me: "I see my sexuality as a gift from God. I don't think it's just some sort of strange thing that happened to me—like a part of creation where God just wasn't really looking out for me or paying attention. He uses all things. You know there's that place where Paul writes about the thorn in the flesh. Well, who knows what Paul is really talking about, but it has been an encouragement for me, and I guess for people with all manner of struggles. If someone could wave a magic wand and make this all go away, would I? My gut says no. One of the most meaningful things my wife has said to me was when she said that she was grateful for this in my life because it has made me who I am. I was blown away, because I felt really known. We're grateful even for our wounds."

It's difficult for me as a gay man to hear my sexuality described as a wound, as an imperfection. Yet I understand that this is how Jake sees it—how he *must* see it, given his worldview. Nor are his words, his beliefs, his understanding of his sexuality, and his gratitude for it born from naïveté. Hear the short version of Jake and Elizabeth's story—gay guy wanted to be super-Christian, struggled, and got married—and it's tempting to say, "Wow, he's repressed." And yet hear the long version, sit with them, listen to their struggle, understand the incredible work they've done to unpack and analyze and process and reevaluate, and things look different.

Will this marriage work? If it doesn't, it will not be for lack of candor. If it does, it will be because of their faith, the keystone of their lives individually and their life together. The great Danish theologian Søren Kierkegaard wrote extensively about how, in the realm of faith, absurdity has a central, even essential place. Faith is not about reason—in fact, reason obstructs faith, and it's not until we set aside the former that the latter's possibility becomes clear. In his book *Fear and Trembling*, Kierkegaard writes about the mind-twisting challenge that such divine trust presents: "For who would not easily understand that it was absurd," he says, "but who would understand that one could then believe it?"

Jake baked a loaf of fresh bread for our last breakfast together. After we sit at the table, he opens his Bible to Psalm 62. It was written by King David when he was under assault, and the first part of it could not be more appropriate for this couple's journey:

> *Truly my soul finds rest in God;*
> *my salvation comes from him.*
> *Truly he is my rock and my salvation;*
> *he is my fortress, I will never be shaken.*
> *How long will you assault me?*
> *Would all of you throw me down—*
> *this leaning wall, this tottering fence?*
> *Surely they intend to topple me*
> *from my lofty place;*
> *they take delight in lies.*
> *With their mouths they bless,*
> *but in their hearts they curse.*
> *Yes, my soul, find rest in God;*
> *my hope comes from him.*
> *Truly he is my rock and my salvation;*
> *he is my fortress, I will not be shaken.*

# CHOOSING CELIBACY

Kevin Olson

*St. Paul, Minnesota*

In the fall of 2010, a Wheaton College graduate named Wesley Hill published *Washed and Waiting*, a book about his struggle with homosexuality. He concludes that his same-sex desires are a manifestation of human brokenness and that, as part of God's universal call to purity, he must choose celibacy. The book's title refers to being "washed" by the blood that Jesus shed on the cross and "waiting" for the freedom and full healing from the shortcomings of this life—including homosexuality—that will come in the next. "Our hope is focused on God's glorious future, in light of which the affliction we now carry—a disordered sexuality and the loneliness that goes with it—will appear slight and momentary," Hill writes. "We long for the end of longing, the end of our loneliness."

"It very much grew out of personal writing—almost journal entries," Hill tells me when I telephone him in England, where he is pursuing a Ph.D. in theology at the University of Durham. "I intended to show it to a few friends, so I wrote it conscious that it would be read not just by me. What it was meant to say was 'This is the way I am trying to conceive of my faith and sexuality and the struggle involved in that.'"

*Washed and Waiting* was a minor sensation in some evangelical circles, especially among younger Christians who bristle at being labeled homophobic, are open to the notion that homosexuality isn't a choice, and yet hold that homosexual behavior is sinful. Kristin Tabb, writing in the Christian magazine *Relevant* (tagline: "God. Life. Progressive Culture"), called the book a "rich and moving theological meditation" that "will pave the way for new territory in evangelical conversations regarding homosexuality." She praised Hill for not "offering pat answers in a removed manner, or perpetuating the same 'love the sinner, hate the sin' mantra that tends to dominate evangelical conversations regarding homosexuality."

Hill's theology is pretty orthodox for an evangelical. But his embrace of gay identity is unusual, as is his invitation to his nongay readers not to empathize but to sympathize. Many of them will never have encountered such a personal and detailed story from a gay Christian man, especially one who is the articulate expositor of an argument that they'll find attractive: While same-sex desires may not be a choice, how to handle them clearly is. In other words, this temptation may not look like yours, but it's not fundamentally different—no better, no worse. "It was evident that he was desperately seeking to be accurate and faithful to the Scriptures," wrote Aaron Armstrong at Blogging Theologically, for whom the book's takeaway was this: "The real question is whether or not someone can live an unrepentant life and still be a Christian. And the answer to that is no."

When I read Hill this review, which he says he hasn't seen, he insists that this is not *his* conclusion. He claims not to be judging other gay Christians, though in his reading of Scripture, there are only two permissible options: marriage between a man and a woman, or celibacy. "The book was written as encouragement for myself, and I thought, There are probably other people in my shoes who could use the encouragement," he says. "It was written for celibate, gay Christians."

At one point in *Washed and Waiting*, Hill quotes an email that he wrote to a friend "at a time in my life when I was feeling especially lonely":

The love of God is better than any human love. Yes, that's true, but that doesn't change the fact that I feel—in the deepest parts of who I am—that I am wired for human love. I want to be married. And the longing isn't mainly for sex (since sex with a woman seems impossible at this point); it is mainly for the day-to-day, small kind of intimacy where you wake up next to a person you've pledged your life to, and then you brush your teeth together, you read a book in the same room without necessarily talking to each other, you share each other's small joys and heartaches. Do you know what I mean?

You don't have to be gay or Christian to know what he means. You simply have to have experienced being alone during humanity's mating season. But there's something especially profound about the loneliness of someone who believes that this life will bring no partner to share its burdens and its joys; that you'll attend every wedding knowing that you'll never have one of your own; that the space next to you in bed will always be empty.

When I finished Hill's slim volume, I realized, though, that I would rather have read *Washed and Still Waiting*, the book that he might be ready to write three decades from now. It's one thing for someone in his twenties to declare publicly his choice of celibacy— admittedly, a difficult, unorthodox, and bold thing. It's entirely another to stand by that decision thirty years on. What are the effects of this kind of long-term chastity? What would life look like for the homosexual who, in his relative youth, chose this?

To find out, I went to Minnesota to spend three days with a fifty-seven-year-old man named Kevin Olson.

Kevin suggests we meet at the Mall of America. Weird, but whatever; I'd never been. And so on a late summer day, just outside Nordstrom, I find him: tall and sturdily built, with a ready smile, a firm handshake, spiky white hair, and skin so pale that I imagine he's what a polar bear might look like if it morphed into a human.

As we wind our way through this uniquely American monstrosity—past the Build-A-Bear Workshop and the Moose Mountain mini-golf course and the Nickelodeon Universe theme park, with its SpongeBob SquarePants Rock Bottom Plunge—he begins his story.

Kevin was born in 1955 in St. Paul, and when he was seven, his family moved to Oakdale, a suburb just to the city's east. The farmland there was being retilled to grow tract homes, and the Olsons found a tidy new house in one of those postwar suburban subdivisions built on green fields and promises: A safe place for your kids to play! A prosperous future for you and yours!

It was, he says, "a good home." Kevin's father was a warehouse worker at a cold-storage facility for thirty-eight years, and his mother was a homemaker until Kevin was eight or nine, at which point she went to work as an office manager. There was always food in the fridge, and what passes for domestic tranquility: "My parents didn't really fight."

Kevin, the second of four kids, was the elder of fraternal twins, though he wasn't raised as one; his twin brother suffered severe brain damage at birth and was institutionalized. Kevin was a B student— "just a little above average," he says—who particularly liked his drafting classes, theater, and music. He knew early on that he wasn't as interested in girls as his friends were. "I guess I wasn't thinking it would be a lifelong situation."

The Olsons' home life was "not faith-based by any means," Kevin says. "My father was raised in the Catholic tradition and my mother was Lutheran, but I have zero recollection of my parents being in church for anything other than a wedding or a funeral." As a youngster, he did attend vacation Bible school at a nearby Lutheran church and went to some Sunday services there during high school, but he says his first real encounter with what he calls "the love of Christ in action" was at JCPenney, where he worked after high school. He was assigned to the shoe department, and one day, he had lunch with a guy named Jeff, who worked in men's. "Before we ate, he prayed out loud. In a public place!" Kevin says. "It was a sign of someone who didn't care what anyone else thought, and that was impressive to me."

Jeff invited him to a Pentecostal revival service. "I felt intrigued not so much by the theology but the camaraderie. I felt part of something important and worthwhile," Kevin says. "I felt like I belonged." Within a year, Kevin had been baptized. He went to Bible college and earned a bachelor's of theology in apostolic studies.

"Basically, it's a worthless degree," he says. But the education was valuable in that it helped him develop and confirm his identity: "I am defined by who I am in Christ, not by my homosexuality," he says. "My relationship with God is stronger than my feelings." So he chose celibacy. "For me, homosexuality is not God's plan for His creation. He made male and female for a reason, in his image. That's his perfect plan, his first choice for creation, even if it's not politically correct."

Celibacy means different things to different people. In the Roman Catholic Church, it refers to not marrying. (*Continence* is that church's term for refraining from all sexual activity.) For Kevin, celibacy means "refraining from sexual intercourse, but masturbation has been an on/off issue for me. I would be less than honest if I said there weren't a couple of isolated incidents where I yielded to temptation."

I ask some questions with the word *gay* in it. "*Gay* infers a lifestyle choice," Kevin says finally. "I describe myself as homosexual-oriented. It's a subtle thing that may not mean much to a lot of folks, but it does to me." He mentions that he has done a fair amount of community theater, and though there's nothing effeminate about Kevin, his mannerisms, or his speech, his cast mates would probe about his sexuality. "I've never really come out and said it, but you know how gaydar is," he says. "I say, 'No, I'm homosexual-oriented.' And then, well, they don't really question it, because they want to be polite. They're Minnesota nice. So you just smile."

I ask about his theater experience. He lights up, rattling off a list of productions he has been in, including *Cats* and *Seven Brides for Seven Brothers*. His favorite show of all time is *Les Miserables*—"it's the story of redemption," he says—and his favorite *Les Miz* song is "I Dreamed a Dream."

"You know, when I was younger, one of my dreams was to be a singer in a gospel quartet, but I was never good enough," he says. "Sometimes I get nostalgic for that dream." He pauses and looks away momentarily, before turning back toward me with a smile. "You know Susan Boyle? I love that story. That's magical. That's dreams coming true. You know the words of the song?" He begins to sing softly: "*Now life has killed the dream I dreamed. . . .*"

Thinking of his singing ambitions, I ask if the lyrics feel true to his journey. But he takes the question differently. "Yes. There's the feeling of being cheated out of being intimate with someone," he says. "Of course you long for that connection."

There are plenty of solitary creatures in nature. The Tasmanian devil, for instance, spends most of its life alone, though it defecates in a communal location and will occasionally dine with other devils. Black rhinos get together only to mate. The crown-of-thorns starfish, whose body is totally covered with spikes, is particularly antisocial, but fortunately, it can reproduce asexually.

*Homo sapiens* is not on this list. The biblical creation story establishes relationship as the model; Genesis 18 says: "The Lord God said, 'It is not good for the man to be alone.'" The Pew Research Center, which has polled Americans extensively on their happiness, has consistently found that a significantly higher proportion of married people than single people claim to be happy. And while such studies on marriage and happiness only identify correlation, not causation, a longitudinal one by Michigan State University psychologists has found that long-term singles report a steady decline in happiness over the years, but married people do not.

Kevin has built something of a moat around his social life. "Male friendships are a particular challenge for me. Because that line exists, for accountability, I make sure they know. I want to be held accountable if I cross that line. So I just come right out and say it: 'I am homosexually oriented, and this is something I've dealt with all my life.'"

That candor has a cost. Kevin has never felt outright rejection from his friends, who are almost entirely Christians. "But I do feel a wall of 'I don't know how to handle it.' They don't know what to do," he says, "because it's never talked about in the church." He has also stopped going to men's Bible study groups, "because I don't want to make people uncomfortable."

Not that people outside of the church have been much better. He no longer does the community theater he used to love, in part because of those awkward questions—voiced and unvoiced—about his "homosexual but not gay" identity. "I don't want to cross that line of having to explain myself to them," he says. "It's such a foreign concept."

He knows of no friends who struggle with the same issue—"It would be nice to know other homosexually oriented men and women who choose not to live that lifestyle." He did open up to one relative who identifies as a lesbian and what he got was a lecture: "She made it clear she felt I wasn't being true to myself."

His voice is entirely even, seemingly emotionless, as he recounts all this. "So," he says, "I've lived pretty much on my own."

I ask Kevin to take me to the places that have meant the most to him, so we get into his burgundy Chrysler New Yorker for a driving tour of the Twin Cities. Our first stop is Hope Church, the Evangelical Free Church congregation that he has attended for nearly twenty years. Inside the lobby of the low-slung modern building, we run into John Larson, the head pastor, who ushers us to a small table, where we sit and chat for a few minutes.

I tell Pastor John about my pilgrimage, and he reflects on the ways in which the issue of homosexuality has unexpectedly become a focal point of his ministry. A good friend in high school turned out to be gay. So did a confidant from freshman year of college. Another buddy was gay and eventually died of AIDS. Then there was a good friend when he was doing youth ministry. "Early on, I realized I have got to figure out what's going on," Pastor John says, "because these are my friends, whom I love dearly."

So he read extensively—he cites one book in particular, *Slaves, Women & Homosexuals*, by the theologian William Webb—and concluded that while he could not support homosexual behavior, he had to be more loving than people in his precincts of the church typically were.

Recently, Pastor John's lesbian niece emailed with the news that her partner was being ordained. "Do you have any words of encouragement as she goes into ministry?" she wanted to know. "So am I going to punish? Am I going to not say anything? Or am I going to love?" Pastor John muses. "My daughter says to me: 'You've got an opportunity here.' In other words, don't blow it! And so I wrote back to her as I would write to anyone going into pastoral ministry, sharing some of what I have learned. I cannot give up my theological basis, but I am deeply committed to loving as best I can."

Pastor John then mentions the theologian Miroslav Volf. An Episcopalian who grew up in Croatia, Volf has built a career that defies the traditional boundaries of church and academy. He is conservative enough to have taught at Fuller Seminary, the evangelical school in Southern California, yet has enough secular academic cred to teach at Yale, where he heads the Center for Faith and Culture. In his powerful 2002 book, *Exclusion to Embrace*, Volf explores, perhaps as only one who has profoundly experienced being an outsider can, "the problems of identity and otherness. . . . How should we live as Christian communities today faced with the 'new tribalism' that is fracturing our societies, separating peoples and cultural groups, and fomenting vicious conflicts?"

"He says brilliant things about what it's going to take for us to talk in a culture that is so polarized," Pastor John says. "If we don't figure this out, we're going to war—a social war. And we're going to be killing a bunch of people along the way. But the church ought to be leading the charge to talk."

We fall silent for a few moments. Then Kevin says to Pastor John: "Over the years, you've really proved that you care." He begins to reminisce about his suicide attempt in 1997. It was set off by a bizarre set of circumstances: He was struggling with his sexual identity. He was just getting over a crush on someone he had been carpooling with: "You spend thirty minutes going to work, thirty going home, in a confined space, and you talk. Proximity bred this, but when we talked about it, our friendship suffered." And after not seeing his twin brother, Kerry, in thirty-eight years, he had tracked him down in the Minnesota state system—but Kerry died a month later. "It was just too much," Kevin says. "Too emotionally difficult."

So one day at work, just before swallowing a bunch of pills, he called the church office, and Marlene, the secretary, answered the phone as usual. "I was checking out. I was not in a good place. I said, 'Tell Scott and John goodbye,'" Kevin says, smiling a little. "Poor Marlene!" (A coworker called 911, and Kevin's stomach was pumped at the hospital.)

As Kevin and I get ready to leave the church, the youth pastor, Zach Boardman, bounds in and greets us effusively. As we say hello and goodbye, Pastor John asks if we might pause for prayer, and so the four of us form a tight circle. He prays for grace, for perseverance, for strength, for wisdom—for Kevin and for me.

Back in the Chrysler, Kevin revisits his childhood and his relationship with his father. "He didn't involve himself in my life. He just wasn't active. I don't think he has ever told me that he loves me," he says. "I don't think that's necessarily the reason why I am homosexually oriented. I can understand that it might have contributed to it. But I don't necessarily believe you're born gay—the jury's still out. I do know I didn't choose this. I certainly didn't. I don't have a choice as to who I feel attracted to. But I do have a choice as to how to respond."

We turn down Grospoint Avenue, a neat street lined by simple, not-too-big, not-too-small homes. Suddenly he points to a house on the left and says, "That's where I grew up." But I have time only to note that the ranch, where his father still lives, is red and white, because he doesn't slow down.

A few minutes later, we pull into the small parking lot of a dull office park with the usual assortment of suburban service providers—an insurance agent, financial managers, doctors. One office is not like all the others. It has a small banner out front featuring the letter *B* and a quotation from Proverbs 22:1—"A good name is more desirable than great riches"—and there is a NO MEDIA sign on the front door. "That's Bachmann Associates," Kevin says, pointing to the counseling firm owned and operated by Republican congresswoman Michele Bachmann's husband, Marcus.

Pastor John and Hope Church have sent many people to Bachmann & Associates for all manner of counseling, and a couple of years ago, Kevin began meeting with a therapist here. He says that his sessions were explicitly faith-based, but he never heard a word about the reparative therapy that has been written about in the press. That wasn't what he wanted, and that's not what they offered him. "They have a good reputation in the Christian community here," Kevin says. "For me, it was very caring, very much from a faith-based perspective. I would recommend it to anybody, with the caveat that this is the way they come at it."

Then we drive to a restaurant called the Little Oven, which, in defiance of its name, serves enormous portions. "Hey, Dawn!" he says to one of the cooks as we walk in, and after we settle into a booth, he tells me about his plans to go to China. He has already visited six times to teach English—every time, going to Guizhou Province, in the country's southwest—and he plans to go back soon to study Chinese. Kevin believes that he's being called to China as an unofficial missionary. "I'm convinced that God has a purpose for me there. My friends say that when I talk about China, my eyes sparkle," Kevin says. "In fact, I've seen God systematically dismantle all my excuses for *not* being in China. All the things that have hindered me from going. I lost my job. I lost my house. My cat died. You know, I haven't felt more peace about anything in years."

Perhaps God really is calling Kevin to China—but I also wonder whether one push factor is a desire to escape his current life.

On my final morning with Kevin, he tells me there's something he really wants to clarify. That first day, when he was talking about the times when he was physically tempted? "I have never had sexual intercourse," he says. He falls silent. "It's hard for me to talk about."

"You don't have to talk about it," I reply, but he doesn't seem to hear me.

"Let's just say I needed physical intimacy, but we didn't get in bed together. There was something comforting about being with somebody, but I was disappointed afterward," he says. "There was a fleeting moment of enjoyment, but the disappointment in myself that I felt afterward was not worth it. Did I feel horrible and beat myself up over it? No, I didn't do that. But did I regret it? Yes. Did I condemn myself? No. Given the circumstance, would I make a different choice? Most likely. But I knew God would understand. He will forgive me. He knows we are fallible. He knows we fail. And there is no condemnation in Christ."

I ask him what the takeaway should be from his story.

"I know that my life has not been easy. I know that my answers may seem, to some people, dishonest with who they think I should be. I know my choices seem outwardly ridiculous or, to some people, obviously silly. But that doesn't really matter. I don't live my life according to other people's standards," Kevin says. "I've chosen this path because it's what I believe is pleasing to my God. Pleasing him is more satisfying to me than pleasing myself or being happy. It's about contentment, which doesn't mean being fine. It means peace about who you are. Sometimes, I do feel cheated because I haven't been able to experience certain things in life, but then I remember that it's not about me. As a believer in Christ, you accept that this isn't all there is to life. There's a life to come. That will be a happy time. So a little suffering here isn't agonizing. It's just a minor inconvenience."

Then he turns his focus outward, as if he were filming his own version of an "It Gets Better" video.

"If you're feeling hopeless, I would say to you, 'There is hope.' It's not necessary to despair. If you haven't come out yet, find someone you trust to come out to. It may be hard to do that. It may be someone outside the church. But get it out. Talk to somebody. Share with someone. It's the first step," he says. "You have to get it outside your own head. Don't be just on your own."

Just before I leave, he goes to get his laptop, telling me that he wants to play me a song by the Christian singer Chris Rice. "There have been times I've had this on a constant loop—it's during the most difficult times," Kevin says. "It expresses how I have felt about this life, with its ups and downs and its difficulties and all the things you don't understand and how every day is a day closer to being with Christ."

Notably, it never mentions Jesus by name. And with its generic soft-pop beat and Rice's pleasant but unremarkable voice, it seems as if it could slot right into any easy-listening station's rotation. But if you listen to the words, you realize why it never will: It's so damn depressing. It's all about wanting this life to be over and the next to begin. It describes how every minute on this earth feels like an hour and every inch of life a mile. It begs Jesus to come soon.

As the song plays, Kevin closes his eyes and softly nods his head to the beat. "It's like a modern psalm. It brings me comfort," he says when it is finished. "It's called 'Smile.'" Which, at that moment, is pretty much the last thing I want to do.

Before I met Kevin, I thought of celibacy as an extended period of inaction that follows a choice, albeit a monumental one. If you could describe it as an act, it would be one of rejection, of pushing away sex and intimacy. There were certainly moments during my time with Kevin where I felt what I think is one of the worst, most condescending, most damnably judgmental human emotions: pity. But I came away from St. Paul humbled. I realized that, if anything, Kevin's lifestyle was not one choice but an active and constant series of them: the choice to resist his desire for companionship and closeness with men; the choice to set aside his perceived physical wants in favor of his perceived spiritual needs; the choice to sacrifice his earthly happiness for the eternal joy that he is convinced has been promised to him by his God. To him, celibacy hasn't been an act of fencing himself off; rather, it has been one of opening up, of embracing the sanctuary that he believes his Lord provides.

When I got home from Minnesota, I grabbed my copy of *Washed and Waiting* off the bookshelf and flipped through it until I found this passage:

> When the earliest Christians spoke of their experience of God's love, they described it as just that—an experience, with a profoundly emotional quality. "God's love has been poured into our hearts through the Holy Spirit," wrote Paul (Romans 5:5). . . . "Though you have not seen him," another early Christian wrote to fellow believers, "you love him. Though you do not now see him, you believe in him and rejoice with joy that is inexpressible and filled with glory" (1 Peter 1:8).
>
> In some profound sense, this love of God—expressed in his yearning and blessing and experienced in our hearts—must spell the end of longing and loneliness for the homosexual Christian. If there is a "remedy" for loneliness, surely this

must be it. In the solitude of our celibacy, God's *desiring* us, God's wanting *us,* is enough. The love of God is more valuable than any human relationship.

And yet we ache. The desire of God is sufficient to heal the ache, but still we pine, and wonder.

Maybe my desire for God is too small. Maybe I chose the easier road. But that first night back at home, I said a prayer for Kevin, I gave my boyfriend an extra kiss, and I said a prayer for him, too.

# TED HAGGARD

*"I am being resurrected."*

Colorado Springs, Colorado

In 2005, a masseur and prostitute named Mike Jones claimed that Ted Haggard, the pastor of New Life Church in Colorado Springs and president of the National Association of Evangelicals, had employed his services and bought methamphetamine from him. Haggard lost his job at New Life, which he'd built into a congregation of fifteen thousand members, and gained a spot in the annals of religious hypocrisy.

I wanted to talk with him about what has happened since his public disgrace. For months, he demurred, but finally, he agreed to meet me for breakfast in Castle Rock, halfway between Denver and Colorado Springs.

Within the first ten minutes of our breakfast, the rawness of Haggard's wounds became clear. He feigned empathy for the media: "It's in a tough spot," he said. "They knew I had never been the right-wing, anti-gay, bigot preacher they made me out to be. But they needed me to be a hypocrite."

He continued in this vein for a few minutes before turning things personal, calling me "insignificant" and "lowly." He said he'd googled me and I wasn't even one of the top Jeff Chus. "Clearly, you haven't had much of a career." Then he said I was "dishonest. All journalists are liars." "So why did you agree to meet me?" I asked. He replied that he wanted to give me a break.

I told him that he could judge my insignificance, but I wouldn't allow him to question my truthfulness. I rarely get unnerved in interviews, but I was shaking by this point. I went on for a while, and slowly, he got this weird half smile on his face. Finally, I said we were done and he could go on back to Colorado Springs. Then he said: "Now we can talk. I just wanted to see your passion."

With that, he became a different Ted Haggard—expansive, less defensive, loquacious, not terse. He said his position on homosexuality has never changed. He believes it "is not God's design" but favors civil unions for gays and lesbians. The doors of his new congregation, St. James Church, in Colorado Springs, are open to all. And his story, he insisted to me, wasn't about his sexuality but about his redemption.

---

How many guys have gone to get a massage and at the end get masturbated? I'm the one who got caught. Do you realize the price I paid? I'm not saying it was right. I'm not saying my mind didn't go a thousand places. But that is the price of leadership.

Here's an interesting thing: Christians have been incredibly helpful and supportive and forgiving. The contrast between Christian people—who just want to obey God and obey the Bible—and Christian leaders has been like night and day. Christian leaders have a responsibility to do image management and damage control, and that leads them to a natural tendency toward Phariseeism. Modern Christian leaders are trained to think in terms of creed, doctrine, and obedience, not mercy, kindness, compassion, love, and healing. The higher you are in leadership, the less and less candid you are—and that's true no matter what religion you're talking about. If a Christian is kind to me, they're just acting Christian. If a Christian leader is kind to a guy like me, they're accused of compromising. I understand that.

---

I tell young men not to go into ministry—don't do it. I regret going to a Christian university. I regret going into ministry. I wanted to serve the Lord and I fell short. I'm broken. I'm despised. I'm hated. To the degree I did good, I was punished—punished for serving the Lord. All of it ratcheted up my prestige so that I could pay for it. I'm very sad I wasted my life the way I did. If I were to do it again, I'd do a military career. If I'd had a navy career, I could have spent my life on an aircraft carrier.

But I'm here to finish the story. Let me give you two parallels. Richard Nixon, when he got into trouble with Watergate, he went to Yorba Linda and died.* He is an unending pillar of shame and misappropriation of power. But Bill Clinton kept going. The Monica Lewinsky story is less and less and less significant. It's just a paragraph in his story.

Here's another one: Judas and Peter both denied the Lord. Judas repented and in his grief he killed himself. He built a pillar to his failure. That's what he is remembered for. Peter, on the other hand, repented and received forgiveness and continued preaching. Peter's denial is just a small part of his story now.

Every thinking person has ideals in their life; they achieve some, and they don't achieve others. But this will be the number one set of questions that I have to answer for the rest of my life.

Not too long ago, I was on Larry King with Jennifer Knapp, the singer, and a pastor from the religious right. At the time, Larry King was contemplating his seventh divorce. Jennifer Knapp was coming out as a lesbian. What's the difference between us and the religious-right pastor? His sins are just respectable. Today, because of the religious right, the unpardonable sin is homosexuality. For my parents' generation, it was divorce and remarriage, but that's not an issue anymore— and I don't think homosexuality will be an unpardonable sin in a generation.

After Larry King, I got lots of mail from people on the religious right saying that I had compromised. I was disappointed,

* Actually, former president Nixon died in New York in 1994, several days after suffering a stroke at his New Jersey home. His funeral was held at the Nixon Library in Yorba Linda, California.

but I wasn't surprised. Let's say my sin is lust, resentment, and anger, and yours is homosexuality—assuming that's a sin. Which of us needs Christ less?

---

A lot has been written about falling from grace. The one time it's in Scripture—I believe it's in Romans—it refers to people who are righteous in themselves and don't think they need redemption. It's not in reference to the sinful guy that got embarrassed. If someone looks at you as a gay man and he feels superior as a heterosexual, that person has fallen from grace.

One time, I was talking to an angry pastor, and he was saying to me, "You are the scum of the earth." I patted him on the shoulder and I said, "Tell you what, pastor. I'll take all the blood of Jesus you don't need." He just smiled. Lovelessness is a huge sin in the church. The four primary personalities in the New Testament—Jesus, Paul, Peter, and John—all four of them say that love is the most important thing. But the only time love really counts is when something unlovely happens.

At this point, if people think I'm gay, that's fine. If they think I'm bi, that's fine. If they think I'm straight, that's fine. I am so out of image-control and damage-management mode now. The people at St. James Church will accept me for who I am and I will accept them for who they are. I am the "chiefest of sinners," as Paul says.

Many of the Christians who come to St. James are persecuted. It's an authentic meeting of believers—saints by faith, sinners by fact. We are certainly not the congregation of the self-righteous. We are the congregation of the gratefully redeemed. We are not in a position to judge one another; we're in a position to encourage. We know what it's like to be the despised and the rejected. I teach our church that the Holy Spirit is the one who convicts us of sin. The Scripture never says we are to judge and convict; it's the Holy Spirit's job, and the Holy Spirit's process in your life is different from the Holy Spirit's role in my life.

Nobody is perfect. But no matter what, you can be okay. You don't have to live in shame. You don't have to go through the worst experience of your life and let that define you. All of us—gay, straight, bi, Republican, Democrat, megaministry leader—are in need of redemption. I always say—and I have always said—that all people are equally in need of Christ.

We're back in Colorado Springs to finish the story. Jesus ministered in Jerusalem, was crucified in Jerusalem, and was resurrected in Jerusalem. I ministered in Colorado Springs. I was crucified in Colorado Springs—though I deserved it. I need to resurrect in Colorado Springs. And it's happening. I am being resurrected.

# THE MINISTRY IS THE CLOSET

## Ben Dubow

*Hartford, Connecticut*

On my bookshelf, there's a black, three-ring binder, a bit taller and wider than an index card. The pages within are filled with row after row of Chinese characters, inscribed by my paternal grandfather in his tidy hand. This binder is one of the only things I inherited from him, but I like to think that, to him, there were few things more precious. Certainly, there was nothing else into which he poured more of himself and his God-fearing soul. He was a pastor, and these are his sermons.

Occasionally I take the volume off my shelf and flip through the yellowing pages. I don't read Chinese nearly as well as I speak it, so the binder has become more a talisman for me than a text. When I spend time with the words, I invariably think of solitude. That may seem an odd thing to think of when looking at sermons, which are words that gain potency from being preached. But my grandfather's life was one of remarkable aloneness, despite his sixty-year marriage to my grandmother and his five children and his seven grandchildren and the numberless faithful whom he taught and pastored over the decades. Even in childhood, he was set apart. Southern Baptist missionaries from America converted him to Christianity when he was growing up in rural China, but finding the Christian God meant losing at least one familial connection: His new faith so infuriated his grandmother, I was told, that she threw him out of the house.

Many of my memories of Grandpa are silent films. He could be garrulous with church people, and he was never more eloquent than when talking to God. But with me and with the rest of the family, he was the personification of taciturn. I remember holding his hand as he walked me to and from school nearly daily when I was young, yet I struggle to recall a single conversation with him. As I got older, I noticed that all the talking he did with other people was about them, not him. I gradually began to suspect that he had no earthly confidants, and the more I learned about other pastors, it seemed that many of them, too, were surprisingly alone.

I say "surprisingly" because that profession appears to be incessantly social. The word *pastor* comes from the Latin for "shepherd," and a congregation is like a mass of needy, bleating sheep. Everybody wants something: visits, prayers, advice, your ear, your shoulder. Even when you're not with people—talking, meeting, praying—you're thinking about them, prepping sermons, or praying for the things they have asked you to pray for. All those church folk seemed to care about him, but who cared *for* him? And who truly knew him? I can't say I did. But when one of my middle school teachers told me that she prayed regularly that I would feel the call to the pastorate, I cringed and countered her prayers with my own: I never wanted that life.

Years later, stories like Ted Haggard's reinforced that un-calling. If I thought then that the pastor's life was lonely, how much more so would it be if the pastor were closeted? Or if some once-secret sin came spilling out? Or if some circumstance led his flock to shun him?

Well, if you really want to know, you can just ask a Connecticut man named Ben Dubow. Once a pastor, he now works as a sous-chef.

———————

If you had visited Ben's parents in 1974 and asked them what their newborn son might be when he grew up, "Christian minister" would not have been on the list. Actually, "Christian" wouldn't have been, either—the Dubows are Conservative Jews. "I would describe our family as observant but secular . . . kosher in the house, but not at all outside it," Ben says. "Growing up, there was never a real sense of spirituality or talk about God. Like a lot of families, I think it was about memory and preserving peoplehood and Israel and the politics that go with that. My grandmother survived the Holocaust and lost much of her family, so my dad grew up in the shadow of that. To this day, I have no good sense of whether my parents believe in a god in any meaningful sense, but Judaism is very important to them."

The Christian youth organization Young Life was active at Ben's high school, and he decided to write an article for the school paper about how it was a cult. "In the process, I was struck," he says. He abandoned the piece, but not Young Life. When he was sixteen, he began going to an early morning Bible study, telling his parents he was just going out to breakfast. "I knew they'd be really upset," he says. "So it was just easier."

By the following summer, during the Dubow family's annual vacation on Martha's Vineyard, Ben was reading *The Fight: A Practical Handbook to Christian Living*, by the British-born evangelist and psychiatrist John White. Late one night, he was out walking by the water after a party—"I was probably still drunk," he says—and suddenly he realized that he had just prayed for the first time. "And I just knew that prayer had been heard by Jesus," he says. "It wasn't me just thinking my own thoughts. There was another participant in the conversation." The next morning, he hiked out to the beach, sat, and read the Gospel of John as the sun rose on his first day as a self-identified follower of Christ.

When Ben's family found out about his new faith, "to a large extent, my siblings and I thought it was a phase," says Molly Dubow, the fifth of his six sisters and brothers. "He was always fascinated with religion.

There was no reason to believe this was the one he would stick with. Just before this, he was very vocally an atheist." But as the phase continued, it became clear that they would have to adjust. At one point, one of Ben's brothers asked what he thought about their eternal fate: "He was like, 'Yeah, I love you all very much, but I think you're going to go to hell,'" says Molly, who notes that Ben did add that he hoped they'd all find Jesus before that happened. "My thought was Wow, that's intense to believe that about your family!"

Ben went to Clark University, the liberal arts school in Worcester, Massachusetts, but when he told his parents that he'd decided to go to a Christian summer camp after freshman year, they threatened to stop paying his tuition. Ben wondered if they might be bluffing, but he also saw it as a faith-defining moment: "Do I really believe what I say I believe? If I really believe he is Lord, then a hundred thousand dollars is not a big deal."

They weren't bluffing. To pay his sophomore year tuition, he opened a pizza business, working twelve hours each night and attending class during the day. But it was unsustainable, and for his junior year, he transferred to the University of Connecticut, in Storrs, about an hour from his childhood home. "That," he says, "is where I sensed a call to ministry."

After graduating from UConn, Ben founded a chapter of Young Life—the very ministry that had introduced him to Jesus—working as a line cook to pay the bills. "I don't know an organization in the world that's more effective at authentically reaching kids who are lost and far away from God," he says. "I saw dozens if not hundreds of kids meet Christ through this ministry in northeastern Connecticut."

Then Ben got a surprise job offer: a Jesuit at a local Catholic church asked him to be the parish's youth pastor. For two years he taught confirmation and learned about liturgy and the sacraments, before doing a stint as an interim pastor at a small rural church and then becoming an associate pastor at a larger nondenominational congregation.

All this, in Ben's view, was prep. God had bigger plans: In 2004, Ben and his Young Life colleague Vince Gierer started their own church, St. Paul's Collegiate, with ten people meeting in a living room.

Evangelists view New England as the toughest territory in the United States. New Hampshire, Vermont, Rhode Island, Massachusetts, and Maine rank first, second, fourth, fifth, and sixth in the nation, respectively, for worst church attendance. (Nevada is third.) That makes the early growth of St. Paul's even more remarkable. Within five years, St. Paul's had five services, attracting hundreds of people each weekend. The church hired architects for a $15 million building project.

Ben was adequate in the pulpit—one of his former parishioners says he was "not great but certainly able to communicate and think through a sermon"—but he shone beyond his public speaking skills. "Ben was gifted in vision," says Tom Andrix, who chaired the St. Paul's church board during Ben's tenure. "Having vision is being able to forecast the future and spark passion in the followers. He coupled vision with leadership, and added a sense of how to carry out something in a very practical manner. Those gifts mark Ben as one in a million—maybe one in ten million."

But throughout his entire journey, Ben had been struggling with his sexuality, mostly privately. Some nights in his late teens, after he became a Christian, he'd cry as he read the seventh chapter of Romans, in which the Apostle Paul discusses his own struggle with (unspecified) sin. "I have the desire to do what is good, but I cannot carry it out," Paul writes. "I do not do the good I want to do, but the evil I do not want to do—this I keep on doing." Then Ben would read on, into Romans 8, which remains a touchstone for him today. There, Paul adds: "We know that in all things God works for the good of those who love him." In other words, it's all going to be okay.

For more than a year while Ben was at UConn, he went to William Consiglio, a Christian counselor who wrote a book called *Homosexual No More* and specializes in reparative therapy. "We talked a *lot* about family dynamics. We talked about healthy living," Ben says. "He never forced an agenda on me. We got to a point where I remember him saying, 'Change is possible for some people but not all people.' But I didn't have a sense that change was possible. So we ended counseling there."

Ben, who didn't have a car, would rent one from Enterprise to get to Young Life staff meetings. The Enterprise office happened to be next to an adult bookstore. Going and hooking up with guys there became a habit. He started meeting people via Craigslist. By the time Ben was leading St. Paul's, he was in full double-life mode. "There was always instant guilt and instant confession, praying as I would go home," he says. "But there was always this sense of God's grace as boundless."

During his time with Young Life, Ben met a guy we'll call Max, who later joined the team that started St. Paul's. Max was also struggling with his sexuality. "We became really good friends," Ben says. "I was one of the first people he came out to. And in the midst of that friendship, we crossed the line on a handful of occasions and acted out together sexually. But it's not like we were dating. We just crossed the line."

This was all well and private until Max went to counseling and then to a Christian boot camp. At that six-day camp, Max did a full-disclosure exercise, and the boot camp leaders told him that he had to resolve his relationship with Ben. "He comes back from the treatment, essentially doesn't talk to me for a week, and then calls and says, 'You need to tell the elders of the church what happened, or I will.'"

What followed was a week of back-and-forth, but even after the first phone call, Ben knew that nothing good could come of this situation. There was no satisfying—or at least job- and face-saving—result. "So I asked him to give me time to pray and think," he says.

Max gave him a little time, but he also told his counselor, who, with another pastor, came to Ben's house to confront him on Memorial Day weekend of 2009. They were gentle but firm: Something had to be done, and quickly. And so it was.


After Memorial Day, Ben had fled to his parents' house. He had lost his best friends, his job, his professional future, his faith community, even his house—he'd been asked by his roommates to leave. He knew, though, that he always had the other Dubows. "For a lot of people in my situation, the hardest dynamic would have been the family dynamic: *How am I going to tell my family?* But I never doubted that homosexuality would not be an issue with my family," he says. "It was weird. They were so supportive. They were actually thrilled I was getting out of full-time ministry, but they recognized it was really complex."

As Ben thought and prayed about his predicament, he realized he needed to talk to someone who might understand, "someone who would not be shocked, someone who had heard it all before." A name surfaced in his mind: J. R. Mahon, who heads a ministry called XXXchurch, which both reaches out to the porn industry and works to combat the prevalence of porn use among Christians. Ben sent him a message via Facebook, and within two hours, J.R. had called him back and told him to get in the car, drive to Cleveland, and spend a few days at the Mahon home.

Even in the weird world of Christian ministry, J. R. Mahon stands out as an oddity. When I phone him for his take, he shouts: "I don't care what hole you are attracted to. It doesn't bother me and it doesn't bother Christ!" J.R. sees no contradiction between his theological conservatism ("anything outside of God's intended purposes—man and woman—is sexual immorality," he says) and his opinion that one of his friends, a retired male gay-porn star who's married to another man, "is definitely not going to hell. I have no doubt there is love in this guy's heart for the Lord. And I am not going to rip his eternity away."

In Cleveland, J.R. told Ben to separate the issue of his sexuality from the matter of the cross. "We didn't need to have gay conversations. No! What we needed to talk about was 'Where are you with Christ? Do you feel he hates you? Has he walked away from you, or have you walked away from him?'" J.R. heard Ben out, heard the remorse, heard his desire to make things right. "He shouldn't have done what he did. Everyone agrees with that. But they could not wait to crucify him. How can a guy be in a community loving Christ and they find out there's sin in your life and you gotta go? You're gay and you're out? That's not Jesus!" J.R. says. "Once I heard Ben say, 'Yes, I'm going to have purity and holiness in my life,' I did start to understand there was repentance for what happened. This is not about the gay issue. We all need to control the body, control lust, control all those things that get us into hot water sexually."

Ben next went to visit Cincinnati pastor Bart Campolo, who is the son of the respected evangelical preacher and teacher Tony Campolo. In their time together, Ben and Bart talked about how to move forward: Ben would have to decide to integrate his faith and sexuality, because it was the hiding, the attempted compartmentalization, that had screwed everything up. "He told me that I was going to have to learn to love God *and* like myself," Ben says. "This was the first time where I thought it was possible that there might be a legitimate answer other than what I'd always assumed. Bart helped me realize that I had already made a shift in almost every other social issue, except homosexuality. I was never 'those evil gays,' but I was a party-line evangelical conservative on the issue. Really, it was a 'thou doth protest too much' issue for me. I was publicly crystal clear, because I had to be."

On his return to Connecticut, Ben resumed and expanded his efforts to make amends. He wrote blog posts and sent numerous letters and emails begging the church for forgiveness. Max, with whom he had the affair, wouldn't speak to Ben and has left Christianity. Many others from the church cut off contact as well; when I ask how many people he has maintained ties with, he says softly, "less than a handful."

Tom Andrix still regrets how St. Paul's responded. "In my mind, if we're talking about the DNA of Christians, forgiveness should be the number one thing," he says. "People would say, 'Well, how do we know he's really repentant?'" Tom spoke to J.R. and Bart and two other counselors who spent time with Ben. "They all said, 'This guy is doing great.' Ben was doing this, that, and the other to make amends. But it was never enough."

Early in 2011, nearly two years after the furor erupted, Ben finally got the St. Paul's board to agree to a meeting, where he apologized again, this time in person. "For there to be healthy closure, the biblical model is to seek reconciliation," Ben says. "I wanted to be forgiven for what I'd done. I had asked, but that had been met with variations of 'Well, we're not ready to do that yet.' Or they were just ignored."

The meeting "was a freaking disaster," Ben says with a laugh. Not only did he not get the forgiveness he sought, but he also almost walked out. "I was thinking, I will never speak to anyone in this room again." But in the parking lot after the meeting, several board members came up to him to make amends privately. Then he went for a bite to eat with Vince Gierer, who was now leading the church on his own.

"How did you feel about the meeting?" Vince asked.

Ben replied: "I still haven't received any forgiveness."

Vince, seeming skeptical, said, "Well, what is it that you would like to hear?"

Ben said, "That you forgive me."

"On behalf of the board," Vince said, "we forgive you."

Vince's statement "felt a little forced, but it did help," Ben says now. "Words matter. Whether they were fully felt or not, I felt unbound."


One fall day, I meet Ben for lunch at the Hartford microbrewery where he's working at the time. As we eat and talk, it occurs to me that the different people in his congregation who witnessed his fall must see him in different ways. Some will see the sin of homosexuality. Some will see the sin of deception. Some will see the sin of hypocrisy, of not practicing what he so forcefully preached.

"I believe sin is real. There are consequences to it. And Jesus paid the price for our sins. But my sin is not that I'm gay," Ben says, insistently but not stridently. The permanent softness in his round face and the embodied earnestness in his intense gaze keep him from seeming overly preachy. "Having a sexual relationship with someone in your congregation and as a single pastor—that was wrong. I would call it sinful. But the fact that it was with a guy doesn't make it worse than if it had been with a woman. Whatever happened as a result of that is because I did something wrong. But it's not wrong to be gay."

That he is even comfortable saying "gay" distinguishes today's Ben from the Ben of his St. Paul's days, when he used what he now calls "bizarre code words" like "same-sex attraction." Ben, now a self-described "progressive evangelical," believes "the Bible is not black-and-white." On sexuality, he's still processing. "It's undeniable there's a negative bias against homosexuals in the Scriptures," he says. "I'm very comfortable saying the passages aren't what they may seem. The question is What does that mean for people today? How do we apply it? What is being said? What is not?"

Ben does much of his processing on his blog, Faith Autopsy, with a bracing and rather daring candor. He's trying to live out what he calls "a spirituality of transparency. These days, I'm pretty much an open book, the opposite of how I lived my life for seventeen years. I did everything to keep a huge part of my life hidden. It was constant image control. But it's not a functional way to live. As Christians, all of us are entitled to a private life, but not a secret life."

On Sundays, he attends Riverfront Family Church, a small congregation in Hartford that welcomes gay people. "We are a welcoming and affirming American Baptist church," the head pastor, Nancy Butler, tells me. "My associate pastor is gay. And if people don't like it, that's too bad."

Butler, who met Ben when he was a Young Life leader, recalls a conversation with him back when he was still at St. Paul's. "I asked him, 'How do you deal with your gay members?' He gave me the usual evangelical song-and-dance, saying, 'We're welcoming, not affirming.' There wasn't room in his church for an openly gay person in leadership. I really challenged him on that. I said it was a load of crap, and I said he was doing damage to those gay members."

When Butler compares the Ben she knew then with the Ben she knows now, she sees a cautionary tale with two lessons. The first is that pastors are called to counsel and support to their flocks, yet they don't get care and guidance themselves. "It is a lonely profession," she says. "Who pastors the pastor?" The second is about the resilience of faith. "This is a hopeful story," she says. "He's going through a time of working in the secular world and reassessing his theology. I would not be surprised if, when he gets himself reconstructed, he goes back into church ministry. He knows the evangelical world so well, and I think he's equipped to help reform it."

Ben is agnostic about whether he will return to ministry— sometimes he dreams about opening up a New American restaurant of his own—but he agrees that he's still in a season of theological exploration. He is still not willing to give up his evangelical identity, even if it looks much different than it once did. "I have friends who think I am crazy, trying to jump through hoops to maintain my evangelical credentials," he says. "I have people who are conservative, who think I have become a crazy liberal who doesn't believe in the Bible anymore.

"I am comfortable with where I am," he concludes. "Well, I am ninety percent of the time. There's still that ten percent. There are moments where you think to yourself, What if I am totally wrong? I wish I could say it's one hundred percent, but we all have those days. So I just wake up in the morning and talk with Jesus. We're good, and that's enough for me these days."

Ben had told me earlier that the Sunday after Ted Haggard was exposed in 2006, he preached a sermon that he still calls "one of the best I've ever preached." The topic was the hypocrisy of leaders—and the necessity of grace. Out of curiosity, I ask him about his sermon on that Memorial Day weekend, before everything was revealed. He stops for a second. "The last sermon I preached?" he says. "How God is greater than your worst failures. I think it was ironic. And I think it was also grace from God. God is grace."

# AGREEING TO DISAGREE

## The Evangelical Covenant Church

*Chicago*

For his first twenty-seven years, Andrew Freeman followed the unofficial life plan of the poster boy for the Evangelical Covenant Church. He was destined to become a pastor in the Covenant, as its members affectionately call the Chicago-based denomination. Swedish immigrants started the church in the late 1800s, and Andrew's family—he is of 100 percent Swedish heritage—has been in the Covenant for generations. Andrew's grandfather was a Covenant pastor, his mother worked for the denomination, and his godfather is the Covenant's treasurer. At North Park University, the denominational Covenant school in Chicago that Andrew attended on a full scholarship, he was elected student body president and, during Geek Week, Geek King. After undergrad, Andrew continued at North Park's seminary and won the preaching prize.

When he was twenty-six, he went to Gothenburg, Sweden, to volunteer at a church there and boost his ecclesiastical-nerd cred to unprecedented levels. "I wanted to learn Swedish so I could study Scandinavian hymnody," he says when we meet for coffee on a cold morning in Chicago. "Also, I was running away, and I thought if there's ever a place to find a beautiful woman, it's Sweden. Then I got there and I thought, Oh shit, this isn't helping anything. Sweden has beautiful men!" When he admitted to himself for the first time that he believed his homosexuality was unchangeable, the implications for a Covenant career clanged cymbal-like in his mind: He could either choose a lifetime of chastity or "live a double life. I call it the Ted Haggard syndrome. That's what happens when people, in order to protect a reputation, suppress a truth about themselves, something that needs expression."

On June 29, 2010, the day that he was formally consecrated as a Covenant missionary, Andrew told his parents about his homosexuality. A few months later, on the day he appeared on the denomination's missionary prayer calendar, Andrew launched a blog called Coming Out Covenant to share the stories of gay Covenanters and their allies. "This is a space for those who hold to the conviction of our Covenant forebears who insisted, 'How can we turn away from the Table those who Christ has already made welcome?'" he wrote in his first post. "If Christ has already made room for us at his Table, must there not, then, be a place for us in his Church?"

Its supporters see the blog as the beginning of a push to make that explicitly true, by changing church policy on homosexuality, especially its rules for pastors—in the Covenant, as in every other major evangelical denomination, sex is officially reserved for heterosexual marriage. They also see the blog as a new and necessary platform for dialogue. Its opponents claim that no such thing happens on the blog, which attracts almost exclusively pro-gay Covenanters, and that in fact the blog has sown untruths and division.

Everyone agrees that the blog—which has tallied about one hundred thousand visitors in its first two years—has stirred debate in the Covenant. In fact, it might be the most open and candid conversation on homosexuality in any of America's conservative denominations, Protestant or Catholic, which have never counted candor among their chief or even desired virtues. Coming Out Covenant has compelled hundreds of members to declare their stance on the gay issue in the church. Perhaps more significantly, many more members have had to acknowledge their ambivalence on a topic that, one Covenanter told me, "is going to be the biggest issue for us in the coming years."

The Covenant, which has about 850 congregations and 125,000 members, is not one of America's larger or better-known denominations—its most famous son might be the former Green Bay Packers coach Mike Holmgren—but its struggle is really that of the entire evangelical wing of American Christianity. Its fold includes mostly small community congregations but also America's second-largest church, Edmond, Oklahoma–based LifeChurch.tv, which has average Sunday attendance of more than thirty-five thousand people. The denomination is much less hierarchical and more congregational than the mainline Presbyterians and Evangelical Lutherans, the most recent denominations to liberalize policies on homosexuals. It's still growing, especially among Hispanics and Asians. And there's also a pretty clear generational divide on the gay issue, with younger people tending to be less restrictive.

The case of the Evangelical Covenant Church is a test of how big the tent meeting of the church can be. What's a deal-breaker issue, both for gay believers and their allies as well as for those who believe a shift on homosexuality is tantamount to heresy? Can an evangelical American denomination like the Covenant continue to be, for someone like Andrew Freeman, not only a spiritual home but also a place where he can minister, yet at the same time meet the ecclesiastical needs of those who believe that folks like Andrew are damned to hell?

It doesn't take much to join a Covenant church. "Fellowship and membership in a Covenant church is open to all people to who confess Jesus as Lord and believe the Bible to be God's word. That's it," says Howard Burgoyne, who, as the denomination's East Coast Conference superintendent, oversees Covenant churches along the Atlantic seaboard. "We've been very ecumenical from the beginning, even though we've had a growing diversity of thoughts and opinions about the understanding of Scripture."

For the most part, the Covenant has been able to agree to disagree—a principle and practice written into the denomination's doctrines. *Covenant Affirmations*, a 1976 booklet that summarizes church teachings, says the key to this unusual freedom "is to be 'in Christ.' By his grace he is able to make a person, as Luther says, into a perfectly free 'lord of all, subject to none.' At the same time, he is able to make that person 'a perfectly dutiful servant of all subject to all.' . . . This freedom has kept Covenanters together in times of strain when it would have been far easier to break fellowship and further divide the body."

That has been important on some big issues. For instance, regardless of whether a Covenant pastor believes that infant baptism or adult baptism is "right," he or she must agree to perform both. Another controversial topic: women's ordination, which is permitted in the Covenant and must be affirmed by its pastors. But congregations also have the freedom not to call a woman to the pastorate. "There are clearly churches within the Covenant that don't call women as pastors," says Rebekah Eklund, a pastor and theologian who served on the denomination's executive board until 2010. "It's sometimes really positive flexibility and sometimes it's really weird."

In 1996, the annual meeting of the denomination adopted a resolution reaffirming a traditional view of sexuality: "God created people male and female, and provided for the marriage relationship in which two may become one," it said. "A publicly declared, legally binding marriage between one woman and one man is the one appropriate place for sexual intercourse. Heterosexual marriage, faithfulness within marriage, abstinence outside of marriage—these constitute the Christian standard. When we fall short, we are invited to repent, receive the forgiveness of God, and amend our lives." Resolutions in the Covenant do not create a line one is expected then to toe; it's just a statement of what the majority believes.

On this issue, there's hope among liberals that the generational divide found throughout America is also growing in the Covenant. "At least one younger clergyman has called me and said they're waiting until us old guys die off," says Dale Kuehne, a Covenant minister who is a professor of political science at St. Anselm College in New Hampshire and wrote the 2009 book *Sex and the iWorld: Rethinking Relationship beyond an Age of Individualism*. "People over forty would tend to stick with the more traditional view of how we understand sexuality. Those under forty and especially under thirty would be much more likely to see sexual relations, so long as they're in a marriage or a committed relationship, as more acceptable."

Kuehne says that the likelihood of a shift is being lessened by the big growth of the denomination in more conservative Hispanic and Asian communities. But over the past decade, a more politicized right-wing flank of the church has sought to secure an insurance policy of sorts, proposing a series of additional resolutions, and in 2003 and 2004, Jeremy Males, a delegate from Evanston Covenant Church in Illinois, proposed that the denomination adopt a binding policy on sexual morality requiring both clergy and congregations to affirm a traditional understanding of sexuality (and prohibition of homosexuality) to "maintain standing within the Covenant."

Males's motion was "narrow," says Howard Burgoyne. "It was single-issue, based on fear. These people wanted a litmus test. They wanted to fence the Lord's table." Burgoyne, as a traditionalist, agreed with the theology, but not the approach. "It deeply troubled a lot of denominational leaders. We had coexisted for over 125 years without that being a litmus test." While a binding policy was not approved, the church leadership did create a task force to do a theological study and report to the denomination on human sexuality, which ultimately reaffirmed the 1996 resolution.

Coming Out Covenant has been just as unwelcome to many denominational leaders as the Males proposal, especially as proponents of liberalization have rallied around it. One fear is that their actions will spark reactions from the conservatives who pushed the defeated motion, and portend some kind of public confrontation and even a schism in the church. "What we say to people is 'You don't under-stand how much freedom there already is,'" Burgoyne says. "You're going to provoke a fight with people who are less comfortable, feel-ing like you're trying to re-center the church. We've watched many denominations do this, and every one split down the middle. We'd like to not split. We don't see the need."

There have long been gay people in the Covenant, and there have long been Covenant congregations that have embraced them.

Charlotte Johnson's family emigrated from Sweden to the town of Washington in western Connecticut in 1888 and helped start Salem Covenant Church, which she has attended all her life. "As a child, I loved it—all of it," she says, her voice swelling with affec-tion. "I was brought up with Sunday school, Sunday school picnics, Christmas stuff, Bible camp in the summer, and it was just such an integral part of our family. The word is *saturated*. You know when you put bread in that egg dip to make French toast? That's what the Covenant was like for me growing up."

Charlotte is perhaps the most plainspoken person I have ever in-terviewed. Maybe it's her Swedish heritage, but there's probably also an element of an "I don't give a damn anymore" spirit that has grown in her over her seventy years. God knows she wasn't always so open. When she was eight or so, she realized she was drawn to girls, not boys, and that "I had to hide what I was." Which was easy. Her class-mates at public school thought of her as a square. "I was a Christian! So I didn't go to dances. I didn't go to movies. I didn't wear makeup. I carried my Bible with me! I was pretty ornery, and when I think about it, I just cringe. But I tell you, it was a good way to hide."

For Charlotte, the only possible college option was North Park—she told her parents that if she didn't get accepted, she just wouldn't go to university—and the career options were to become a nurse or a secretary. At North Park, she first became sexually involved with a woman. "I thought, Oh, God, I am a lesbian. That was really bad," she says with a laugh, sounding like it was really not that bad at all. "There was a wretched psychiatrist at North Park who really believed he could cure gay people. The whole thing struck me: I am not going to change, so I am going to go to hell. Like most good Christian kids, I thought, Why wait? So I attempted suicide. I was maybe twenty-one. And I ended up in the psychiatric hospital." Almost as an aside, she adds: "You know, she's still in the closet."

The hospital, Charlotte recalls, "was a really nice one," and being committed was oddly liberating. "I was a very angry person. I told everybody I was queer, and that's why I was there," she says. "But when you're locked up in a mental institution and you tried to commit suicide, you can say anything and do anything because you're nuts! It was very freeing. Also, I reached a point where I was thinking that the only difference between those of us locked in and those carrying the key was a matter of degrees."

After six weeks, she was let out. It was 1966, and free love was in the air. The following year, she met a schoolteacher named Joan Gauthey, whom she has been with ever since (and who in 2005, when gay marriage was legalized in Connecticut, finally became her wife). They settled back in Charlotte's hometown, where they continued to go to Charlotte's home church. "It was like, 'Don't ask, don't tell.' We never brought it up in church, except when this one awful minister came," she says. "He opened up his office and said to everyone, 'Come and talk with me!' We'd never had that before."

Charlotte believes he used information he gathered from those talks to try to get her fired from her job. "When I was hospitalized for a bad reaction to medication, he went to the nursing staff I worked with and said, 'Do you know she's gay?' They said, 'Yes, and what are you doing talking about it?'" She chuckles. "So I called the superintendent of the Covenant, and I said, 'If you don't get rid of the son of a bitch, I'm going to sue the Covenant for everything I can get.'"

"Every minister we've had since that psychopath was here, every one has been supportive. Every single one," Charlotte says. "They say, 'God loves you and we love you.'" The current pastor, Paul Corner, has been particularly supportive of Charlotte and Joan, contributing a blog post to Coming Out Covenant that cited them. "I think that this church may be a good example of a way forward for the Covenant church," he wrote.

> What I mean is, there is no Biblical and theological consensus in this church on homosexuality. There are some who hold very traditional understandings, and there are others who hold a more open theological position. But where there is consensus is on the commitment of this church community to love and welcome these two sisters with open arms, to receive communion from them without any hesitation, and to listen to one of their voices sing beautifully from our choir loft. Their sexual orientation is different from the rest of us, and that is a challenge for some of us, but we are still *us*. We are the body of Christ, we are the church, and we commit to loving one another regardless of our mutual brokenness and frailty.

Because of Charlotte and Joan, Salem Covenant has become a welcoming congregation for others, too. "We had a fellow in our church for a while who was—oh dear, what do you call it? Transgender? He went from being a man to being a woman. Really, it wasn't too successful. He was an ex–football player!" Charlotte says. "Anyway, he came to our church, and people were basically very accepting, even though, well, she was still so much of a man! It's just the way it was. There was another fellow who said to us, 'Well, we know why he's here! Because you are!'

"Sometimes I feel like Joan and I have stayed in the church to be a burr under the saddle," she says. "We won't leave."

The Covenant's official position is that homosexuals may serve in the denomination as long as they remain chaste. In practice, the policy may be somewhat stricter. After Andrew launched his blog, he was called to denominational headquarters and told that his missionary status would be changed to "inactive." "They said they couldn't send me out," he recalls. One of the main issues was how the Covenant's sister churches abroad, particularly in more conservative countries in Asia and Africa, would respond. "They said, 'We love you. We support your gifts. But . . .' 'Don't ask, don't tell' might not be our written policy, but that's basically what we have," he says. "I told. And now I have a better shot of firing a gun in the U.S. military than preaching the peace of Christ in the Covenant Church." (Technically true, if a little melodramatic.)

"One friend said to me that they'd almost rather be excluded and that religious rejection is preferable to religious persecution," Andrew continues. "Better to be told to go away than to be treated as second class, like a defective heterosexual." This is bad logic; in both cases, you're being treated as second class. It's just that in one case, you stay and in the other you don't.

In any case, Andrew the layman has not been rejected; he serves on the worship team at Resurrection Covenant Church, in Lakeview, on Chicago's north side. One blue-sky Sunday, I join him at ResCov, as its members call it, for worship. Andrew—gangly, bespectacled, with a mass of tight dirty-blond curls—meets me in the church's small foyer, wearing a short-sleeve black-and-white gingham button-down atop crimson pants. It's Pentecost, and red is traditionally the color of the feast—the day on the Christian calendar when Jesus unleashed the Holy Spirit on the church. "Nice pants!" someone says to Andrew. "Thanks!" he replies. "Liturgical fashion! When I bought these, I thought, I am wearing *these* on Pentecost!"

Before the service begins, the sanctuary buzzes with catch-up conversations against a subtle soundtrack of Andrew on the ivories. His choices for liturgical music can be eclectic and unconventional, injecting the profane into the sacred. Once, he slipped a sample of Katy Perry ("Firework," if you must know) into an offertory medley (which did not go unnoticed by the worship pastor).

"I definitely have my moments when I think, What is the point of all this? Why didn't I just leave and go someplace where this issue isn't a big deal? Even at my church now, though I am welcomed in and I play the piano every Sunday, I still live with the sense that there will be questions if I start dating. Will it be an issue? Will it be okay? And why am I not going to a church where I don't even have to think twice about it?" Andrew says. "I feel like I have to defend being gay, and yet I don't have time to enjoy being gay." His sexuality has become so much of a public cause for him that it has almost entirely ceased to serve any private purpose.

Sitting two rows in front of me at ResCov is a middle-aged couple, John Knoff and Eva Sullivan-Knoff, and their teenage son Benjamin, whose head is topped by a carefully combed shock of red hair. Eva is an ordained Covenant minister who currently works in private practice as a spiritual director. John, a former Roman Catholic who became a pastor in the mainline Baptist church, now works as an accountant for nonprofit organizations. And Benj, an aspiring play-wright, is, when we first meet, enduring the torturous last days of high school.

A couple of months later, I come back to Chicago to spend some time with the Sullivan-Knoffs, and over lunch at the Art Institute of Chicago, Benj tells me about growing up in the Covenant. He was baptized into the church as an infant, was confirmed at thirteen, and, during junior high and high school, went to a Covenant camp every summer. Faith can be such an abstract thing, but that camp, on Michigan's Upper Peninsula, made Benj's belief visible and the closest to concrete it has ever been. "It was where I've felt closest to God," he says. "My friends and I would lie in an open field, and you could see all the stars. It was the first time I understood why it was called the Milky Way, because you could see it all. You could see God's glory at work."

When he's talking about serious things—faith, family, rela-tionships, memory—Benj has a tendency to speak pretty softly, matter-of-factly, and without much inflection. When he talks about the landscape at camp, his words are picturesque, but they march out of his mouth in almost eerily even formation. On some summer mornings, he says, "there would be this fog over the lake. If you were standing at the very edge of the lake, you couldn't even see the lake. It was like a wall of fog."

Which is not a bad metaphor for being a teenager, even if you don't have this little problem of uncertain sexuality to sort out. Benj says that as his understanding of his gayness grew, "of course" he had questions about his faith. This is partly because he is a self-labeled "big overanalyzer and super Type A perfectionist control freak," and partly because these are just tough issues. "I was concerned about the religious standpoint. I didn't want this to be an issue with God," he says. "I had assumed it was sinful—no one had ever said that. It was just understood."

Yet even if he questioned how God felt about homosexuality, Benj says he somehow eventually felt reassured about God's love. "Here's how I came at it," he explains. "If God made people inherently sinful, that would be unfair. He has to give us a choice between right and wrong. And if I didn't have a choice to be gay, how could it be wrong?"

His reasoning echoes what I heard from many gay Christians I met on my journey. And whether or not such arguments pass theological muster—does an omnipotent God *have* to give us anything?—they have allowed Benj to sustain his faith. His sexuality and his religious belief are not "either/or" but "and." "Religion and homosexuality need not demand two dissimilar worlds. Many LGBT people are deterred from Christianity (and other religions) because they are taught that they can only choose their love for their Creator or for their same-sex loves, and that they are unworthy of God's love. But God loves all of His children, regardless of whom they love," he writes in his Coming Out Covenant contribution, which he titled "Paradox." "I am living, tangible proof that a Christian can live without gay guilt."

That guiltless integration—that emotional, spiritual object of my envy, I confess—is on full display in Benj's poetry. After lunch, we go for coffee and I ask if he'll recite his poem "Ways I Want to Be Kissed" for me. He says yes, but refuses to do it in the crowded quarters of a café. So we wander into Millennium Park, in downtown Chicago. It's a sweltering day, with no clouds to shield us from the sun, but we manage to find a quiet, shady spot away from the tourist hordes.

I plop myself on a bench, and as a couple of butterflies flit about, Benj stands in front of me to perform. He's skinny. Whether he's sitting or standing, his frame usually seems slightly stooped, even folded in on himself, as if he's trying to contain something within. But as he prepares to begin his recitation, his spine straightens and his body opens up. "Ways I Want to Be Kissed" is playful and poignant. It's a list of fifty ways, yet it somehow feels freer than that form should be. And the words feel authentically Benj—quite young, romantic, a tad rebellious, with shades of maturing manhood.

I liked Number Seven ("in church, for they could not tell us it was wrong"), Number Twelve ("in the mid-to-high branches of a sycamore tree, where bravery just begins to wane"), and Number Twenty-Four ("like Spider-Man"). I loved Number Nine ("as if a war had kept us apart") and Number Fifty ("with the promise of again").

Benj came out to his parents in 2009, during his sophomore year in high school. One night—"it was a regular night, and we had watched some movie"—he went into his parents' bedroom just before they were to turn out the lights. "I told them I had something to tell them, and then I said the words: 'I'm bi.'"

They were the ninth and tenth people to find out—and, according to Benj's ranking, John comes first, "because he understood it a few seconds before her." As Benj remembers it, John started smiling and said, "I'm proud of you." Eva said, "What?" Benj had to repeat himself, and then John leaned over to whisper to her: "Bisexual." (When

I asked her about it later, she explained, "I'm not a night person. For anyone to tell me anything at night, it's just up for grabs.")

Eva was then working as an associate pastor at a Covenant church in the Chicago suburbs, and not long after she found out about Benj, he tells me, "she told me I couldn't come out publicly. She would get fired. So I just shut up about it. I had to protect my mom."

Hiding part of your person to save your mom's job deserves be-atification. At one church dinner, Benj found himself making small talk with an older man, who asked what Benj intended to major in at college. "Theater," Benj replied. The man then said, "That's where a whole lot of gay people go." "I couldn't say anything," Benj says. "I had to sit there. And then I excused myself so that I could go fume outside the room."

That summer, Benj went with his youth group to a weeklong Covenant high school conference in Tennessee. On the Wednesday night, the speaker gave a talk about hiding, about authenticity and secrets and the downsides of maintaining false fronts. Even before she was done speaking, the facades he had maintained to hide his homosexuality—for his mother's sake, but also for his own—had crumbled. "I was like, I just can't do this anymore," he remembers.

Another thing had happened during the talk: "My mom had texted me." When he got outside the auditorium, he read it: "Benj, I had spiritual direction today. I am not worried about my job any-more, only you. I honor you." Benj smiles when he tells the story. "This is one of those moments when I knew God was looking out for me."


That night, I meet John and Eva for dinner. John, who is slender, with a face shaded by light gray stubble, saves his words until they matter. Eva is more expansive, radiating warmth and maternal hug-gability. We get to talking about when they found out about Benj being gay. They had wondered for a long time, and John says it's one of those situations where you know before you really know.

John acknowledges, "while I am fairly liberal on most things, there is something about the reality of this that jarred me. It was a process for me to get to where I am now. You kind of have a vision of what it's going to look like when your kids grow up, get married, have kids. So I wondered, What does this mean? What if he wants to get married? What if he wants kids? How is extended family going to react?"

Coming to terms with Benj's sexuality was much more complicated for Eva. "It all revolved around me being ordained in the Covenant," she says. "They were going to fire me in thirty seconds if they found out that I had a gay son." The curious thing about Eva's reaction is that she has, as an ordained woman, directly benefited from the Covenant's big-tent ethos. When she was a child growing up in San Diego, she started going to Sunday school at a Covenant church. The people of the church essentially adopted her. "They treated me like I mattered, like I had great value, like part of the family," she says. If things were tough at home—and they often were—she could always find a haven at church.

Eventually she felt a call to ministry. And though the church she grew up in did not approve of female pastors, they helped subsidize her theological training, telling her that they knew her and had seen God's hand in her growth. "They were so intentional about relationship with God, about building community, about this saying we have: 'For God's glory and neighbors' good,'" she says. "They lived that out." John looks tenderly at his wife and adds: "The impact of that church, their encouragement of her as a woman leader, helped her become who she is."

"I knew, when he first told me, that at some point, it was going to come down to my willingness to lay down this dream. This church is not only where I am credentialed," Eva says. "It's family to me." But it took a little time for her to wrestle with who her son is and who he might become, as well as her role in—and response to—that equation. She went back to the Scriptures about sexuality, which she says she had never studied carefully. She sought counsel from friends and her spiritual director. She prayed and prayed and prayed.

She came to realize that she was being selfish. "One of my great sins and failing was that when he said he wanted to come out, I said, 'I could lose my job! My vocation! My ordination! How can *I* be who *I* am, in this place, and be your mom?'" she recalls, her voice faltering. When Benj got home from Tennessee, she apologized in a tear-filled conversation, saying: "Did I make you carry all this? I didn't mean to do that. I cannot tell you how sorry I am. I wish I could take it back. And if I have to, I will walk away from all this."

I'm not sure the Covenant would strip Eva of her ordination. When I ask one denominational official, he says that he doesn't think that anything would happen to any pastor purely because of what he or she believes privately, but preaching a line on homosexuality that differs from that of the denomination might be another thing. Still, Eva has stepped away preemptively. She now works as a spiritual director, doing one-on-one counseling. At moments she has been tempted simply to withdraw her ordination before they can take it away from her.

Our conversation turns to the future. Benj told me earlier that day that his mom was still overcompensating for her earlier disapproval. She texts him multiple times a day. She asks him about dating. And when she couldn't make it to Chicago Pride—John went—"she apologized like six thousand times for that."

Benj also told me that he's not sure he's going to "do the marriage/kids thing. I just don't know." Whatever he decides, John says, "I would like to see a day when he doesn't have to worry about being attacked for getting married or having kids."

But Eva can already hear the wedding march and see her son standing at the front of the church. "Benj has asked me to officiate when it happens," he says. "I told him I probably wouldn't have my ordination by the time he gets married, so I'll have to go online, pay the twenty-five dollars, and do what I have to do. I love this denomination, but I love my son more."

———————

Andrew says he and his allies aren't trying to pick a fight. While they haven't made formal moves to change Covenant policy, this is about as believable as if Lenin had said in 1917 that he was just gathering a few friends for a nice chat. At the denomination's annual winter conference in January 2011, Freeman organized a guerrilla session on homosexuality that attracted a crowd. These kinds of activities make even some of their would-be allies nervous. "I really admire their courage for telling their stories," says one former denominational official who is sympathetic to Coming Out Covenant but requested anonymity to avoid offending friends on both sides of the issue. "But my worry is that if the question of whether we should ordain openly gay, practicing homosexuals were brought to a vote at this point, it would fail in a huge way. Right now, there's some sort of flexibility and openness in the Covenant position. Do we want to lose that? What if there was conservative pushback?"

While the blog has provided an online home for liberals on the issue and a place to tell their stories, it has not necessarily created conversation across ideological lines. First, says Howard Burgoyne, some of the blog posts contained what he believed to be inaccuracies. For instance, a Covenant pastor named Leah Klug blogged about how, in 2009, the denomination cut off her Seattle start-up congregation financially after it officially announced that it would be an open and affirming church. "Here's where the proverbial poo hit the fan," Klug wrote. "In the ECC, ministers are allowed to believe privately in open and affirming theology. They are not allowed to share in any public capacity that they believe homosexuality is something to be celebrated."

"None of the superintendents wants to go on the website and post, 'Well, that's not the way it happened,' because it gets to nitpicking," Burgoyne says, but he seems perfectly willing to nitpick with me. He denies that the congregation's position on homosexuality was the deciding factor in the denomination's withdrawal of support, though he allows that it was a factor. "Some of what the post says about why the plant failed is not really what unfolded. But it's how they told the story. I'm not saying people are out there intentionally mischaracterizing how things happen, but there's always a different angle."

Second, he says, the comments section at the bottom of a blog post isn't well suited to real dialogue. He knows because he tried. "I responded to a couple of posts. I want to have a conversation," he says. But the heat directed at anyone who disagrees and the inability of the typed word to convey complex emotion undercut his efforts. "You need to see the tears come down my face," he says, "rather than just the text."

Dale Kuehne, the New Hampshire minister and professor who, like Burgoyne, maintains a conservative view of sexuality, says he has reached out to some Coming Out Covenant supporters—to no avail. He has become convinced that neither side is truly interested in dialogue. "Both sides want to establish whether you're on their side before they want to talk. There's not a lot of cross-pollination going on, and I don't get the impression there's a big desire for it on either side." He studies presidential politics, and notes that there are pretty good parallels between what's happening (or not) in the church and what's happening (or not) in Washington.

Rebekah Eklund, the former denominational executive board member, believes the two sides "are almost having two different conversations. The conservative side wants to talk about the Bible. The other side is sharing stories. You can tell stories all day long, and they're wonderful and they're valuable, but for people who think the Bible says no to this issue, it's not going to change anything," she says. "I want to believe we can have this conversation in a spirit of grace that doesn't hurt people on either side. It's just really hard to do."

Can this denomination—or any—do it? How could they forge dialogue about an issue as polarizing as homosexuality that would satisfy both sides? That question, Kuehne believes, has serious implications for the future not just of the Covenant but of the broader church. "I don't actually think people under the age of thirty are demanding that the church agrees with them on everything. They just want to have an honest and reasonable discussion and decide if it is a place they want to be. I don't think the number one issue is whether the church agrees with my sexual views or not. I think it's: Can I develop a relationship with Christ and his body in this place?" he says. "We owe each other a dialogue and a discussion."

Burgoyne would agree. "What kind of a church do we need to be where it's actually possible and desirable to come into a community to process these issues together?" he asks. "Quite frankly, right now, the church is perceived as the last place you'd want to go."

Andrew Freeman had been unemployed for more than a year when a friend told him about a job opening at All Saints Episcopal Church in Chicago. The parish administrator, who doubled as music director, was leaving, and the rector had commented that she'd have to hire two people; after all, how many people out there could do both church administration and music? Andrew's friend said, "I know someone who could!"

It seemed like a dream job for Andrew, who has both a seminary degree and one in finance; who collected hymnals and prayer books in college, and also maintains a website; who recites from the Book of Common Prayer as part of his personal spiritual regimen, and samples from the Top 40 in his piano-playing at church. He sent in his resume, and though he had a twinge of concern that Episcopalians might judge someone from the Covenant to be too retro, he hid neither his Covenant background nor his sexuality. "While I consider myself thoroughly Covenant in my roots, I have discovered myself to be thoroughly ecumenical in my convictions and practice," he wrote to the rector. "Perhaps this is part of the hidden gift in being born into an evangelical tradition and being born gay: It requires you to creatively seek truth and beauty in otherwise unfamiliar places."

Six weeks later, Andrew had the job.

"I haven't become Episcopalian . . . yet," he tells me two days before he starts at All Saints. "I don't have to be there on Sundays. This means I can continue to attend ResCov and be involved in conversations that are beginning to take place there about sexuality. That said, this job does mark a clear shift in my denominational loyalty. Not that I am now loyal to the Episcopal Church, but it clearly sent a signal to people that I am not afraid to leave the ECC."

That he even mentions what kind of signal his new job sends shows how Andrew has internalized the public element of his struggle in the Covenant. But he is also weary of it. During his interview with the All Saints staff and search committee, he commented that he had begun "to feel that sitting around and talking about whether God actually loves gay people is quite uninteresting. There are far more interesting things in our faith to discuss, and far more important work that our faith requires of us."

"To be able to work in a church where the obstacles that once impeded me are completely taken off the table is both healing and liberating for me," he tells me later. "They are doing amazing ministry that I want to be a part of, and they happen to not care one bit that I am gay."

# BENJAMIN L. REYNOLDS

*"Brothers, I think the church needs a season of prayer."*
Chicago

From the beginning of this pilgrimage, numerous people encouraged me to explore the unique tensions in the African-American church. "It is different," said Vanderbilt sociologist Richard Pitt, who grew up gay in the Church of God in Christ. "If church is almost compulsory for black people generally, it's as compulsory for black gay people. But the black church is a little schizophrenic in its approach to gays. Gay-bashing sermons follow choir selections by the clearly gay minister of music at black churches all over the country. There's a kind of 'don't-ask-don't-tell' phenomenon."

So I tried to engage with that world, but it turned into the most fruitless reporting endeavor of my entire career. I sent hundreds of emails. I begged people for sources and stories. Few of my calls were returned. The phone appointments I did manage to make were mostly broken.

As frustrating as the collective silence was, I also understood: I'm an outsider. Why should I be trusted? I realized eventually that the silence was part of the story. And when this issue has been forced into the open, as in the case of Baptist minister Benjamin L. Reynolds, the fight has often been painful and ugly.

———

My family used to call me "Church Boy." Even when I was quite young—five, six, seven years old—I wanted to preach. At every opportunity, I wanted to go to church. I would take the opportunity to preach from my Sunday school book to my younger siblings, wearing one of my older brothers' choir robes. And when my siblings didn't want to hear it, I'd preach to GI Joe and Barbie.

Even as a child, my parents were concerned about my sexuality. When I was five years old, my aunt Betty came to visit our family. She had around her neck a beautiful strand of pearls. I told her they were very nice, and she took them off and put them around my neck. I heard my father coming down the hallway and I yanked them off. The strand broke and went all over the floor. My father whipped me. He told me the reason he did it was not because I broke them but because I had them on.

When I started preaching, my family was able to take a sigh of relief and say: "That's why he's different, because God deals with him differently." My first sermon was July 20, 1975, my fourteenth birthday. The title was "A Real and True Christian." It was taken from Acts, the eleventh chapter, from the verse where it says: "They were called Christians first at Antioch." There was something about Antioch, as I recall, that drew the people to a place of community. Not just oneness, but community. They were trying to follow the teachings of Christ. They were trying to actually do what Christ did—which was to go against what the culture was doing. And that is how they got the name "Christian."

I was nervous. But I had also been given advice that if I wasn't nervous, I should be scared. Any preacher going to the pulpit to preach should be afraid, because you are carrying the word of God. But I was encouraged, because that night, our church was very crowded. People seemed to be swinging from the chandeliers and standing along the walls. They had come to hear this child wonder, who claimed he was called to preach. The congregation received this message.

Most African-American churches are the place where you have voice. If you're not able to speak at school, if you're not able to be who you are at home, the church gives you voice and an opportunity to speak publicly. The pastor at the time— whom I call my father in ministry—was very careful to lead me to navigate, as best he knew how, the waters of ministry. I preached every three months or so after that. And when I preached, other churches said, "We want him to come and speak to the youth of our church!"

I knew there were gay men in my church. I wouldn't have called them that then, but there were several men who sang in the choir who you might say I had an affinity toward. I would look at them very closely—not in the way of lust, but I would say, "I want to sing like ____!" or "I want to play the piano like ____!"

When I was sixteen, we went on a trip to Denver to another church. A chaperone on that trip was gay. He was unattractive, and he was flamboyant. I remember him asking me in the church van if I was gay. I was just like, "Are you kidding me?" I was really disturbed. How could I possibly be gay if I was a preacher? My older brothers, who I knew were active sexually, I would preach to them and judge them. It is a sin to be having sex out of marriage!

When I was twenty-four, I moved to Dallas, where I lived for ten years. I worked with a Baptist congregation there and later served as the director of singles ministry. I was very clear that our dating ministry was not a dating game. That was the only way to get males there—they had to feel like every woman was not there to get at them. I was in denial about my sexuality, but I was dating guys and engaging intimately with guys and repenting later. Sometimes I'd go to a park that I knew guys would frequent and engage them, but true to who I am now, I would go through this process of trying to get to know them. I was afraid, but I found camaraderie with people like me. We did not say we were gay. We were all afraid that anyone would know. We would take a pill—anything—to get rid of it. We were afraid of being discovered.

In 1992, I moved back to Colorado because I was hired to be the pastor of the church I grew up in. One interview still stands out in my mind. We were gathered around the table—and my father was at the table because he was part of the pulpit selection committee. The question comes up: "How do you feel about homosexuality?" I think the way I answered was to say, "I think that God feels about homosexuality the same way he feels about people who are liars, people who are adulterers, but somehow, God still loves them. The jury is still out." Whatever I said, they let it alone. I am telling you, they knew I was gay—or at least had gay tendencies. But they didn't have the nerve to ask. Instead, they asked how I felt about it. That's a different question—and I think I was being truthful.

Around 1997 or 1998, a reporter from the *Colorado Springs Gazette* approached me for an article she was writing about the black church and homosexuality. I was quoted on the front page as saying, "The jury is still out. God does not condemn homosexuals." That started a storm in my congregation. *We have a pastor who is not clear about whether homosexuality is a sin!*

Several years before, I had married a woman from Dallas. She already had a child, and I think I was more attracted to becoming Daddy than I was to being married. Ultimately, that marriage died in 1999. While I was getting the divorce, I came before the congregation on that issue. But there were other rumors flying. My daughter—she had become my daughter—comes to me one night and says, "The people at school and church are saying you're gay. If you are, I still love you." But I was still hidden.

In 2001 or so, I invited a dear friend of mine named DaVita McCallister to come preach. She is an avowed lesbian, but she and I had a conversation and decided we would not include that in her bio in the bulletin. I told her I was going to edit it out and send it to the secretary for the bulletin.

On Saturday, I picked DaVita up at the airport. I told her I was going to go by the church and get a bulletin. So we open the bulletin and in it are the words "She is an avowed lesbian." I think I sent the wrong version to the secretary, but the truth is, DaVita *is* an avowed lesbian. The church loved her preaching, and I hoped that was the thing that would guide.

Sunday morning came—Palm Sunday. The first service started at 7:45, and people responded very well to her preaching. There's a break in between that service and the next, and she and I are having breakfast in my office with other people. I have no sense that a storm is brewing. She preaches. The congregation receives her, and fellowships with her after the service.

Monday morning at 6 a.m., the director of operations of our church calls me. All night, people have been calling her about what is going on. Her husband, a minister, is leaving the church. She is crying. Other people made decisions that they were leaving the congregation, too. I kept saying things like "You loved this woman before you found this out. What happened? You think her theology is good. What happened?" People are making appointments to see me. They're calling me. I'm running into people in the grocery store. They are saying, "It is a sin. And you know it is a sin."

That Easter was the lowest-attended we ever experienced. In African-American churches, when the minister is preaching, the congregation is usually very responsive. But that Sunday, they were mad as hell. It was icy. And it just kept growing icy. It never came back.

My own family was on its way to turning the corner by this point. My brother who was two years younger than me was also gay and had died of AIDS. I believe God seized that opportunity in order to help me have voice about sexuality. My brother had been very clear that, when I eulogized him, he did not want me to say he died of some mysterious disease. He wanted me to say he died from complications of the AIDS virus, so I did. My youngest sister is a lesbian; she came out in the late 1980s. And my parents came to this place where they're just trying to love our family. But I don't think they were ready for me to say: "Guess what? One more!" So I decided I still had to be hiding. I knew I was gay, but I was teeter-tottering on whether I was going to hell.

The crowning jewel happened in 2006, when I became vocal about issues pertaining to LGBTQ community. In Colorado, there was a Referendum I, which would have given same-sex couples legal protection in the event of sickness or death. I was leading a number of clergy who were very vocal about this issue. There was a press conference in Denver, and they asked me to be one of the speakers. Our youth minister, Reginald Fletcher, went with me to that meeting. He and I had gone to seminary together, and I had come out to him. Driving up to Denver—it was a Thursday—I remember saying to him, "What if I'm at the microphone and my picture lands on the cover of the *Denver Post?*" We laughed about that, but that in fact is what happened.

On Saturday morning, I had a deacons' meeting. We gathered in a circle as we typically did, beginning the meeting offering prayer requests. This morning, these men were very icy. I would say, "Deacon So and So, how are you today? How is your soul? How is your spirit?" They would reply curtly: "Blessed!" "Fine!" Not normal. Then they started saying things like "I think we need to pray for our church." Finally, as we come around the circle, seated on my left is the chairman of the deacons. He says he's "blessed," but he's concerned about the church. He pulls out the article. He says, "Are we becoming a gay church?" I said, "I don't know what a gay church is. But brothers, I think the church needs a season of prayer."

We scheduled a meeting for September so that I could tell the congregation the direction in which we were headed. In the meantime, I'm contemplating: "God, where are we going?"

Hours before I went before the congregation on September 29 to declare the journey, I believe God spoke to me. The spirit and I decided that it was time for me to go. The room was packed out, and I felt a lot of love. I resigned from the congregation that night, and I came out to them about my sexuality. The plan was that I would be with the congregation through the end of the year to help with the smooth transition to the new leadership. I asked that night that they not try to respond to me that night, but listen to me and hear my heart. I apologized to my parents, to my ex-wife. I said to them, "Some may say I need to repent. What I need to repent from tonight is that I have not trusted God with who I believe God has made me to be in the first place."

Some people left mad. There were tears. Some people hugged me and loved me as best they could, but some also became hostile to me. One of the deacons said, "Pastor, everybody knew you were gay, but I'm mad as hell you told us." In African-American communities, we can know something. But it's the telling that's problematic.

Sometimes I think about a young man in that congregation. I brought him under my wing and nurtured him. The night after I resigned, he was the first person to call me at home. And he called me by my first name. Benjamin is my name, and I love my name. But I recognized that a decision was made to reduce me by not calling me "pastor" anymore. That young man, he is ostentatiously gay. People know. He goes to clubs. He's at Pride. He and I have had conversations since my coming out. At night, he is supportive, but he is also a part of them. How can we keep this charade up?

I hold on to some tenets of being Baptist, but it was also the Baptist church that excluded me because of my sexuality. I want to be in a denomination that accepts the totality of who I am. So I am in the process of transferring my credentials to the United Church of Christ. In the end, the white church is who affirmed me. I no longer have a desire to be in an all-black church. I need to be in a setting that more resembles the reign of God, more of a multicultural setting.

The UCC is not quite home yet—the word *home* sounds a little too comfortable. But I think I am getting there. I'm still learning the denomination. I'm trying my best to better understand who they are and help them to better understand who I am. Hopefully the twain shall meet.

# WHAT PRICE, UNITY?

## First United Lutheran Church

---

*San Francisco*

Because I am a lifelong Protestant, every church I've ever attended has in some way been the product of not just one split but a string of them. My current denomination, the Reformed Church in America, has its roots in the Reformation, when the teachings of Martin Luther and John Calvin swept Europe. The Southern Baptists walked away from their northern brethren in 1845 over slavery. The Presbyterian Church in America seceded from mainline Presbyterianism in the early 1970s in response to growing theological liberalism (the PCA website cites, somewhat hyperbolically, the denial of "the deity of Jesus Christ," as if all Presbyterians except for those who left had stopped believing in the Messiah as anything but a good man). When I was in graduate school in London, I went Anglican. The Church of England has the most spectacular split story: king wants son, queen can't produce, church won't annul, king creates new church.

The history of Christianity is a history of rifts and rivalry. There's a moment back in the earliest days of the church when, according to the Book of Acts, "all the believers were one in heart and mind. No one claimed that any of their possessions was their own, but they shared everything they had. . . . And God's grace was so powerfully at work in them all that there were no needy persons among them. For from time to time those who owned land or houses sold them, brought the money from the sales and put it at the apostles' feet, and it was distributed to anyone who had need."

The church's honeymoon period did not last long. Within a few years, Paul was publicly admonishing Christians to quit fighting and sort things out. In his letter to the Church of the Philippians, he calls out two women in particular, Euodia and Syntyche, pleading with them "to be of the same mind in the Lord." Unfortunately, we never find out if they listened. Instead, we're left with the impression that, while those who call themselves followers of Christ may invoke the name of the same Lord, from nearly the beginning they've followed him in all different directions and fought over how to read the road maps.

At least in this way, America has always been a Christian nation. From the earliest days of European immigration to the New World, people have bickered about God, Jesus, and the Scriptures—and the Pilgrims settled what became New England because of the fight. In popular myth, they crossed the ocean for religious freedom. This is true inasmuch as they wanted their own religious freedom, but they never intended it for anyone else. Dissatisfied with the level of reform in the Church of England, the Puritans sailed westward to build what the preacher John Goodwin called "a nation of saints," based on their strict theology and exclusive of other interpretations of Christianity. But every generation, every nation, has its renegades and its rebels, too. Within a few years of the 1628 founding of the Puritan-dominated Massachusetts Bay Colony, there were dissenters to be banished, and theological rifts preoccupied the courts.

Every denomination in this book and in this world, with the exception of one, has resulted from someone's conviction that there needed to be a new church. And while Roman Catholicism can proclaim an intact line of leadership going back to St. Peter, it's not as if Christianity's meiotic tendencies have left it untouched—it's the establishment church from which others have repeatedly split. Today there are at least two thousand Christian denominations in the United States, and the fastest-growing part of the American church is the nondenominational, in which each congregation could be seen as its own little stand-alone denomination, answerable to no one else.

We live in a new boom time of ecclesiastical and denominational divorce—and issues related to sexuality are huge catalysts in the split process. These kinds of issues, more than, say, the virgin birth or papal infallibility, are the ones we are fighting about. Over the past five years, as mainline denominations have changed policies regarding marriage and ordination of gays and lesbians, more conservative congregations have been departing. The issue of homosexuality has helped to cleave four new denominations from the Episcopal Church of the U.S.A. and splinter the worldwide Anglican Communion in spirit, if not in practice. Despite repeated pleas from Archbishop of Canterbury Rowan Williams, head of the Communion during most of this fracturing period, to remain together in grace, unity has proved impossible, given that the conservatives see the liberals' position as heresy and the liberals see the conservatives' as hate. "I don't see unity as a great virtue if you're unified in allowing something that's evil," says retired Episcopal bishop John Spong, a liberal-church hero and, to conservatives, a theological goat. "You don't unify the church around unity. You unify it around what's right. The Episcopal Church has done what's right. The problem is, people don't understand that prejudice isn't something you debate—it's something you counter."

Bishop Thad Barnum of the Anglican Mission in the Americas (AMiA), an Episcopalian splinter church, says that to focus on homosexuality and gay rights, as Spong does, misses the point, which is really biblical truth. The Episcopalians' failure to uphold that truth became clear to the AMiA's leaders during the tenure of Presiding Bishop Frank Griswold, who helmed the Episcopal Church of the U.S.A. from 1998 to 2006. Barnum, who's highly skilled in the art of faint-praise damnation, calls Griswold "a consummate diplomat and politician" with "great authenticity." "The thing I appreciate about Griswold is that he saw that you don't take Scripture and force it to agree with you," Barnum says. "He said, 'I'm not going to do that. I'm not going to follow your linear thought. I'm going to create a new thought.' It's not 'We're trying to make Scripture sing a different song.' It's 'We're saying God is speaking in a different voice now. He has changed his mind.' Griswold went beyond liberalism. It's revision. It's a new gospel."

If you had any doubt as to Barnum's views of the theological legitimacy of this, he puts it to rest thus: "That's like Mormonism!" He pauses momentarily and then says, "I am thankful for this argument."

You'll hear similar rumblings in the Presbyterian Church (U.S.A.), America's third-largest Protestant denomination. In the summer of 2011, the PCUSA voted to allow the ordination of non-celibate, openly gay and lesbian ministers. The following January, a group of conservative-leaning Presbyterian pastors and congregations announced the creation of a new denomination called the Evangelical Covenant Order of Presbyterians (ECO). The effort was led by the pastors of some of the biggest, wealthiest Presbyterian congregations in America, including the PCUSA's largest, Peachtree Presbyterian in Atlanta.

The timeline has led plenty of outside observers to conclude that the vote on gay ministers was the cause. The ECO's leaders protest that it's not about that decision at all—but it is, a little bit, insofar as it provided one final data point, one last proof that there has been a long-term denominational shift in how Scripture is interpreted and rules on Christian behavior are written, rewritten, and understood. "This is not really fighting about gay sex and it's not politics," says John Crosby, senior pastor of the fifteen-hundred-member Christ Presbyterian Church in Edina, Minnesota, and an ECO leader. "This is about hermeneutics. Whether it's the salvific work of Christ or the uniqueness of Christianity on sexuality, society is pushing us to accept that all positions are true."

There are few things everyone, no matter where they are on the theological spectrum, can agree to be true, but one is this: These splits have caused pain. People who used to sit next to each other in the pews every Sunday have found themselves in rival congregations and denominations. Families have been split along theological lines. Any semblance of church unity has been eviscerated.

A prime—and unusual—case study of the trauma of denominational division is a small San Francisco congregation called First United Lutheran Church. In recent years, the typical pattern has been that a denomination will move in the liberal direction and conservative members will flee. Not so in First United's case. Once part of the Evangelical Lutheran Church of America (ELCA), it was ejected from the denomination in 2000 because the congregation was *too* liberal, having broken church policy by ordaining a gay man as associate pastor. But in the summer of 2009, the denomination came around to First United's position, voting to legalize the ordination of noncelibate gays and lesbians. Then the ELCA sought to convince the people of First United, all twenty-five of them, to return to the Lutheran fold.

"The wounds are deep," current pastor Susan Strouse says. "This congregation wants the ELCA to understand that. It's not just no harm, no foul. This horrible, horrible divorce happened, and they're wondering if there can truly be reconciliation. They want guarantees, but of course there can't be. We have to live in faith, and it can't be fear-based. We talk a lot about not living in fear."

Among the world's Christian denominations, the Evangelical Lutheran Church of America is a relative toddler. It was formed on January 1, 1988, when three denominations, the Lutheran Church in America, the American Lutheran Church, and the Association of Evangelical Lutheran Churches, combined. Lutherans hailed the merger as a triumph of Christian unity. However, for three openly gay seminarians in the Class of 1988 at the Pacific Lutheran Theological Seminary in Berkeley, California, it was troubling. The Lutheran Church in America and the American Lutheran Church, the more liberal partners in the new denominational trinity, had earlier approved all three for call to ministry. Until that point, the typical practice in most synods was a form of "don't ask, don't tell"; gay and lesbian seminarians would be quiet about their sexuality as part of a gentlemen's (and ladies') agreement with the bishops, who would allow their ordinations to go forward.

But after the ELCA formed, "the bishops of the new church had a kind of anxiety attack," says Jeff Johnson, one of the three gay seminarians. It issued guidelines requiring openly gay and lesbian candidates to commit to celibacy. "The three of us weren't interested in observing the old agreement, and we were not interested in not taking our church up on the approval they had granted us before the new policy." Johnson and his two gay classmates opted for alternative careers. He ended up pursuing work in social services.

One day, the pastor of First United took Johnson to lunch. Liberal Lutheran pastors around the country had been circulating a petition stating their objection to the celibacy rule, and Johnson was told that First United wanted to go a step further: It hoped to call Johnson as its associate pastor. The church, founded in 1887, had long seen itself as a beacon of progressive theology and practice, and this would be an intentional act of righteous rebellion. "I told them they couldn't, because it was illegal. He said they knew that," Johnson says, noting that there's some irony in a Lutheran celibacy requirement. One of Martin Luther's complaints against the Roman Catholic Church was that it insisted on priestly celibacy, a requirement that he said had no biblical basis.

For the next eighteen months, First United's leaders and members thought and contemplated and mulled and debated. They knew there would be denominational consequences for such a defiant move. But eventually, they decided to go ahead and call Johnson. They also recruited allies: another San Francisco congregation, St. Francis, decided that it would ordain two lesbian ministers at the same time.

On January 22, 1990, at a joint service with St. Francis that drew a thousand people, Jeff Johnson, Ruth Frost, and Phyllis Zillhart were ordained. In response, the ELCA declared the ordinations "valid, but illegal," which to most people sounds like "Yes . . . but no!" In other words, everything had been done by Lutheran protocol, with one exception: The local bishop had not approved the ordinations. So the two churches were sent letters informing them that a disciplinary board would be convened. At First United, "the congregation was pretty much of one mind. There may have been one or two holdouts at the beginning," Johnson says. "When the denomination put the congregation on trial, everybody just rallied. It unified the congregation. People felt like the reason for their actions was justified and the reason for the expulsion was not."

Johnson says the church still thought there was a chance to avoid discipline. "We hoped there would be people moved by what we interpreted to be the Spirit and that they would change their minds," he says. "We hoped that the real-life experience of these openly gay pastoral candidates and all the people who gathered to support us would be powerful enough to help people deal with the prejudice of heterosexism and homophobia." Not only had the bishops of the ELCA not changed their minds, but they also insisted that St. Francis and First United change theirs by reversing the ordinations within five years. Of course they declined, and in 1995, both congregations were expelled from the Evangelical Lutheran Church of America.

On the day that First United was kicked out, it celebrated. "We called it the Feast of the Expulsion," says Orion Pitts, First United's music director, a lifelong Lutheran who was then one of the church's newest members. "It was celebratory because we had not compromised on our integrity. We had a worship service as we would celebrate the Easter vigil or Christmas Eve—hymns, Scripture, the whole thing."

According to Martin Luther, when bishops and priests refuse to do what the Gospel requires—they "have grown quite indifferent," he wrote in 1520—then the congregations must. And Johnson saw his now-former denomination as having done the opposite of what, in his interpretation, the Gospel requires. "I think gay and lesbian people have rightly abandoned the church for decades because the church was the enemy. The institutional church was the enemy of our own liberation, our own freedom," he says. "The stories—the foundational stories of our faith—are stories that don't serve the status quo. They serve the liberation of LGBT people—and that's the problem for the church. Some people call it salvation. I call it the liberation of humanity. It's taken time, but we know what the trajectory will be. Over time, churches like Westboro Baptist will become fewer and fewer and more and more isolated and alienating—kind of like strong coffee that sits on the burner too long. It will become not palatable because everybody else has moved on."

St. Francis and First United were the only two congregations ever expelled from the Evangelical Lutheran Church of America over this issue. Other churches also ordained gays and lesbians—the next such ordination took place in 2000 in Kansas City, followed by fourteen more over the next decade. But for those congregations, punishment never went farther than a letter of censure, the church discipline equivalent of a public wet-noodle flogging.

"What does it mean to be the church in this day and age? Instead of moaning and groaning, how can we be creative?" Pastor Strouse says when I meet her for coffee in Berkeley, where she lives.

First United has had to be creative in the years of its exile. This was especially true when it needed a new pastor in 2000. (Its previous lead pastor had retired, and Jeff Johnson had moved on to the University of California, Berkeley, where he still serves as the Lutheran chaplain.) Any minister on the official ELCA roster would risk discipline by accepting a job at a renegade church.

First United's pastoral search committee called Susan Strouse, a brainy cradle Lutheran and native of upstate New York who was then studying for her Ph.D. in interfaith studies at the Pacific School of Religion, also located in Berkeley. She was an unorthodox choice, given that she had no interest in heading a congregation. "I made a list of why I should and shouldn't take the job," Strouse says. "The 'shouldn't' was a long list. I didn't want to be in a congregation. And what would it to do to my pension, because I am on the ELCA roster? The bishop warned me not to do it. Plus, the church's finances were so bad that they could only afford me half-time." But there was one compelling item on the very short "should" side of the ledger: "I felt like I was being called."

Under her leadership, First United has become a "church without walls." In 2007, the church sold its half-century-old building on Geary Boulevard. (The buyer was a Buddhist temple.) The decision was less financial—San Francisco's celestial property values won't drop anytime soon, and the church could have found a wealthier buyer than the Buddhists—than philosophical: The congregation committed to being a more visible part of the community. So it got rid of its literal walls, selling the property and shedding the forbidding stucco walls that set it apart.

Today it meets in a Unitarian church, drawing about twenty-five attendees on a typical Sunday. It's about a third gay, a third straight families, and a third straight singles and couples. It's "a little bit too white," Strouse says. "We should do better." Most of the people who were in the congregation at the time of the ELCA expulsion have moved on.

Strouse is straight, and with Johnson at UC Berkeley, First United was technically no longer in violation of the ELCA's rules. An odd courtship began. "For five years, the synod would dangle a carrot in front of us, trying to get us to come back. They said, 'You are now in compliance!' But they kept raising the bar," she says. At times the church has been tempted to rejoin. At one point, the members told Strouse that they would rejoin the ELCA for her sake, so that she could get the benefits that First United couldn't afford. "I said, 'No, no, no, no!'" she says. "Unless the policy that caused all this changed, we were not going back."

In the summer of 2009, after two decades of contentious debate, the policy did change. The new statement on sexuality passed by one vote.

Jeff Johnson had a few dozen people over to his East Bay home to watch the vote on television. When Presiding Bishop Herbert Chilstrom announced the results, a cheer shook his house. The next day, he was talking to a neighbor. "I tried to find the game yesterday," she said, "but I had no idea what it was." Johnson replied: "It was a church convention!"

The following spring, the Sierra Pacific Synod, which includes San Francisco, passed a resolution inviting St. Francis and First United to rejoin the synod as well as the broader church. Johnson and six other gay pastors whose calls had not been recognized by the church were also officially validated in what the church called a "rite of reconciliation." Within months, St. Francis had decided to return to the official Lutheran fold. "People in this congregation have a very strong sense that the church is bigger than the congregation," St. Francis pastor Robert Goldstein said. "We look forward to participating in the wider church."

But First United resisted. "Everyone on the outside was asking, 'What are you going to do?'" Strouse says, "I convinced the members they had to talk about it. And so we entered into a time of discernment. We had a couple of people from St. Francis come over and talk about the process and why they did what they did."

The local ELCA leadership has sought to rebuild ties to First United. On Palm Sunday 2010, Bishop Mark Holmerud, who leads the Sierra Pacific Synod, came to worship at the church. A few months later, he sent one of his subordinates to spend some time with the congregation. Ahead of her visit, she asked to see a copy of the church's constitution. This has been one of the key obstacles for First United. Its constitution has two provisions that violate the ELCA's strict guidelines: one articulates First United's support of same-sex marriage, while the other codifies its commitment to inclusive language. Rather than the traditional "Father, Son, and Holy

Spirit," First United says "Creator, Redeemer, and Sustainer." Pitts, the music director, walks me through a verse of the traditional Lutheran hymn "Jesus Shall Reign Where'er the Sun," highlighting words that are unacceptable at First United. "*Reign*. That's holding dominion over. That's hierarchical imagery. Hierarchy is one of the big problems with organized religion. And '*his* successive journeys run.' We avoid as much as possible the male pronouns, even when referring to Jesus. So where it says, 'His kingdom stretch from shore to shore,' *kingdom* definitely we would not use."

When the associate bishop got to the church, she surprised the members, telling them that she read the constitution en route and that she thought it was "great." But her approval is ultimately irrelevant; to rejoin the ELCA, the more conservative bigwigs at denominational headquarters must approve the constitution. When St. Francis went through the readmission process, it accepted the traditional "Father, Son, and Holy Spirit" language, relegating its preferred words to a footnote. That has seemed like a cop-out to the people of First United.

But these are mere details. The bigger issue is whether First United wants its future to be within the ELCA or not. "If the church decides not to rejoin, we might look bad. So if they decide not to, I want them to have a really good rationale," Strouse says. "But whether or not it rejoins, this congregation has survived for twenty years outside the denomination and has retained its theology, its creativity in worship, its integrity, and its commitment to social justice. It has done well. Whether or not they go back, it will still be a wonderful, Gospel-centered church."

As Strouse has tried to guide the church gently through the process of answering that question, the congregation has divided into two camps.

The "why bother?" camp sees little upside to rejoining the denomination—and plenty of downsides. There's greater bureaucracy, a return to the hierarchy and the officialdom that they fear could cramp their San Francisco style. And there are some significant unanswered questions, such as fears about what might happen to the church's commitment to gay unions. During the brief period when gay marriage was legal in California, two couples in the church were wed; would First United be disciplined because of that?

The other camp, which includes mostly cradle Lutherans, misses being part of something bigger—especially something with the history and tradition of Lutheranism.

When I ask Strouse how she personally feels about rejoining, she seems almost startled and thinks for a long while. "I have mixed feelings," she says finally. The denomination "moves slowly. It's sad it took so long, but I'm happy it has happened, and I am thrilled that our own synod, with all these congregations threatening to leave across the country, has said to them: 'We will send you with our blessing. The door will always be open to you.'"

Then she widens her lens, expanding the conversation to take in the balkanized whole of American Christianity. "Many people will say that there's this split between progressives and conservatives. There is, and to my way of thinking, it needs to happen," she says. "If people feel they cannot accept this interpretation of Scripture, this interpretation of theology, then you have to say, 'You go with our blessing! You need to be where you're comfortable.' We have to accept we're not going to change people's minds. There was a time back in the days of the Evangelical Lutheran Church when they were always talking about unity, unity, unity. We were worshipping at the altar of unity—it became an idol. But sometimes divorce on good terms is the right thing to do if you can't live together. It would be great if we could be together, but sometimes, at some point, it's not happening and it's not the right thing."

Yes, sometimes remarriage is right, Strouse acknowledges. And there's another consideration beyond what the church can get out of rejoining: What can First United, this little band of liberal believers in San Francisco, bring to the broader church? At a congregational meeting, one member gave an answer that seemed to satisfy most of her fellow parishioners, philosophically if not yet actively: "We do have something we can give to the rest of the church," she said. "We can show them what the power of forgiveness looks like."

I have no idea which side I'd be on if I were a member of First United. As I toyed with the merits and demerits of both sides, I did some reading on church unity over the years, and I came across a letter written in the way that people sometimes use when they're dressing up their words to be more impressive—a tuxedo of prose comprising an "indeed" here, an extra adverb there, not to mention words like *comprising*:

> Amongst the great evils of our century must be counted the fact that the churches are so divided one from another that there is scarcely even a human relationship between us. At all events, there is not the shining light of that holy fellowship of the members of Christ, of which many boast in word, but which few seek sincerely indeed. In consequence, because the members are torn apart, the body of the church lies wounded and bleeding.

These words could have been written yesterday, such is the polarization of the Christian churches today. But they actually come from a letter that the sixteenth-century reformer John Calvin wrote in the spring of 1552 to Archbishop Thomas Cranmer of the Church of England.

"So far as I have it in my power, if I am thought to be of any service, I shall not be afraid to cross ten seas for this purpose, if that should be necessary," Calvin wrote to Archbishop Cranmer. But there were theological seas he would not cross—especially when it came to the Roman Catholic Church and what he believed it had done to the one true faith. In another letter, to Cardinal Jacopo Sadoleto, who had written to the people of Geneva urging them to return to Catholicism, Calvin alleged that real Christianity was "almost destroyed by the Roman pontiff and his faction." The church ought to "humbly and religiously . . . venerate the word of God, and submit to its authority."

There's the core of the problem: In our millennia-old game of religious telephone, we have come to hear that Word spoken in possibly irreconcilable ways, such that people of good faith are really people of different faiths. When I asked Orion Pitts, the First United music director, what he believes, he referred to the collection of twelve tattoos on his right arm. Among them: a symbol that Muslims know as the hand of Fatima and Jews would say is the hand of Miriam; an alpha and an omega; an Egyptian ankh; and a yin-yang symbol.

The faith he describes would be unrecognizable as Christianity to Calvin or Luther. "Our Christianity recognizes other faith traditions as equally valid," he says. "As the Hindus say, there is one God, but it is called by many names." Actually, Pitts doesn't even call himself a Christian right now—"but I can't say tomorrow I wouldn't. That's part of the journey right now. It's the reason that many people have: That word has become so co-opted by influences that I do not consider Christian. I am not willing to use it or categorize myself in that way."

So which Gospel are we talking about? Translated and retranslated into modern American English and its myriad religious vernaculars, it sounds less like good news and more like the frustrating, polarizing words of spiritual discord that drive people away from the church. And I say "the church" knowing it's wholly inaccurate. If there's anything that a case like First United shows, it's that such a unified thing no longer exists.

from: Jeff Chu
to: Gideon Eads
date: Tue, Jul 26, 2011 at 1:21 PM
subject: Re: Hi, "Chuck" from Twitter

Gideon,

Sorry for the break in communication. I had a crazy, busy weekend. What does your family think of your interest in cake decorating? Have they been supporting your various pursuits? Do you feel like you "fit in" with them? Do you think they suspect at all that you might be gay? When you were reviewing one of the books for me, you referred to the argument that we focus on religion of tradition and the religion itself so much that we lose sight of everything else (Jesus, for instance). Can you tell me a little bit about your family's relationship with faith? Do you think it falls into that trap as well?

That's it for now. Let me know if you have any questions for me!

Best,
Jeff

from: Gideon Eads
to: Jeff Chu
date: Tue, Jul 26, 2011 at 8:07 PM
subject: Hi

Hey Jeff,

Do I feel like I fit in is a complicated question. . . . It's both yes and no, but only a few years ago it was totally no. The rest of my family are pretty much in the same mind and spirit on everything, and I've always been different in taste, opinions, views, and obviously my sexuality. When it began to cause conflict, I kind of forced myself to fit in. So within the place I've created to exist I do fit in, but that place is the straight shell of me. I don't think my sexuality will ever fit in with this family, but I long for them to know (even if they disapprove and reject me) the real Gideon. On the same note I also long for them to know the real Gideon AND realize it's the same Gideon they've loved and fellowshipped with their entire lives.

I'm not sure if they suspect I'm gay, sometimes I think it's guaranteed that they've at least thought about it. I mean, my best friends growing up were girls, I played house and dolls with my little sister when I watched her, I never showed any interest in dating girls or even talked about girls. I decorate cakes, I like to paint, I care about my hair and hygiene, and I never ever take part in their put-down conversations about gay people. Do they notice me watching and drooling over muscular guys the same way men do over woman's breasts? My brother who is now 30 years old has also never officially dated, but he talks about woman and wanting to find one, and has often expressed desire to find a nice girl.

When I was 15 years old, a few years after electricity service was extended to our house and we no longer ran off of a gas generator, we began to slowly acquire modern technologies, phone lines, computer, and finally the internet. I had never used the internet except a few times at the public library in town, and I really did not know how the thing worked. The more I realized what the internet was, I began to wonder if I could find information on my sexuality. At the time I did not know what a morally dangerous place the internet could be. One day when I was alone in the house, I typed in a few simple keywords "Gay men" hoping to find information, and what I got was list of gay pornographic websites. I was brave and clicked on one just to see and the images that began to flood the screen both horrified and excited me. I quickly tried to close all the browser windows but apparently one of them contained a virus. My family did not even know computers could get a virus nor did we even own any virus protection.

In a panic I figured out how to delete the browsing history and thought all was well. The virus however began to infect our computer, and eventually we figured out that we needed to use some software to scan the computer. My mom has always been funny with computers, I still don't think she understands them after using them for so many years. She sat down and watched the software scan every single file. It was like 6 hours! To my horror, she saw the various "xxx" and "Gay" items that were planted somewhere on the system. She sternly questioned me and I denied anything. I was scared out of my mind! During this time, I had been writing in a devotional journal. I tried to write things in a way that was honest but not going to give me away should my siblings find it. About a week later my brother came across the book and read the entire thing to my mother. The moment I saw her holding my journal I was scared out of my mind again. The hate I felt from them was unbearable, though at the time I may have confused their hatred of the sin for hatred of me . . . I'm not really sure.

I never said I was gay, but I did tell them honestly that it was a PRIVATE journal of things I had been talking to God about, I was not a sexually active person, or was in danger of being "lost." They didn't really speak to me that day, and later on when we took a trip to town, as we pulled into the parking lot of Walmart, Mom hit her palms against the steering wheel and said in that tough stern voice, "Gideon, the websites and the book. Do you have a problem with this stuff?" I remember wanting to tell her that I was gay, but that I did not have a problem with sex. But the only thing I could do was to shake my head no. She continued, "If you have a problem with this kind of stuff you need to stop it, and repent of it. I will not be having this kind of crap in my house, do you understand?" I nodded my head and I don't think I spoke another word the entire day.

Do they remember this day as clearly as I do? Did they even fathom that their son could have been dealing with homosexuality? Or did they just think I was trying out porn? I honestly do not know.

Take care and God bless.

—Gideon Eads

---

from: Jeff Chu
to: Gideon Eads
date: Sun, Jul 31, 2011 at 8:39 PM
subject: Re: Hi

Hi Gideon,

Tell me more about what you believe you are being called to. I would be interested to hear more about that, even though I understand your thoughts are not really fully developed. Also, do you think that your family views homosexuality as worse than other sin? If so, why do you think that is?

Hope you had a good weekend!

Jeff

---

from: Gideon Eads
to: Jeff Chu
date: Mon, Aug 1, 2011 at 1:27 AM
subject: RE: Hi

Hi Jeff,

Good to hear from you, I've been very busy this weekend. I had two special cakes to make, one for a dear member of our church who is facing cancer and moving away, she will probably not return before she passes away. The other was a cake for my dad's birthday.

I feel like God is calling me to come out here very soon. I was thinking maybe by my birthday in December, but I kind of feel like it needs to happen sooner. Primarily I was going to wait until some very large cake orders are finished in the next few months, I did not want to risk losing that business if they knew I was gay. I feel however that God may be asking me to trust Him with all those situations no matter how they turn out, and come out sooner than I planned.

I would have to say my family thinks homosexuality is the worst sin. Though they may not say it is more sinful than "regular sin" because they do believe all sin is sin in God's eyes, the way they treat it shows what they think about homosexuality. Just today, I was driving home from church, and my sister made a statement about not listening to a particular artist any longer, because one of the videos had [a] gay person in it. This horrified her, and she swore to find alternative music.

We finally got a good rainstorm today, it's been SO humid and hot, church was enjoyable and we just went to go see the smurfs movie. I hope you have a great week!

—Gideon Eads

# RECONCILING

---

"Then said the Shepherds one to another, Let us here show to the Pilgrims the gates of the Celestial City, if they have skill to look through our perspective glass."

−PART I, THE EIGHTH STAGE, *THE PILGRIM'S PROGRESS*

# NEW COMMUNITY

The Gay Christian Network

---

*Raleigh, North Carolina*

Sometimes I wonder, What if I had had Google when I was a teenager? We did have a computer, on which I sometimes played Oregon Trail. (I loved dying of dysentery.) But there was never any temptation to click over to the Internet, because it didn't exist. I'm part of the last generation to have grown up in the days of card catalogs and *Encyclopædia Britannica*. Playing a video meant popping a cassette into the VCR, and "it gets better" referred only to getting past the part of the tape that was messed up, not to a genre of online encouragement.

But just as connectivity has transformed how we watch TV, how we eat, and how we fall in love, it has revolutionized faith, giving the seeker new tools and new opportunities for community. If I'd had the Internet when I was a confused, hormonal teen in gay denial, I might have done what I did years later, as a confused, hormonal twentysomething—search out all manner of homosexual sites, not just porn but also discussions of theology and scientific research into the origins of homosexuality.

One day in late 2004, when I was still pretending publicly to be straight, I typed the words *gay* and *Christian* into Google. The first link led to gaychristian.net—the online home of the organization that controversially hosted Alan Chambers at its annual conference, the Gay Christian Network.

Justin Lee founded the Gay Christian Network in 2001, when he was twenty-four. With his bald head (alopecia), politely cheery manner (Southerner), and geeky tendency to exclaim semi-square, age-inappropriate things like "Oh, goodness!" (inexplicable), Justin could be Dr. Evil's cuter, cheerier younger brother. He radiates openness, and it's hard to imagine anyone who wouldn't respond in kind. Yet as he struggled with his faith and sexuality through his teens and into his twenties, people didn't. Which is why his website has a big-theological-tent ethos: All are welcome, no matter their theology or views on gay behavior.

Justin was sometimes called God Boy in his youth—with good reason, he tells me when I visit him in his hometown of Raleigh, North Carolina: "I was the kid with the Bible in his backpack, ready to witness to everybody at school." Occasionally he got bullied. On the bus one day when he was thirteen or fourteen, a bunch of kids started a conversation about why Justin never cursed. "It became this *thing*," he says. "They wanted to know, like, why it was a big deal to me. I had never ever uttered a profanity in my life. And they were trying to goad me into it, daring me, trying to see if they could get me to say something. I wouldn't do it. I was the good Christian kid!"

In my experience, to be the good Christian kid is both a horrible blessing and a wonderful curse. There's comfort and fear in the fortress of faith that you build around yourself, and there's excitement and terror in the weaknesses that you—and only you, or so you think—see in its walls. Invariably, at some point, you have this epiphany: that those walls you imagined were built of emotional and psychological Jerusalem stone were actually made of plastic, of Legos, of things that can quickly be dismantled or obliterated.

In Justin's case, he was such a good Christian kid that when he noticed he had no feelings for girls, he could almost convince himself it was because "I respected girls so much." But on some level, he knew that was a lie. Because he had feelings for boys. At fifteen he began crying himself to sleep. "I was just begging God to take this away from me," he says. "I was trying harder and harder to not feel this. At no point did it ever occur to me that I was gay, because that was a lifestyle that was anti-Christian—it might as well have been Wiccan! I just had weird feelings that wouldn't go away. This was the secret I would take with me to my grave."

When he was eighteen, he went to a Jars of Clay/Michael W. Smith concert—with his girlfriend, "whom my friends thought was really hot," he says. "She was holding my hand. And then I caught a glimpse of this guy in the crowd who walked past, and I just felt really drawn to him. Suddenly I wanted to know everything about him. This random guy! I had never felt for my girlfriend what I felt for this random stranger. I felt this attraction deep within me. I started crying."

These were the Internet's early days. The *News & Observer*, the local paper, was offering high school kids free accounts for its new online chat service, NandoLand. Justin began chatting with a friend of a friend, who seemed just to understand him in a way that other people didn't. "It was sort of like gaydar," he says. "Finally, he says, 'I guess there's something I should tell you: I'm bisexual.' I just completely broke down. I was bawling at my computer. I realized at that moment that I was bisexual!" He pauses. "I'm not. But gay was just too scary. So I realized I was bi."

He told a friend, who said that he should just accept it and be a gay Christian. "I was horrified," Justin says. He told his girlfriend, and that was the end of that. He told another friend, who introduced him to a secret ex-gay group. "It became very obvious to me very quickly that these men were not becoming straight," Justin says. "That was the first time I had a twinge of doubt." He also told his parents, whose response was "We're going to love you and we're going to help you beat this," he remembers. "Which was what I wanted. I would have done anything to become straight."

So he went to ex-gay conferences and tried to get into ex-gay groups, but one turned him away because they didn't know what to do with a teenage virgin. He went to counselors. Finally, "I went back to God," he says. "I stopped praying, 'God make me straight,' and I started praying, 'God, show me what you want me to do.'"

By this point, enough people knew about his struggle that they were gossiping as church people do—which is to say enthusiastically. Justin had volunteered for a couple of summers as a counselor at a Christian camp; the parents of kids he had counseled stopped letting them talk to him. People in his Christian fellowship at Wake Forest University and even at church shied away from him. "They treated me like a heretic," he says, "and I wasn't even doing anything!"

When he ventured online, into a couple of gay Christian chat rooms, he found them full of people who had no doubt gay sexuality could be reconciled with Scripture and wanted to talk only with those who shared that conviction. "I really wanted to understand how they came to that," he says, "but they didn't really receive my questions very well. They thought I was some gay basher, pretending to be gay. Or they'd give a nonanswer."

When he went to the campus LGBT group, they too kept away: "They didn't know what to do with this good Christian boy. And I never felt as alone as I did at that point. I was thinking about suicide all day, every day. I was only staying alive because, as a Christian, suicide was wrong. I don't think I really wanted to die. I just didn't want to live as I was living."

One day he came out to a discussion group on a Christian music site that he frequented, though nobody knew his real name. He started a website where he posted his story, more as an exercise in truth telling than to spur responses, because who was even going to read the thing? Then his inbox began to fill with messages of encouragement, with other people's stories, with pleas for help, with requests for advice. The emails came from all over the country, from people (mostly men) old and young. One came from a closeted pastor who was struggling with his sexuality. "I have kids and a wife and a congregation," he wrote. "What should I do?" The memory still makes Justin laugh: "I don't know! I'm a college student!"

After graduating from Wake Forest, Justin took some time off, waiting tables at Applebee's and trying to deal with his issues. In 2001 he was chatting with a guy in California, and they got on the subject of creating a place for people to connect with each other, sort of an online support group for Christians who happen to be gay. Says Justin: "I couldn't keep answering all those emails."

The term *safe space* conjures for me notions of self-serious shrinks, corporate retreat trust falls, and overbearing HR people who have no intention of keeping your secrets, but a safe space is exactly what Justin wanted the Gay Christian Network (GCN) to be. For so many Christians, your position on committed gay relationships is a theological litmus test—the very thing Justin was sure he did not want for his site. "I wanted it to be a space where people felt welcome, wherever they came down on the issue," he tells me as we sit on the black leather couches in his apartment, which is decorated in the masculine postcollege style. "That is and was the most important thing."

GCN was to be a place for other Justins, a place where they could boldly ask the questions that are hard to ask even without the fear of judgment. And despite the fact that Christians sometimes recoil from doubt as if it were the devil himself, GCN would be a place to recognize that, while some of us might think we have the answers about the Bible and homosexuality, we can't know for sure.

The site "opened up a whole new world to me," says "Johnny," a Southerner and military brat in his late twenties who requested that I use a pseudonym because he's seeking ordination in a denomination that wouldn't ordain him if it knew of his sexuality. At college, Johnny confided in another guy in his dorm who was also struggling with his sexuality, and that friend recommended the Gay Christian Network. For a few months, Johnny lurked on the boards; it was nearly a year before he "began to join in conversations and to talk to people," he says. "Here were LGBT people who were also Christian, and they had sincere faith. I had felt so alone and suddenly I had a community of people to talk to and grow with."

Offline, Johnny, who is in his last year of divinity school, leads what he calls a "half life in public, pretending to be single. I have to lie sometimes so that I am allowed to answer my calling. It breaks my heart that we lose good people who would have been great clergy or have clergy that are forced to hide a whole part of who they are [and] sometimes even the person they are spending their life with." But on GCN, he can be wholly himself. "GCN has provided me that safe place I needed to deal with the world that was not supportive of me," he says. In fact, he probably wouldn't be pursuing a career as a minister if not for this community, because it "allowed me to develop the esteem to truly believe I was right in the eyes of God."

One of Justin's key early steps was to create a forum on the site for "Side A," people who believe that homosexual relationships are biblically permissible, as well as one for "Side B," those who don't. "We should be able to be bluntly honest without worrying about offending the other side with our questions," he explains. There's also a link on its home page to "The Great Debate," as its known on GCN; Justin has an essay up arguing for Side A, while another longtime GCNer, Ron B., takes Side B.

Other Christian-based organizations have sprung up that seek to push a particular agenda or address a certain demographic— Soulforce promotes gay rights on college campuses, the Marin Foundation tries to make amends for wrongs done to the gay community by Christians, The Evangelical Network (TEN) ministers to gay Pentecostals—but GCN's effort to welcome people from across both spectra is unique. It's a spirit that Justin has fostered not just online but also off. When I visit, his staff of three includes a Baptist-raised evangelical (himself); an operations director who was reared Congregationalist and is now Methodist; and an administrator who was raised Methodist, then joined the Assemblies of God, and finally converted to Roman Catholicism. And the annual conference that GCN has hosted since 2004 has featured speakers who approve of homosexual behavior within committed relationships (such as the late Harvard chaplain Peter Gomes, in 2009); some who oppose it (2012 keynoter Misty Irons is a straight woman whose husband, an Orthodox Presbyterian Church pastor, was disciplined for an article *she*, not he, wrote in support of legalizing nonchurch same-sex unions); and some who decline to state a position (Christian author Philip Yancey, a 2011 keynoter, refuses to take a public stance on the gay issue and declined my interview request, saying, "Every time I touch on it, I end up answering emails, blogs, and radio cranks").

Justin's decision to welcome Exodus president Alan Chambers to the 2012 conference was perhaps the most incendiary decision he'd made in the entire life of GCN. But it reinforced his commitment to dialogue—not merely for the sake of talking, but in the spirit of understanding that is too often missing from the church. "We are in the middle of the debate," Justin says, and he intends to stay there, as uncomfortable and costly as balancing on that middle ground may sometimes be.


After I began telling friends and family about my homosexuality, I quickly realized that some of them viewed me as a changed person. I was: I was finally being honest about an aspect of my life that I'd hidden, not only from them but also from myself. But that's not how many of them saw it. In their perception, I somehow morphed from a multidimensional character who loved the San Francisco 49ers and collected stamps and hated marzipan and listened to bad pop music to this Gay Person who listened to bad pop music. (At least and at last there was an explanation for that.)

I was never more than a wallflower at GCN. At times I saw it as a place where the members only talked and thought about "gay" things. I was wrong. While its core mission may be to provide a forum where people can discuss faith and sexuality, the greatest testimony to the community is that it has grown into a true community—a place where people talk about all the stuff of life, not just their faith and not just their sexuality.

On GCN, people seem to feel free to be vulnerable and curious, earnest and teasing, expressive and weird—in other words, themselves. They discuss *Dancing with the Stars*. They gripe about pet peeves. They share poetry. They play games—in one sub forum, a game of Geography has been running for eight years and 3,600 posts.

The flowering of GCN's online fellowship has also reaffirmed that humans crave connection offline. GCN members—it now has more than twenty thousand—meet locally and regionally, organizing Bible studies and bowling nights and camping trips. Each January, hundreds gather for the annual conference, where they sing, listen to speakers, pray, and hang out, with few giving a thought to who's Side A and who's Side B. And increasingly, GCN has sought to build offline dialogue and multimedia understanding through film, lectures, and podcasts. "I had a little hobby," Justin says, "that grew into this."

I stop by the world headquarters of the Gay Christian Network, a small suite of offices in the basement of a dull building in suburban Raleigh. The spartan setting befits the bare-bones operation. The organization operates on about $200,000 a year, cobbled together almost entirely from members' donations—a budget built, Justin says, from "the widow's mite." Justin, whose official title is executive director, has never earned more than $28,000, and when the economy crashed in 2008, donations declined with it, prompting him to ask the board to cut his salary to $22,000—less than his two staffers.

Even though GCN began as a website and its message boards are central to its work, it has never had a dedicated IT person. Nearly all the videos on GCN were recorded in Justin's living room. And when the organization produced the documentary *Through My Eyes* in 2008, to tell the stories of a handful of its members, Justin chose not to include any credits. If he had, they would have read:

DIRECTOR: Justin Lee

CINEMATOGRAPHER: Justin Lee

EDITOR: Justin Lee

LIGHTING: Justin Lee

UNIT PUBLICIST: Justin Lee

"There are so many misconceptions in the LGBT community about Christians, and so many misconceptions in the Christian community about LGBTs. It's important that the groups understand each other a little better. That's a good starting point."

When I hear these words, I almost do a double take, because they're coming not from a thirtysomething bald gay Christian but from a twentysomething long-locked lesbian agnostic named Annie Bolton. Annie is the president of the Gay-Straight Alliance at Georgia State University in Statesboro, and we're sitting in the student center, chatting on a warm autumn afternoon. She grew up unreligious in Marietta, near Atlanta, "except for when my parents went on some kick when I was ten and we went to church across the street every Sunday, but that lasted only a few months. My parents never taught me about religion. I'm still discovering what I believe in."

Last spring, Annie got an email from the Gay-Straight Alliance's faculty adviser. The Gay Christian Network was interested in sending its executive director to campus to talk about communication and conversation between the gay community and the Christian community. Would they be game? "I thought it was a really cool idea," Annie says. "If it worked out, it could do a world of good for respect on both sides."

That's the goal, anyway, when Justin comes to Georgia State to do a two-night duet of talks. The visit is part of a series called "Transforming the Conversation," which, really, could be the name of his entire life project. Georgia State is the third campus he's hitting on this tour—eleven universities in all, scattered across the South—a journey funded by a $77,000 Arcus Foundation grant, the largest outside gift GCN has ever received. On the first night on each campus, he speaks to all comers—while the Gay-Straight Alliance is the official host, it's asked to invite members of the public and specifically all the Christian fellowship groups. On the second night, he speaks more directly to alliance members.

When I ask Justin what he means by "transforming the conversation," he answers, "We need to move beyond conversations where we say, 'We should be more loving!' Many of us agree on that, but we don't agree on what that looks like," he says. "The question is, how do you do that and how do you address the disagreement?"

For starters, you get people who disagree vehemently to sit down together, and on Justin's first night at Georgia State, some fifty students gather in a fluorescently lit classroom to hear him. About two-thirds of the audience raise their hands when Justin asks who believes that gender doesn't affect a relationship's morality (in other words, gay's okay)—he tells them they are on what is usually called Side A—and just shy of a third believe "sexual relations ought to be between a man and a woman" (Side B). Two students bravely raise their hands when he asks "who's torn or still not sure," and one shoots his arm up when Justin says, "How many people as a matter of principle never raise their hands when people ask you to raise your hands?"

After telling a short version of his life story, Justin orchestrates what one might call a vigorously moderated, relentlessly polite debate. First, he says, "I want to give you a chance to ask a question of the folks in the room who are on the other side from you." At first, the students just sit there, but slowly, the questions come: "Without using the Bible, what arguments are there against homosexuality?" "What do you do with the parts of the Bible that seem to contradict each other?" "Do you feel you were born this way, or does your sexuality have something to do with the influence of people around you?"

This last question draws out some of the most personal, revealing, and funny answers of the night. While most of the gay students who respond say that they were born this way—"I remember in third grade, I just had the hugest crush on another girl in my class," one woman says, "but never once did I have a crush on a guy"—one guy confesses, "I honestly don't know. I'm bisexual, and I thought when I hit puberty, I was just really horny." He pauses. "Whether I'm born this way or because I was an air force brat, I caught something in Europe—well, your guess is as good as mine."

Justin offers few personal thoughts. Instead, he redirects and re-interprets questions. When one Side B student begins sermonizing on homosexuality, arguing that "gay is not who you are. It's a sin upon you," Justin gently says: "I want to zero in on this. Side A folks, is it frustrating for you to hear Side B folks say, 'This is just like any other sin, like lying or adultery'?" When another Side B student talks about his own (heterosexual) lust and his need to "sacrifice his desires to the Lord," Justin once again recalibrates the conversation's tenor. "It's interesting," he says. "One of the things I notice when I have these conversations is that we often use terms differently. For instance, I hear folks on Side B say homosexuality is like lust. That's a very broad term.

"It's not always clear what we mean by homosexuality. . . . My guess—and tell me if I'm wrong—for those who identify as gay, it's not who you have sex with but who you are attracted to. In that sense, would it be fair to distinguish somebody who is gay from somebody who is gay and lusting?"

"Tell me if I'm wrong."

"Would it be fair . . . ?"

"It's interesting."

"What I'm hearing you say is . . ."

With these slight verbal directives, Justin repeatedly pushes the conversation back to a less charged center. And two hours into the evening, when he draws things to a close, the chatter doesn't end. Side A students seek out Side B counterparts for post-meeting chats. I listen to debates about biblical translation and the death penalty, Osama bin Laden and the definition of evil. One self-described conservative Christian girl asks a gay guy what compels him to stay in church. In another corner, a small group of students is wrestling with the nature of heaven. And as the room buzzes with questions and answers and more questions, it occurs to me that such conversation—open and candid and mostly not defensive—happens too rarely, whether on college campuses or in our churches or at our kitchen tables.

"I really did learn some things tonight," Annie Bolton tells me later. "For instance, I had never thought about Christianity and the Bible being so core to their identity before. I can understand better why, because of that, they wouldn't want to accept that I'm gay. One of them told me he didn't understand, but that he wanted to try. I just really appreciate them trying. I know it's hard." By the time she goes to bed that night, several of the students from the Christian fellowship have friended her on Facebook.

In her book *Alone Together,* Massachusetts Institute of Technology psychologist Sherry Turkle, a keen observer of online life, writes that "these days, insecure in our relationships and anxious about intimacy, we look to technology for ways to be in relationships and protect ourselves from them at the same time. . . . We fear the risks and disappointments of relationships with our fellow humans. We expect more from technology and less from each other."

Many gay people have been conditioned to fear risk and disappointment. There's good reason for that; after I began telling friends about my sexuality, some relationships faded away, while tensions grew in others. "You make me sad," one friend told me in one of the more delightful moments of my coming-out ordeal.

All this makes me wonder if technology might play a different role for minorities than for the general populace. For most GCN members, the Internet has been additive. Their online community didn't replace something offline; it's provided interaction that they'd never had before. In some cases, it has even brought love.

Justin has always been adamant that GCN isn't a hookup site. But it happens. It's a well-policed community, thanks to the sizable number of doctrinaire folks who seem constantly ready to call someone else out for sin, whether it's smoking or swearing. "But just like the church is about the people, not the building, GCN is about the people, not the interface," one member told me. "People share their stories and then sometimes they meet each other, too! And there's nothing wrong with that."

"Dave," who grew up Roman Catholic in Illinois but has attended mainline Protestant churches since college, had been active on the site for a few months when posts by "Shane," a Canadian, caught his eye in a discussion forum called Waiting for Marriage. "I had seen some posts from Shane in that forum, and I recognized that we shared similar values about sex, about marriage, about relationships," Dave tells me one night when we connect over Skype. "A little later, he posted some photos of himself, and I saw that he was a fun-loving guy. I just really liked the way he articulated himself and his values."

A comment on one of Shane's photos led to private messaging, which led to Skyping. Eventually Dave found that he'd come home from work every day, open Skype, and have dinner at his desk with his computer—and, by fiber-optic extension, Shane. Six weeks after they started Skyping, Dave and Shane had their first in-person date. Less than a year later, they wed in a civil ceremony in Ontario, and a few months later, they had what Dave calls "a wedding wedding" in Maryland. Both ceremonies were well attended by friends from GCN.

A story like Dave and Shane's can be read whichever way you like. Those who believe homosexual behavior is a sin might say that, via the site, Christians have been led astray and encouraged to indulge their same-sex temptations. Those on the opposite side might see Dave and Shane's marriage as a triumph; what better illustration could there be of God's desire for us to find true relationship, of his commitment to conquering isolation and loneliness, than the journey of two believers who come together as Dave and Shane did?

If GCN were a church and something like Dave and Shane's wedding happened within the congregation, it might be enough to cause a schism. It says something about the online network that disagreement on such an issue is seen not as a sign of the community's weakness but as a mark of its strength.

After Statesboro, I drive down to Florida to meet a GCN member named Sandy Bochnia, who joined in January 2005. "Like everybody else, I googled *Christian* and *gay* and came up with GCN," she says. And like everybody else, she lurked for a while, nervous about registering. At the time, she says, "I was a mess." Unlike everybody else, she's not gay. But her son Stephen is.

The GCN staff strives to avoid making GCN what Justin calls "a gay Christian ghetto." "We want to encourage dialogue in families and in the broader church," he explains. "There's a lot of good that comes if a son brings his parents to his conference, for instance." Or, as Sandy's journey shows, if a mother joins the community to learn more about her son.

Sandy's son did not come out of the closet so much as she pulled him out of it. The Bochnias live in Madison, a town of ten thousand a few miles south of the Georgia-Florida border, with lots of churches and no claim to fame. For months, Sandy had been hearing rumors around town about her son and his best friend. "But they just swore up and down: *No, no, those are rumors!*" she recalls with a wan smile. Then she confirmed the best friend was gay, but her son still denied that he was. "We can be friends with gay people!" he said to her. "And I said, 'Well, yeah. That makes sense.'"

But the rumors kept coming. Her son's best friend worked in a little shop in town, and Sandy's niece worked next door. The best friend's coworker told the niece that Stephen was gay, too, and then the niece told Stephen's sister, and Stephen's sister told Stephen's mom. "Finally, one day, I was doing laundry, and I looked at Stephen, and I just said, 'If you had the balls, you would admit if it's true,'" she says. "And he said, 'Okay, I am.' I just started laughing, and I said, 'Really?' He said, 'Really.' I stopped laughing real quick."

"My first thought, my first worry and concern, was, Is he going to go to heaven?" she says. "What if he died right now in a car wreck?" Sandy begged God for answers, and she found them online. "I would pray, and he seemed to say, *Listen to what I have to say through these people,*'" she says. "On GCN, I would just throw out all my questions, and they were really kind. They didn't get mad at me for asking dumb questions. One day, when I was really in a mess, I said, I don't know what it's going to take, but maybe I'll just fast. I'll have nothing else but me and God. By noon, everything felt as if a weight had been lifted. I felt God say, *It's okay. Don't worry about who is right or wrong. Continue to learn and listen.* And you know, when you feel God has answered your prayer and is speaking to you, you just know when you know. I began to understand."

There are times we understand things because we want to understand things—we know what we want to know. "I wanted to find answers, but I wanted them to be positive answers," Sandy admits. But she's sure that they came not from her own wishful thinking but from her God. And she's firm in her belief that GCN has become her ministry. Certainly, it quickly became less about information and more about community—something she felt she was losing offline as she became more accepting of Stephen's sexuality. Distance was growing between her and her friends at the Southern Missionary Baptist church she had attended since she was three, "this little-bitty white church in the country. All the literature there about homosexuality is negative, and any picture of anybody that's gay is snarly-looking."

Eventually she felt that she couldn't worship there anymore. "I just can't hold hands and pray with Christians who have blinders on and won't open their hearts," she says. "After Stephen told me, one of the church ladies came over to talk, wanting to know why I wasn't in church. She's so sweet. She brought me flowers. She's sitting there and saying, 'Oh, honey, I'm so sorry. You are a mess!' And I said, 'No, I'm not! Nice people like you do not understand.' She said, 'I'm going to pray for Stephen. The Lord will change him, honey.' That's the kind of people we have around here."

In time, Sandy began to spend less and less time with the church ladies and more and more on GCN—two, three, four, five hours a day. Her online friends began to call her "GCN Mom," and she served on the organization's board for three years. Occasionally, she'll talk to other moms who need wisdom and support. But she'll also talk to a guy who just wants to talk about his boyfriend. Or one who wants to understand his mom and dad. "I don't do anything special," Sandy says. "People just need someone to talk to, to feel a little glimmer of hope."

Sundays are still hard. "I have a craving for the Christian fellowship and the worship—just sitting down and reading through the Bible with a group of people," she says. "I miss all that. But I have to find it different ways. GCN. Reading here at home. Lots of praying. Just feeling close to God. I do the best I can."

What if I had found something like GCN earlier?

That question became less important as I spent more time with Justin. Nobody I met on this pilgrimage was more effective at helping me think less about myself and my sorrows. Justin has conquered fear—which I shared—by looking beyond himself. "It's because of my faith, not in spite of it, that I believe the church should love and support gay people," he says. "It's because of what I read in the Bible, not in spite of it. I love the Bible!"

"A lot of people assume that the primary reason I do this is because I want to see gay people more accepted in society," he says. "But I'd say my primary motivation is that, if the church doesn't get this right, it's not going to stop gay people from being accepted in society. What it's really going to do is turn people off Christianity."

It's not just the gay people like Dave and Shane, but also moms like Sandy and siblings and friends.

"If the church doesn't learn how to be loving to gay people soon, the damage will have been done. We'll see a generation of young people who want nothing to do with the church. And that would be a great tragedy."

# DAVID JOHNSON

*"My answer is always the same: God loves you no matter what."*

Anderson, South Carolina

There's been a mini-trend in the evangelical wing of American Christianity lately, as more theological conservatives have acknowledged and apologized for systemic vilification of homosexuals. The Chicago-based Marin Foundation has gone to gay-pride parades over the past several years, holding signs that say "We're sorry." Lead Them Home, a Boston-area ministry led by Bill Henson, assists churches in a process of "posture shift," moving from judgment to love.

The most unusual representative I met from this new generation of reconcilers was David Johnson, a real estate appraiser, husband, and dad of three. Johnson, who grew up in the Assemblies of God, felt called to seminary several years ago. He enrolled in the master of divinity program at Anderson University, near his home. Johnson's decision to focus his ministry on gays and lesbians has produced unexpected ripples in his life and work.

---

When we were told we had to do this project that's almost like a dissertation in order to finish our master's, I thought I'd do something in my field of expertise—real estate. I've been an appraiser forever. But I kept asking, "How does this benefit anybody?"

Then I started thinking about what group of people the church around here seems to ignore. There are a thousand programs for poor people—and there need to be more. There are a thousand programs for abused wives—and there need to be more. I realized that there's no outreach for somebody who's gay, at least in this area. In fact, it's just the opposite: Churches turn their backs on gay people. The church's reaction is "You need to repent! You need to quit being gay and then you can come back to church!" But it doesn't matter if you're gay. God's love is for all of us, not just the celibate or heterosexual. We're not to judge. Sometimes I look at people and think something like, God, why did she wear that out of the house today? That's human nature, to judge. But we shouldn't do that.

I decided what I needed to do was to start a Bible study and call it my project. Hopefully, I can get some people who have same-sex attraction to talk and meet. My goal is not to pray the gay away—I don't think that's something that can happen. But maybe after six months—maybe!—they'll start saying, "Maybe I need to change a little bit." I don't mean that they will want to get out of their relationships or anything like that immediately. I just hope they will draw closer to Christ, and then we'll see what happens.

I knew this was going to be really tough—and not because I don't know any gay people. I do, and I always have. When I was a student at Furman and the University of South Carolina, I waited tables, and in the restaurants where I worked, I was usually the only straight guy working in the place. So I became very good friends with a lot of gay men. They would tease me, call me a "breeder," stuff like that, but they all ended up becoming friends.

When you're faced with their sexuality, maybe it makes you examine your own sexuality. I've never questioned my own. They always respected boundaries. They were just nice guys who had a different lifestyle. I guess I became accepting of it.

For quite a while, I dealt with alcohol. The moment I tasted it, I loved it. I love bourbon. *Man.* But after I got out of college, I realized it was going to cost me in more ways than one. I don't drink anymore. Was I born that way? Hard to say. I don't know if they'd find a gene that says I'm going to like alcohol. But I do know it's something I have to fight. We're all born with things we're susceptible to. It's part of our sin nature. We don't wake up every morning saying, "I'm going to sin!" But we still do it. So we have to fight that sin. It's 100 percent our choice. We can choose to sin or not to sin.

---

We have this hierarchy of sin in our churches, as if one sin is worse than another. But that's just not the case. The Bible doesn't discriminate. Churches that judge you for being gay are wrong. They're not judging the guy who is beating his wife or embezzling from his company. That hypocrisy needs to be dealt with.

I have this other friend, this guy who is what people refer to as a bear. He's a big burly guy who's been living with another guy. They've been together for fifteen years. Honestly, you'd think one was a lumberjack and the other was an auto mechanic. You'd just think they're good old Southern boys. They're not what people would consider "typical" gay, although I don't even know what that means anymore. They're just always in their Carhartts and old boots.

Neither one of them grew up in church. They know where I stand on faith, and when we've talked, I have had to be careful with the language I use. It can send the wrong message. Say you grew up in the church. There are some things you'll absolutely understand. But somebody who hasn't grown up in that, there's a huge divide in what the church actually says. They will wonder: Why is the Bible relevant for me?

Both of these guys consider themselves to be very spiritual. They are good people. One of them has said to me: "Why is the world judging me? There's no reason to be judged." I've told him I don't judge him, but it's a shame the church down the road does. A lot of it has to do with people needing to be taught. What does the Bible have to say about how we serve each other?

The truth is, a behavioral change is required of *all* of us. The Bible does not pick on same-sex relationships. We all have to change to become closer to God. Paul says it all the time: One of the things you have to do is to die daily to yourself. We die daily to our sins. Your sin is not my sin, but none of it is a deal-breaker.

---

As I'm working on this Bible study, I start calling pastors to try to get one to be my project supervisor. I know the line I'm trying to walk is a very fine line; I've been told no by twenty pastors.

This is the Bible Belt, where it's all about good ol' boys and Hank Williams and rebel yells. The majority of men are severely homophobic. A lot of men have issues dealing with other men who might find them attractive. I think the only reason I'm not homophobic is the environment I was in during college, but I understand that a lot of people down here are— extremely. That goes for pastors, too.

With each one, I went down and talked to them and told them about my project. "I'm trying to reach lost people!" I said.

"Oh, that is awesome! That is a great concept!" they said.

"Here's why I am talking to you. I need a supervisor to help me stay in the boundaries," I said.

"Oh, no, no, no! Can't have my name on that! That's a little too toxic a topic!" they said.

These are prominent people! They have lots of building projects! So I guess they think they have too much to lose. But I finally asked a friend of mine who is the pastor of a small Baptist church down the road. He said, "You can count on us to help."

The hardest person to tell about my project was actually my dad. He's old-school, a truck driver, a man's man, with home-made tats—a real good ol' boy who grew up in a rural family in Louisiana. And you know what? He asked how he could help. Which was completely not what I was expecting. My mom? Well, my mom, she said, "Well, that's really deep stuff, Dave!"

I also told my wife. She knows a lot of my gay friends from college, because we were dating then. I had to tell my wife, "If you go on my laptop, I'm just doing research! I don't want you to think I'm cruising!" I've gone to gay websites, and I don't erase my history. She laughed.

Locally, I understand I'm going to meet resistance—Bob Jones University is just down the road, and there are a lot of Bob Jones churches around here—but I don't care. There are a lot of hurting men and women. There's a large gay community in the Greenville-Spartanburg area, an artsy community with lots going on—don't ask me why. But nobody—nobody!—is reaching out. I can reach out and say, "God does love you."

I hope I can do this. I feel like the goal is absolutely right: I want people to draw closer to Christ, to have a closer relationship with Jesus. I know it sounds pie-in-the-sky, and forgive me if it does. But I just want them to have a strong relationship with Jesus Christ. And Christians who are judging, who aren't trying to bring that about, who are ignoring this group of people in America—they are the ones who really need to consider where they're at.

Many of my friends in the gay community are distrustful of anything having to do with the Bible. They don't want to be told they will burn in hell for how they were born. But my ministry is not saying that. And it's not saying, "Quit being gay first, before you come." I am never going to say that. I am never going to teach that.

I am worried no one will show up. My biggest fear is sitting there by myself. In an empty room. I don't care if they show up with their partner. I don't care if they show up in drag. I just want them to show up.

---

*Five months after our conversation, Johnson emailed me an update:*

> *I meet with two men on the phone each Thursday, and we do a short Bible study. Neither is out, and they are scared to death that they may be outed. Both have said they would never attend a Bible study for fear of being outed and it hurting their respective businesses. We are currently talking about forgiveness and grace. Both have such large swings concerning their sexuality— one moment, they are convinced they will burn in hell. Then the next day, they are convinced that since they were born gay, how could that condemn them? My answer is always the same: God loves you no matter what.*

# KEEPING IT TOGETHER

## The Schert Family

*Valdosta, Georgia*

Whan I first saw John Michael Schert's Facebook profile, I had a hunch that this Valdosta, Georgia–born gay guy had grown up in church. John Michael is the executive director of a stellar Boise, Idaho–based contemporary dance troupe called the Trey McIntyre Project, and we began corresponding after I wrote a tiny article in *Fast Company* about TMP partway through my pilgrimage year.

I told him that I was working on a book about Jesus and the gays and warned him that I might ask him about that topic. So when we finally connect by phone, I do just that, and he tells me that, yes, he grew up in church. In fact, though he no longer attends, it was a huge part of his early life, not just Sunday mornings but also youth group (his parents were leaders) and Episcopal church camp.

"But you should really call my mom," John Michael says.

"Why?" I say. *Your mom? But you're the gay guy who grew up in church. And I don't have anyone from Georgia yet.*

"A big part of why I feel the way I do about church is because of how she was treated when she came out," he explains. "I was thirteen."

Aha.

Jan Schert grew up in Jacksonville, Florida, in a family "where you just never missed a Sunday of church." Every summer was chockablock with vacation Bible schools—at the Baptist church one week, the Methodist church the next, and the week after that, the Disciples of Christ church where her mother belonged and her mother's mother and so on.

Seven-year-old Jan would often stand in her bedroom just talking to God. He was as much a part of that place as her bed and her dolls and her nightstand, and maybe even more so, because of his magical mobility. "I just knew he was there," she says when I reach her on her cell phone on a hot summer Georgia afternoon. "I just knew he was everywhere."

The part of Jacksonville where Jan's family lived was, in the 1950s and 1960s, woodsy and semirural. Her maternal grandparents had ten acres, and to the young Jan, if church was sacred, then the outdoors was divine. "My deepest experiences with God—and I definitely identified it as with God—were in nature. Being in the woods. Playing in the mud. Especially climbing the trees," she says. "I'd look up at all the mosses and the lichens growing and I'd sing. There was just this innate need to stand in awe of something larger than myself. It was worship."

But as Jan grew older, what she saw in the world around her began to erode her faith. She was especially struck by the way black kids were treated—integration of the Jacksonville public schools didn't begin until Jan was in ninth grade. "There was just this discrepancy between Jesus's love for everyone and what I saw around me," she says. "What we're told the Bible says is not what I was seeing lived out. At one point, I did say to my mom, 'I just don't get anything out of this. It's hypocritical.'"

The subsequent years were what you might call her "gray period." She went to community college and then on to Florida

State University. After a bad breakup with a boyfriend, she felt empty and adrift—a spiritual shadow of the tree-climbing, faith-filled girl she had been. The night before Easter 1971, "I let go," she says. "I said, 'I need the God in my life I knew growing up—the one I could stand in my bedroom and talk with, the one I could talk with when I was playing in the trees.' And in a flash, it was there again—something beyond the conscious mind, something beyond the tangible."

Ask and it shall be given unto you, and in Jan's case, it seemed to be given and given and given again—in community, in revival, in unexpected gifts. This was the time of the Jesus Movement, the countercultural religious revival that swept American college campuses in the early 1970s, and when the wave hit Florida State, Jan let it wash all over her. "I had been reading in Acts where Jesus, just before he ascends, sends the Holy Spirit on the crowd on Pentecost. People in the group were speaking in tongues and dancing," she says, wonder swelling in her voice. "I thought, I want to experience this."

At one service, some other worshippers laid hands on Jan—and as she tells me the story, amid her touchy-feely speech, I can still hear echoes of the emotion-driven Jesus Movement. "What came out of my mouth was 'I want to receive the baptism of the Holy Spirit,'" she says. "I felt such warmth, like warm oil was being poured over me, in an incredible lubricating-of-my-spirit way. I felt so light. It was the letting-go of the left-brain part of myself, which had held me so tightly. I let go of so much hurt and fear. It was totally a right-brain thing."

Another gift of the movement: a tall varsity high jumper named Dan Schert, who ran in a circle of artsy Jesus freaks. Dan and Jan married ten days after their 1972 graduation. Over the next ten years, they had four kids and eventually became pillars of their church community in Valdosta, Georgia. They led Cub Scouts in the parish hall. On Wednesday nights, you'd find them at the church potluck. Each summer, the kids went to Honey Creek, the Episcopal Diocese of Georgia's camp near Cumberland Island. The Schert home on

Pine Point Circle had an open-door policy, and for years, Dan and Jan were the cool parents.


Jan met Judy at a funeral. For a while, they were just friends. Dan recalls that Jan would develop these intense attachments to other women that would eventually flame out. But this one turned out differently.

Who knows what really happens when two people fall in love? Is it timing? Is it passion? Is it pheromones? Is it need? All of the above?

Perhaps it's less important that Jan met Judy at a funeral than that Jan met Judy at a time of need. Jan's oldest son, Daniel, was off at college. Her second son, David, had been seized by schizophrenia. Her third, John Michael, a dancer like his mom, had just gone to boarding school. Young Kristin Claire was her one remaining anchor to the normality of the domestic life she had known. "I had wrapped all my identity in being a wife and a mother," Jan says. "But that had been eroded. Those tendrils holding me in place, in my marriage, were being severed and released."

It was Martin Luther King Jr. weekend of 1995 that Jan and Judy made plans to go to Thomasville together, for the afternoon. They were sitting in the park, just talking, when Jan noticed that Judy's leg was touching hers. Later, as they walked to get something to eat, Jan blurted: "I want to hold your hand!" Even now, her voice quickens at the memory. "It was electric. I had never experienced that. As a kid, you pine for that feeling of being in love. It was crazy. I felt so alive for the first time since I was twelve years old. That evening, I kissed her. And it was like the first time I kissed anyone in my life."

When Jan got home that night, Dan gave her a funny look. "Come here," he said. "Into the bedroom." He locked the door behind them. As Jan recalls it, he said, "After all the years I have done therapy, I know what it looks like when someone is in love. I know you are in love with somebody, and it's not me.

"Is it Judy?" he asked.

"It's Judy," she replied.

"What does this mean? Are you going to . . . Do you want to have sex with her?"

"I do."

Jan says that as soon as those words came out of her mouth—a very different "I do" than she'd said to Dan twenty-three years before—"Dan was no longer my best friend. He couldn't be that anymore. He just couldn't."

Dan said: "*No!* I will not have this! You are my *wife!*"

But she wasn't, not anymore, not in the sense that she had been; in the way that she had been so reserved that Dan had playfully nicknamed her "Little Mouse."

No one will ever own that part of me, Jan thought. No one has that right.

As I drive up to Dan Schert's graciously restored Valdosta Victorian late on a balmy autumn morning, the front door swings open and he emerges onto the porch to greet me. After exchanging pleasantries, he takes me inside to the cluttered sitting room that doubles as his office.

The grandson of a Lutheran–Missouri Synod minister, Dan comes from a family that he describes as "loving, but liturgical and fundamentalist. If you bought a car, it was because of the Lord." The fervid faith of his mother, Alice, left the biggest imprint on him. "She was this very spiritually strong woman—in an outspoken way. She lived it. I work hard at my work today not because I'm afraid of God but because I'm afraid of Alice." As he chuckles, I think about how curious it is that he calls her Alice, not Mom, as if the familial and familiar would somehow reduce this formidable woman's identity to her relationships.

"Was she intimidating?" he muses. He lets the question linger. "Well, she was six foot tall, but she wasn't intimidating after you learned to deal with her. She was very nurturing. My parents would hold hands and pray together every night before bedtime."

Unsurprisingly, Dan's mother led the loyal opposition to Jan's self-discovery. "The tough side of Alice came out. She threatened Jan with hell and damnation," he says. "I said, 'Either leave Jan alone or I'm never bringing the children over again.' I said, 'What you're doing is destructive and not helpful and you need to stop immediately.' The six-foot-five, two-hundred-and-eighty-pound gorilla in me came out—I keep it locked up most of the time—and Alice softened."

His large frame shifts in his big red leather chair as he begins to tear up. "I'm sorry. I'm still fresh over her death." He composes himself. "All that neo-Pentecostal stuff—*pffffth*. Underneath it all was a wonderful human being."

His brother, Fred, was also adamantly anti-Jan. "He was very angry, angry, angry," Dan says, "about her and about gays."

Fred's wife, Vicki, told Jan before Christmas 1995 that she wasn't welcome at the family celebration, because she was no longer part of the family. And Fred made his disgust clear to Dan and Jan's children. John Michael remembers his uncle saying to him, "We just wanted you to know we still love your mom, but we love her with God's love, which is a tough love, and she can't come around anymore." "I said to my uncle, 'Jesus was the one who hung out with the prostitutes and the lepers. He didn't push aside the people who were different. He brought them closer,'" John Michael says. "My uncle said something lame like 'We try to be like Jesus, but nobody can be Jesus.'"

Eventually, I ask Dan: *Were you angry at Jan?*

At first, he avoids personal language, sounding very much like the clinical therapist that he was for many years. (Today he's a patient advocate for those recovering from trauma.) "The one who finds is always excited," he says. "The one who's left is hurting. That's true whether you're talking about heterosexuals or gays."

He turns away and thinks for a few moments. When he returns to me, he says: "I had this unspoken contract with God. If I did everything right, everything would be right. And I had done everything right. Then this thing called divorce hit me. And what I learned is that pain is part of life. It happens. It's just the nature of the universe. Relationships are relationships—they're complicated. You are going to get bruises, regardless of how hard you work. And she's not malicious. That's just who she is. She has this beautiful energy.

"People were so mad at me. Everyone was saying, 'Jan's a bitch! She's ruining the family! Don't let her bring Judy!' I said, 'Listen, I am not comfortable, even though I look like I am. I am choosing to be open because I want these moments where nobody feels ostracized,'" he says. "I wasn't going to torture the children by saying, 'Your terrible mother . . .' They love their mother. They know she's eccentric. And there was enough love there, enough authentic love, to make this work."

And so it did. David's home, which they called "the Little House," became a neutral gathering place. Dan remarried and brought his new wife, Marti. Jan's parents came, as did Dan's mother. Judy was invited as well, though she didn't always join. Somewhere down the line, Marti's parents, who are divorced, even came along. It was wonderful, and it was weird, and it was totally awkward.

At times, even the kids wondered why Dan was so insistent on keeping the family together. "Maybe," John Michael says, "it would have been easier if it had just ended."


About ten years after coming out, Jan entered a time that she calls "the dark night of my soul." Her relationship with Judy wasn't working, but more crucially, her relationship with herself wasn't working. "I felt so alone in the universe. I'd consciously, maybe arrogantly said to God and to myself that I really wanted to know myself, to the depths of who I was. And when you get stripped down, well, a part of me was open to that. But . . ." Her voice trails off.

She needed to get away. John Michael, then living in San Francisco, invited her to come stay for a while. "I went, saying to myself that who I am as a person is more than my gender, more than my race, more than who I've been as a parent or as a wife, more than my sexual orientation," Jan says.

Coincidentally, Paul Brenner, the pastor who had married Jan and Dan and came out as a gay man years later, was working at St. Francis Lutheran in San Francisco, and John Michael encouraged Jan to go one Sunday morning. She sat in the sanctuary and looked over the order of worship, with its emphasis on gender-inclusive language, on God as "she," on the divine feminine. It was all so San Francisco.

When the congregation launched into a rewritten stanza of the hymn "Praise to God," Jan had to stifle her ridicule. "It was something like 'lesbians and gays, bis and transgender, sing to the Lord a new song . . .'" She hums a bar or two. "I was just trying not to laugh! Oh my goodness! And then I begin to sing, and suddenly I find myself sobbing. I just could not stop crying. I didn't understand, until I sang those silly lyrics, how much I had shut down. I may not be defined by my gender, my race, my sexual orientation, but neither can I block it all out."

After that, her recovery began in earnest. She spent time thinking, writing, praying. She left John Michael's, enrolled at Holy Names University across the bay in Oakland, discovered a community of like-minded spiritual seekers, and moved into a dorm. "What I had found," she says, "was a sense of being able to take a deep breath."

By the time she returned to Valdosta, she had regained a modicum of faith. And there was no more potent symbol of her rejuvenation than her decision to change her name, shedding Jan for her middle name, Lee.

Just after midday on a Thursday, I meet Lee in downtown Valdosta at her church, where she's about to begin a class in a healing movement called Capacitar.

In the center of the room, Lee has placed three candles representing the Trinity. There is a little pile of broken pottery—"earth," she explains. She waves her hand: "There's air." A sprig from a tree represents growth. And two blossoms represent "blooming."

Lee is a slender, fine-boned woman with porcelain features, strawberry-blonde pixie-cut hair, eyes that dance as she speaks, a voice that is soothing. She guides me and the only other student, a stout, nervous woman who looks to be in her late sixties, through the litany of exercises—one called the Circle of Healing Light, another called Shower of Light, a third called Let Go of the Past, a fourth called Fly Through the Air. I have legendarily low tolerance for New Agey, hippie-dippie mumbo jumbo, but I try my best not to accompany each with one called Roll the Eyes.

Afterward, Lee and I walk to a nearby restaurant to catch up over sandwiches. Since moving back to Georgia in 2010, she has been living with her parents in nearby Lake Park. "I am sixty years old, and I am back living with them," she says with a slightly hard-edged laugh. "How sad is that?"

In some sense, it has actually been the opposite of sad. For some time, Lee's relationship with her mother had been strained. But after her mother broke her back, Lee cared for her during her recovery and they reconciled. "We have talked," Lee says. "We've talked about the years of her feeling disappointed in me."

Even in her seventh decade of life, she hasn't lost the desire to please her mom, and as she talks her eyes shine. "I know I still want other people's approval," she says with a half smile. "It's not as bad now as it used to be, but I never realized until recently how much I wanted that."

That realization has given her some pause, even as the reconciliation with her relatives has continued. She recently saw Dan's older brother, Fred, at one of John Michael's performances. He wrapped her in a big hug. "I love you," he said. "I'm sorry. I'm so sorry." He said he'd had his own demons to fight. Then he and his wife invited her to spend Christmas with them again, but she declined. Maybe another year.

After lunch, Lee drives me around Valdosta. We go past the old family house on Pine Point Circle and take a quick stroll through the shady grounds of Christ Episcopal Church. "This was my whole life, this church," she says wistfully as she tries the main door. Locked. "I can't feel any connection anymore. There's just this disconnect. It's puzzling to me. John Michael and Kristin Claire were baptized here. I look at the parking lot, and I think about how many fund-raisers we had. Easter egg hunts. Camping trips. It was such a family here. But there's nothing anymore."

There's an oddly bellicose passage in Paul's Letter to the Ephesians, in which he uses the metaphor of battle gear to describe faith's protective elements. "Put on the full armor of God," he writes, "so that you can take your stand against the devil's schemes." He then runs through a checklist of items, including the belt of truth, the breastplate of righteousness, and the helmet of salvation.

If I were the type to do Halloween, the full armor of God would be high on my costume list. My favorite piece would be the shield of faith. There's something appealing in the notion of carrying this picture of who you are into war. Then when, God willing, you come home, it comes, too, changed, as you are, by the dings and scars of the journey and the battle. Your faith can't emerge unscathed or untouched—not if you've really fought.

Most Sunday mornings, you will find Lee at Christ the King, a progressive and ecumenically minded Episcopal congregation in Valdosta. After all her questioning and exploration and seasons of doubt, Lee has returned to a place where she recognizes what she needs spiritually: "My human condition needs a human God. And my need for that has drawn me back to the religion of Jesus. For me, Jesus is the Way. We are called to love one another as Christ loved us. That's powerful."

Like Lee, Dan still goes to church every Sunday—he has stuck with Christ Episcopal, where he still teaches religious education classes, but he also attends First Christian Church, where his new wife, Marti, directs the choir. Once he would have called himself a fundamentalist, but now he says he's a "Christian liberal with an ambiguous relationship with the church." "That Lutheran/Old Rugged Cross thing is still very much a part of who I am, and the Episcopal Church is very much a part of who I am," he says. "I am still very spiritual and I guess I have to say I'm still religious, even though I don't like that word, because it carries so much baggage."

Dan returns again and again to the promise of Romans 8:38–39—one of my favorite passages of the New Testament, too, for its sweeping generosity—where Paul writes, "For I am convinced that neither death nor life, neither angels nor demons, neither the present nor the future, nor any powers, neither height nor depth, nor anything else in all creation, will separate us from the love of God that is in Christ Jesus our Lord."

John Michael no longer attends church regularly. "I believe there are really powerful forces in the world that are bigger than just me, but I don't have any belief that it has to be channeled through a form of organized religion," he says. He still sees his mom's coming out as a turning point. "My view of organized religion up to that point had been really positive. It had been community and love and people coming together," he says. When he's back in Valdosta for Christmas, "my siblings and I will still go to Midnight Mass at our old church because it's fun to see the people. Later in life, almost all these people have apologized. There has been for a lot of people a recognition that what they did was based out of fear."

One of the last places Lee takes me in Valdosta is a pottery studio on Webster Street, where she has been studying with a ceramicist named Walter Hobbs. Lately she has been trying a type of pottery of Japanese origin called raku—a high-gloss form that's fired at unusually low temperatures in an outdoor kiln.

In the parking lot across the street from the studio, I ask to see one of her pieces. Lee grimaces, but eventually she relents and begins rummaging around the trunk of her car. Eventually she emerges with a ceramic object that couldn't really be described as a pot or a bowl or a vase—it looks more like a tentacled sea creature entombed in clay.

Lee looks embarrassed by the piece, but it's actually quite striking in a sculpturally *jolie-laide* way. Hobbs, she confesses, has been prodding and nagging her, telling her not to be so uptight about what she's making. Apparently, it's antithetical to the spirit of raku, which is a Japanese word that roughly translates as "pleasure" or "ease."

"I said, 'Does it look like I'm going for perfection here?'" She laughs. "He says, 'This is not about controlling the process. It's not about figuring it all out.' I guess sometimes you have to let go. You just have to."

# RETURN OF THE EXILES

Lianna Carrera and Jennifer Knapp

---

*Hollywood, California; Nashville, Tennessee*

The spiritual exile is a frequent motif in the stories I encounter as I travel across America. So many people and even some congregations tell of wandering in a wilderness of the soul. Some do this by choice. Jeff Simunds, the ex-gay counselor, cordoned off an entire year, free of other work and ministry, to reexamine his faith. Many others, though, find themselves exiled. Ben Dubow, the disgraced pastor, got that reflection time by dubious virtue of his work and ministry being stripped away, while First United Lutheran Church was ejected from its denomination. Often, the wilderness experience comes with a physical journey— the lesbian mom Lee Schert went to California and New Zealand, the pastor Jake Buechner to Asia, the lifelong Covenanter Charlotte Johnson to a mental hospital.

These wanderers follow biblical footsteps. In Scripture, the wilderness is depicted as dry and desolate, all thorns and briers, days of heat and thirst, nights of chill and longing. It's a place for castoffs (Abraham's concubine Hagar) and for sinners (the unfaithful Israelites, who were forced to wander for forty postpharaonic years). But it's also for prophets (John the Baptist was the famous "voice crying in the wilderness") and for the redeemed (those Israelites did

get manna and water from the rock). It's a place where God repeatedly shows his faithfulness and provision. So amid trial—Jesus was
tempted by Satan there—there is also comfort. The Gospel of Matthew reports that "the angels came and ministered to him" in the
wilderness, and later, Jesus chose to retreat there for reflection and
prayer. Anyone who has spent time in the desert knows those moments, often just after dawn or just before dusk, when the light is
so pure, so clear, that everything appears startlingly sharp. It's as if
you'd never seen the world with these eyes before, and once you do,
nothing can be the same.

I'm thinking of clear light and radiant sunshine on a misty, murky
gray October day in Lynchburg, Virginia, where I'm meeting Jennifer Knapp and Lianna Carrera. Both women went into wildernesses
of their own. Jen, a college-era convert to the faith, was a star of the
contemporary Christian music scene until she disclosed that she was
a lesbian, while Lianna, a cradle Baptist and comedienne, walked
away from her faith as she embraced her sexuality. Today their wind-
ing paths have led them back to something resembling faith. And
with their talents, these two women are trying to be what they never
had: lesbian role models who are openly wrestling with difficult
questions of sex and soul.

If you asked me where to spend National Coming Out Day, Lynchburg, Virginia, would not be at the top of my list. A couple of centuries ago, it might have been more fun, a capital of carnal pleasures
that a preacher named Lorenzo Dow decried as "a deadly place for
the worship of God." Today it's home to Liberty University, the
bastion of politicized evangelicalism founded by the late preacher
Jerry Falwell.

Ten years ago, when Jennifer Knapp was one of the brightest
stars in the firmament that is contemporary Christian music, Liberty welcomed her enthusiastically on several occasions. Once,
she came on tour with DC Talk, another time with Jars of Clay,

and crowds of thousands cheered her as she sang hits, including "Undo Me":

> *Time to get down on my knees and pray*
> *"Lord, undo me!"*
> *Put away my flesh and bone*
> *'Til You own this spirit through me Lord*
> *I am wanting, needing, guilty and greedy*
> *Unrighteous, unholy; undo me. Undo me!*

But perhaps more important than anything happening onstage were the conversations offstage. "Most of the time in those environments, they just whisper behind your back, point and giggle: *It's Jennifer!*" Jen says. "But I do remember a lot of conversations backstage with the students—intelligent dialogue and general enthusiasm for trying to find a reality to their faith. At the time, and I would include myself in this, we were becoming adults in a faith experience that we'd either inherited or chosen in a rather youthful fashion. You don't really know what Christianity is when you first get into it. The rubber is starting to hit the road, and you start trying to figure out what it means in reality, rather than the fantasy of it. That's kind of the way I describe a lot of those conversations. It's trying to figure out how to get beyond the surface and get into the real tangibles."

Jen returned to the Liberty University campus on October 13, 2011. Since her previous visit, she had done a lot of work to get beyond the surface and get into the real tangibles of her own life and faith. But ironically, doing that and being honest and choosing candor might have cost her the rapturous reception she'd received a decade before. "Now, maybe, just because I identify as a lesbian, that might not be the case anymore," she said in a shaky video that she filmed on Liberty's campus. "Well, I'm here to claim my space. My name is Jennifer Knapp. I'm gay, and I am a Christian."

A few hours after she posts the video on her website, I meet

Jen across town, in the basement of the chapel of Lynchburg College. Lynchburg is the skeptical, countercultural punk to Liberty's
buttoned-down, Sunday-best believer, and it has invited Jen to perform at a special concert for National Coming Out Day.

The gig is part of a series that Jen has been doing called Inside
Out Faith. With Jen on this evening is Lianna Carrera, a Los Angeles–based lesbian comedienne. Inside Out Faith started after
Jen and Lianna did a show together at Vanderbilt Divinity School,
and the organizers asked if, in addition to Jen's songs and Lianna's
jokes, "we might answer a few questions," Lianna recalls. "It was
organic."

Today the format is pretty set: The entertainment comes first—
often it's just Jen performing, but sometimes Lianna will appear
as an invited guest—and then there's a time for conversation with
the audience about faith and sexuality. "More and more, it feels
like the entertainment portion is—the only word I have is *foreplay*,"
Jen says. "But it's preparation for the Q-and-A. The art centers
everybody."

"It gets you connecting," Lianna says.

Jen: "By the time you open up the floor, it's amazing to see the
art and the way we share our stories encouraging people to engage
in the dialogue."

Lianna: "But if you weren't really good at what you do, it wouldn't
encourage dialogue. Good foreplay is necessary."

Jen: "From when we started, I've felt a lot of pressure to tell my
*whole* story—to give some profound block of lessons I've learned
along the way. I guess it's just a personal thing. If someone asks me a
question, I want to answer it, and given the importance of the subject, I don't want to leave anything out."

Lianna: "It's the sense of responsibility you feel not only to the art
but to the conversation. You know, the same thing that makes you an
artist is what makes you an activist."

Jen: "Don't call me an activist! You can call me an advocate—
I'm not going to tie myself to some semi! Anyway, it's the action of

speaking my story. It's not always just 'I am gay. I am Christian.' It's also 'This is how I got here.'"

Lianna grew up in church. "From birth, God was playing jokes on my parents," she tells me a few months earlier, when we meet for drinks and dinner in West Hollywood, California. Born on Christmas Day, she was mislabeled as a boy by a neonatal nurse. Saved at four, she was proselytizing by the fourth grade; she'd collect those AOL CDs that came in the mail offering free Internet time, and burn every one of those thousand minutes in chat rooms, telling gay people to repent because they were an abomination. ("It was definitely my precritical phase," she says.)

In seventh grade, she was the best player on her Christian school's basketball team. But a deacon had a vision that she was going to be a lesbian. He called a meeting with the basketball coach, the principal, Lianna's parents, and the cheerleading coach. A decision was made: She was off the basketball team and on the cheer squad. "You can't play," Lianna's dad told her. "Why?" she asked, genuinely and innocently. "We don't want you to grow up to be like Ellen DeGeneres," he replied.

She lasted just a week as a cheerleader, but for a time it seemed as if that did the trick—or maybe it was her mom's fervent prayers. In high school, she played guitar in a praise band at church. "I was gross," Lianna says. "I was like Mandy Moore in *Saved*.* I did that until God could not take it anymore."

Just before Valentine's Day of Lianna's junior year in high school, she went to her dad to ask for his credit card. She wanted to buy some flowers for her crush.

"Who are they for?" he asked.

---

* If you aren't familiar with the American evangelical high school subculture, this 2004 cinematic masterwork should be required viewing. Sample dialogue: LILLIAN: "I keep trying to remind myself that when Jesus closes a door he opens a window." MARY: "Yeah, so we have something to jump out of."

"Emily," she said.

"I don't want to play games, Lianna," he said. "You need to tell me what you want to tell me."

"Okay, dad," she replied. "I am a lesbian."

Lianna's uncle had been gay, and after her revelation, Pastor Carrera thought of the things he had said to his brother when he came out, things like "Please be careful in front of the kids" and "Love the sinner, hate the sin," which had undermined what little faith he had left. Then he thought of all the things he wished he'd said instead before his brother died of AIDS.

When Pastor Carrera told some other ministers about his daughter, they advised him to get her into a treatment program as quickly as possible. Instead he devised a treatment program of his own—for himself. He told Lianna he wasn't sure if it was a sin, but that he believed she could still be a Christian and gay. He committed to study the issue more. He took her to all different kinds of churches, hoping that she would find one where her faith could continue to grow. And he instructed her to do what he hadn't done with his brother until it was too late: "Follow your heart."


Jen, who grew up in Kansas, did not grow up in church. "My family is not atheists or anti-God or anything like that. My parents just did not raise us with any particular spirituality," she tells me when we first meet, at a café in Nashville, where she lives with her Australian-born partner.

Before becoming a Christian in college, she was a self-described "colossal hedonist. I was a real catch for this evangelical community. I was this hard-drinking, swear-like-a-sailor prize. I was pretty much shagging anybody for a six-pack of beer." But somehow she found herself with a clutch of devout friends. "They were nice enough people, but for a long time, I felt like what they were trying to do was to convert me to some kind of club I didn't want to be a part of. It seemed like surfacey and guilt-ridden," she says.

"But one day, that Gospel story really connected with me. I didn't have this Pauline kind of conversion on the side of the road. It just made sense to me. For whatever reason this story existed, it reminded me that, underneath all of this gunk, I was a person this story was made for. I was potentially a person of great value and great worth whom apparently this God would go to great lengths to preserve."

That was the end of her smoking and her drinking and her carousing and the beginning of Bible reading and churchgoing and ten solid years of celibacy and a period of really annoying her mother in "trying to get her saved. My family just didn't understand the frenzied side of things. I've always felt supported and appreciated by them—just not understood."

It was also the beginning of her musical career. Growing up, she played trumpet and, under the influence of her parents, listened mostly to country—Barbara Mandrell, Kenny Rogers, Crystal Gayle—which probably explains the roots of the intense storytelling in her own songwriting. A music education major who was also studying classical-trumpet performance, Jen was asked to play (guitar) in a Fellowship of Christian Athletes worship band as well as at the American Baptist church she was attending at the time. Some friends suggested that she write some songs, setting her testimony to music, so she did. "I had no idea that such a thing as Christian music existed," she says. "But people kept asking me to play. And this was the nineties, and there was the huge coffeehouse thing, so I would go up to Kansas City and play every once in a while."

Those gigs led to a record deal, which led to the contemporary Christian music version of stardom. Her debut album, *Kansas*, went gold, and from 1998 to 2001, she sold more than one million albums, was nominated for two Grammys, and won four Dove Awards (the Grammys of Christian music). But she also had some crossover appeal, playing Lilith Fair during the summer of 1999.

---

Lianna's coming out, at seventeen, was a transformational moment for her family.

For her dad, it was the end of his career as a church-planting pastor and as a proponent of organized religion. "He started volunteering at hospices and doing AIDS rides with my uncle's picture on his back," Lianna says proudly. "Then he was like, 'Can I march with PFLAG in the pride parade?'" Her reply: "Dad, it's *my* pride parade. That is *so embarrassing.*"

For her mom, it was a sign that she had failed as a mother. At the most critical point in her thought process, Mrs. Carrera was diagnosed with severe diabetes. For her, that was confirmation: "The only way she could understand it is to think she did something wrong," Lianna explains. "The diabetes is her punishment for my being gay." Though she still occasionally nags Lianna about her sexuality, her husband has told her to lay off, and these days, her typical stance is quiet acceptance. "She disagrees, but the Bible says the woman should listen to the man, so she didn't challenge him," Lianna says. "At least she's consistent."

Lianna tells her stories with that "can you believe it?" incredulity that many comedians wear professionally, and like so many in her profession, she distills comedy from life's tragedy. When most people would cry or wallow, she jokes. Usually she's a whirl of fast-moving hands and arms and eyebrows—this is what happens when you mix Cuban and Italian. But when she gets to talking about her *abuela*, her dad's devoutly Presbyterian mother, her whole body quiets and tears flood her eyes.

Abuela took care of her gay son as he was dying, and later did the same for his partner. When Lianna was growing up, she and her grandmother perfected a little litany. "I love you," Abuela would say. "How much?" Lianna replied. "As big as the sky!" was the answer, every time. In later years, in every letter she wrote Lianna, she would write, in her shaky grandmotherly script and shaky grammatically off-key way: "I love you. As big as the sky!"

Always, she told Lianna: "You are a child of God. Don't let anybody ever tell you differently."

But it was easier just to step away from the church. "I knew I was gay without question, but I was so concerned with what others thought. I thought they had a say in what God thought," Lianna says. "The Bible says you should tie a rock and plunge to the depths before you make someone question their faith. And I thought that by asking questions, I would make them question, and I did not want to be a part of that."

Jen's coming out, at thirty-three, was a transformational moment for her. She had met her partner in Australia, and over the years that she was away from Nashville and American church culture, "I was becoming less and less content with living in a bubble," she says. "I wanted to put my faith into practice and not worry about who I offended."

She returned to the United States in 2009. Shortly after her return to Nashville, rumors started to percolate through the Christian music community. "I started to get my inbox filled with people saying, 'If you're gay, just please come out,'" she says.

So she did. She gave long interviews to the *Advocate* and *Christianity Today*, and she appeared on *Larry King Live*. "It was like chum in water," she says. "People went nuts! Inside of a day, there were well over twelve hundred posts on the CNN website." While some people praised her honesty, many of her Christian fans decided that she had abandoned her faith. After she did a surprise birthday gig for a long-time fan, she learned that the mother of the birthday girl had been upset, saying, "Isn't that the Larry King gay Christian girl?" One friend told me that, afterward, when a Jennifer Knapp song came on the radio, his sister turned the dial in disgust, saying she would never listen to "that lesbian's music."

"I don't want to be that gay Christian artist. Who wants that headline?" Jen says. "Oh my God, it drives me nuts. I definitely recognize that there's a segment of the Christian population that says, 'Either you're in the club or you're not.' And I understand that the road I've traveled has separated some people from being able to have a genuine relationship with me and my music.

"Nobody was supposed to remember who I was. In Australia, I was nobody, and I really liked that. I'd left it all behind." But she came back. She couldn't expect to return to the same communities— Nashville, the American church, music—and expect people to say, "And who are you?" But to return to the profession she loves, she has had to reposition herself as an artist, having been largely abandoned by the Christian retailers who helped her sell more than one million albums. "For most Christian artists, your survival and your reward are in the Christian retailers. You're supposed to represent what it's like to be a good Christian. You're the paragon, and their association is your endorsement. But if you fail to measure up to what they want to present, they just don't stock you," she says.

Touring has been a mix of different kinds of new: Churches, especially on the liberal end of the theological spectrum, welcome her as an example of how faith and homosexuality can coexist, and small secular venues are getting into her sound, which is folksy and earthy, a huskier Sarah McLachlan with little bits of Natalie Merchant and Mary Travers mixed in.

In the spring of 2011, she played her first lesbian bar, Sisters, in Philadelphia. "I was actually really scared! I was imagining chains and wallets and groping and *Dirty Dancing* for lesbians." She holds her head in her hands in semi-mock shame. "I just didn't know! It's embarrassing! I mean, I've never been to Paris, either—you build up in your mind what it's going to be like! Anyway, the people there were very nice. They were tickled pink that I was a lesbian-bar virgin."

"I have to build a new fan base in a new market," she says. "Many of the venues aren't familiar with me. So you have to get to know the places, the regions, the culture where you're playing."

She was a little surprised to see that a handful of fans from her pre-gay days came for the show, including what she describes as an "incredibly normal-looking, pretty straitlaced heterosexual couple." After the show, they waited in line for a long time to meet her, and when finally it was their turn, "the first thing out of their mouths was: 'We're fiscal Republicans!'" She laughs. "I took that as a compliment. Maybe it was the closest thing they could say to 'We're straight but we're okay with you!' I mean, they were fans enough that they could go into a place where it might be all dykes and bikes, and they stood in line forever to meet me."

A few months later, when she did a second gig at Sisters, they were there again. "Remember us?" they said. "The fiscal Republicans!"

If you believe in predestination, it's not hard to read the components of Lianna's early life as part of a plan to give her comedy material. Her preacher dad + her mom's total deafness = comedy gold. Once, when she was auditioning for David Letterman's show, she joked about how her favorite childhood game was to follow her mom around the house while she was vacuuming; Lianna would unplug the vacuum cleaner and see how long it took her mom to notice. The booker thought she was making it up—"nobody will believe you unplugged a vacuum cleaner on a deaf woman," he said—and rejected the joke.

Lianna always includes some church jokes in her act, and she started getting emails from people writing to her about faith. Some were the typical cries of sacrilege that you'd expect in response to her irreverent mass slaughter of sacred cows. "I get 'God hates you and you're going to hell,'" she says. But others seemed oddly inspired to unload their issues, as if her stinging jokes were some sort of perverse invitation to dialogue. "I've also gotten a lot of 'I don't know how to stand up for myself. I hate God. I hate church. I hate Christians.' And that just breaks my heart. So it started out with helping them, but I feel like I'm finding my own faith again."

Not that this has put her back in a church pew. "Being a good Christian doesn't mean ten percent in the offering plate and being in church on Sunday and Wednesday. The checklist is not true. Does swearing like a sailor make you less Christian? No," she says. "Jesus said that where two or more are gathered in my name, there I am. He met the outcasts where they were—on the riverbanks, in the community." So she does her shows with Jen. She has volunteered with foster kids and ex-cons, teaching them to tell jokes—"turning their tragedy into comedy," as she puts it. "That's church to me, one kid at a time."

But though Lianna has rarely gone to church since she was seventeen, she has not shed its vestiges. One day during college, she wandered into the student center after class. Lots of girls were hanging around, and there was a guitar lying on the floor. Lianna picked it up and started strumming. "The only songs I know on the guitar are Indigo Girls and praise music," she says. She started playing a song about God's holiness and sanctuary. She looked up and noticed a crowd of girls from Campus Crusade for Christ singing along. A few days later, she got a note from one of the girls: "I hope you know that God is working through you, even if you don't think he is."

When I ask her if she is still a Christian, she gives an answer that seems muddled, but on reflection is totally accurate. "I say that I am Southern Baptist," she says. "And am I an agnostic? Probably."

There are times when she'll be ripping down the 405 and nothing seems more natural and right than to put on the Christian radio station and blast something cheesy, maybe some Steven Curtis Chapman or early Amy Grant. "What's funny about faith is that you can leave it, but it doesn't leave you," Lianna says. "And I am not going to leave the church—they are going to have to leave me." And she bursts out laughing.

If you believe in predestination, it's hard not to believe that Jennifer Knapp was meant to use her music not just to tell stories but also to deliver confidence and invite others to tell their stories back. "People come up to me and say, 'Because of you, I take ownership of my sexuality and ownership of my faith in a way that I never did before.' That's a huge responsibility, and the way I deal with it is that I step back and say, 'It could have been anyone.' I say, 'Gosh, what an honor.' And I'm glad I never intended it to be this way, because otherwise I'd be an unbearable narcissist."

Jen has been conflicted about her role, but she has gradually embraced the opportunity to build a unique platform at the intersection of faith and sexuality, at a time when there's a hunger for voices to speak out on those issues. "This issue is at the marrow of what a lot of people have experienced," she says.

As part of the process of learning how to address this issue publicly, Jen has been doing what she calls "these little straw polls" after her shows. "I ask people, 'What denomination did you grow up in? And what is it you're after in church?' Often, they lead with some kind of story of conflict regarding their sexual orientation. But most of these people tell me they are either engaged with the church or trying to reengage," she says. "They want that sense of belonging to a community, but they want to do it as people of substance. There's been a shift. We used to go in and sit as lambs, and the people at the top would talk down to us, telling us what to think: *Gay is bad! Gay is bad!* But now we are taking ownership. People aren't just taking that *no* as the answer."

Curiously, as her public profile as a gay Christian singer-activist has risen, her church attendance has fallen, especially when she's home in Nashville. At first she tells me that it's because she doesn't "want to be a distraction. My reputation precedes me. It's hard to navigate that in this city." But as we talk, it becomes clear that it's less about them—whoever that may be—and more about her own as-yet-unreconciled faith. "I don't have that easy place where I can come into the sanctuary," she says. "I just don't."

Two or three times a year, though, she manages to escape into a cocoon of her own making. She chooses an album—most recently, it was one by the Nashville-based singer-songwriter Megan McCormick, "a journeyman artist whom I really enjoy. Then I just listen to the music, lights off, headphones on. It takes me somewhere else.

It's definitely a solitary thing for me—I have to be alone and un-interrupted so I can let down my guard," she says. "I can cry about the music. I can dance if I want to dance—not that I usually do."

There's a lovely passage about the pain of spiritual doubt in a letter that Flannery O'Connor sent in 1959 to her friend Louise Abbot. "I think there is no suffering greater than what is caused by the doubts of those who want to believe," O'Connor writes. But I'd add this to that: I think there is no suffering greater than what is caused by the doubts of those who want to believe *and are told by others that they cannot.*

I'm thinking about that kind of power grab—and the conse-quences of it—about half an hour after the end of Jen and Lianna's Lynchburg College gig. At a folding table in the dimly lit narthex of the chapel, Jen is signing books and CDs and greeting fans. Finally, a jittery, wet-faced seventeen-year-old girl reaches the front of the line—and Jen.

"I'm a lesbian, and . . . ," she sputters.

She looks for a moment as if she's trying to choose between talk-ing and holding her tears back, but she completely fails at both.

"Do you have good friends, people to support you?" Jen asks.

The girl nods and wipes her eyes.

"Cry it out, man," Jen says softly. "Some days you've got to let it go."

"You're . . . just very inspiring," the girl says.

"I'm just being me. That's all I can be," Jen says. "Be who you are. That's all you can do." And she reaches across the table to wrap the girl in a big hug.

Later Jen tells me that it's all she can manage to utter a few words of comfort and check her own emotions. "It makes me cry. What are you supposed to do?" she says. "I can only imagine the thousands of things running through that girl's head. It's really heavy, man. Most of the time, I'm just trying to keep my cool.

"You just want to tell them it will be okay, even if it may seem hard or scary. I want to give her permission. I want her to know: You are a person of value. You are a person of worth. If you're crying because this journey has been incredibly painful, cry it out. Let it out. Let it go. And move on to the next step, whatever it is."

Jen hopes that one of her next steps will be a concrete one that will help her recruit more artists like her and like Lianna to work on gay issues in the church. She's starting a not-for-profit that will be both nerve center and clearinghouse—a meeting place and a dispatch center to connect churches and advocacy groups with musicians and writers, comedians and entertainers who can and want to help. "We need to get people who can speak to speak," she says. "I can't do it all myself. There are others who want to help—maybe not for sixty days a year, but four or five. And there are groups and churches who will want us to come but they won't have the money. So maybe this is a way to raise money to make it possible. I've said, I wanna help, I wanna help, I wanna help. Nobody's given me an opportunity."

And so she's making her own.

# MARY GLASSPOOL

*"God said to me: I am bigger than the church."*

Los Angeles

Mary Glasspool, the suffragan bishop of Los Angeles in the Episcopal Church of the U.S.A., is the first lesbian to be elected a bishop in a major American denomination. She was the second homosexual to be elevated to bishop in the Anglican Communion, after Bishop Gene Robinson of New Hampshire.

Her 2009 election renewed the divisions in the worldwide communion. While U.S. church head Katharine Jefferts Schori hailed the vote as "a prayerful and thoughtful decision," Archbishop of Canterbury Rowan Williams stripped the U.S. church of all its seats on Anglican ecumenical boards. A group of conservative archbishops—including the primates of Kenya and Nigeria and the archbishop of Sydney, Australia—also criticized Glasspool's election, saying that it "makes clear to all that the American Episcopal Church leadership has formally committed itself to a pattern of life which is contrary to Scripture."

Glasspool oversees LGBT-related programs in the Diocese of Los Angeles along with ecumenical and interfaith work.

---

I am a cradle Episcopalian. My father was an Episcopal priest who was rector of St. James Goshen, in Goshen, New York, for thirty-five years. He was a very traditional Episcopal priest, and I would say he was conservative theologically. There were no girl acolytes. But I sang in the choir.

In 1972, I went to Dickinson College. At the time, if a woman was to have a career, basically you could be a secretary or a nurse or a schoolteacher. Certainly, in the Episcopal Church, there were no women priests. But at Dickinson, I met an assistant chaplain who was a Presbyterian woman. All of a sudden, embodied and incarnate, I was able to visualize that which I had never been able to imagine: a woman who was a minister in a mainline American denomination.

On July 29, 1974, the first eleven women were ordained in the Episcopal Church, but it was done "irregularly," as they said, at the Church of the Advocate in Philadelphia. For my father, that was the beginning of the end. We argued about it, so it became off-limits to talk about.

Exactly at this same time, I was wrestling with my sexuality. I was scared. Was God rejecting me? I grew up in a typical heterosexual context where *fag* was an insult; that was the way kids mercilessly and cruelly teased each other. In my worldview at the time, it wasn't a positive thing to be. Yet I found myself emotionally and eventually erotically drawn to women more than to men.

In the dustiest, darkest corner of the basement of Dickinson's library, I found some books on homosexuality. I was praying and wrestling and reading—and falling in love with a woman. The very thing I was wrestling with was love: whom I loved and how I loved. I knew I loved God. And I knew I loved this woman in college.

Here is the thing that kept me from tossing it all out: If I loved God and love was good, then God ultimately would not reject me. The culture, it seemed to me, and society and even the institutional church were at that time telling me that homosexuality was wrong—that it was not of God. But the good news I recognized, even then, is that God is not to be equated with the church. God said to me, though not in words: *I am bigger than the church. Do not equate the institutional church with me.* I understood that the institutional church is a tool—a means to do God's work in the world and to spread the message. But it is not to be equated with the omnipotence, the majesty, and the mystery of God.

*[In 1976, the Episcopal Church approved significant revisions in the Book of Common Prayer, including "recognizing" the ordination of women. Episcopal seminarians must be sponsored in their "holy orders" by the rector of his or her parish; Glasspool's father agreed to sponsor her studies at the Episcopal Divinity School in Cambridge, Massachusetts.]*

In 1979, I was one of five representatives from my seminary to the General Convention in Denver. The then-bishop of Rochester, Robert Spears, headed a commission on health and human affairs. They had prepared a report to be given to the General Convention, saying that homosexuals were children of God and entitled to all the rights and privileges thereof.

When the gay community started pushing for gay rights, conservatives said, We passed the [changes to] the prayer book. We passed women's ordination. Enough. Not this. It felt like too much.

I signed up to be one of the people to speak for it at the General Convention. I gave a speech that began, "We gay and lesbian people . . ." After that, the bishop of New York, Paul Moore, came up to me and said: Now that you've come out to fifteen hundred people, don't you think you ought to tell your parents? So I made an appointment to see my father—he was very formal.

I was very scared. For fifty-five minutes, my father and I talked about world peace, the crisis in China, and whatever else we could come up with. At five minutes to 5 p.m., he said, "Your mother will be having supper ready in a few minutes. Is there anything else?"

I closed my eyes and said, "The reason I made this appointment, Doug"—we always called him Doug, though in public, we had to call him Father Glasspool—"is I want you to know I'm a lesbian. I want to know what effect it will have on my 'holy orders.'" There was a long silence. Finally, he said, "I thought so." Then he said, "As long as you don't make this public, as long as you don't create a scandal for the church, you can continue to be sponsored here.'"

Then we went up to dinner. It was like normal. Nothing was said about it. My family was always pretty good at denial. That, we knew how to do.

*[Glasspool worked at St. Paul's Chestnut Hill, near Boston, and then became rector of St. Luke's and St. Margaret's in Boston. There, she met her partner, Becki, a fellow Episcopalian.]*

I've never wanted to be less than honest about myself and who I am. But it's also the case that I've never wanted to be a one-issue person. I wanted to normalize this issue and not have that one aspect of my life be preclusive.

When I interviewed at one church, one member of the search committee asked the question "Are you dating?" I honestly said, "No." The guy started fumbling around and said, "Should we call you here, would you be dating?" I said, "No." If they're going to ask a question like that that is clearly beating around the bush, I'm not going to do the work for them. I eventually said, "I am in a partnered, monogamous relationship." I didn't get called to that job.

At St. Margaret's in Annapolis [Maryland], I was the only female candidate in an original pool of fifty. I was never asked directly about my sexuality, and I did not bring it up—they didn't ask, and I didn't tell.

I was so flabbergasted when St. Margaret's did call me, but I felt I had gifts and skills that they desperately needed. They wanted someone to come and love them into a community. I could do that. But it was a risk for both of us: Because it was a more conservative congregation, I had friends who said, "What are you doing, going to this church?" For Becki, it was too conservative; she went to a Unitarian Universalist church in Annapolis.

It turned out to be a wonderful time, but there were painful moments. We had a lesbian couple coming to St. Margaret's.

One died of cancer, and the local paper, the *Annapolis Capitol*, refused to print the name of the partner as survivor. I got into a screaming match with the editor. It was devastating to me. It doesn't take a social scientist or a believer to see that this is destructive and not loving. Today the two of them are buried side by side in the graveyard at St. Margaret's.

*[On December 15, 2009, the Diocese of Los Angeles elected two new bishops, both women. In Glasspool's office hangs a framed copy of the next day's* Los Angeles Times *front page.]*

We were walking through the airport on the day after my election. Becki said, "I'm going to get a magazine." She came back and said, "You're on the front page of the *L.A. Times*! We have to hide!"

*Lesbian* was in the headline. I have at least a modicum of respect for wanting to post the most attention-getting headline in order to sell the newspaper—it's marketing. But I feel like only one aspect of the complexity of the person I am is being singled out. We've worked very hard—and we still work very hard—to try to articulate our story in the way in which we would like to articulate it, so I don't like that.

Outsiders might perceive a focus on sexuality, but I don't think that's what the Episcopal Church is really doing. Some people say to me, "How can we get more people into the church?" I say, "That's not your job. The job is, How do you meet the needs of the community? The church exists to meet the needs of the world, not to build up the institutional church. I think the Episcopal Church is doing well with that, but it needs to continue to grow in its corporate life of service and mission."

My late grandmother used to say, "Don't criticize. Try something harder." It's very easy to criticize. It's very easy to tear down. What can we do to build each other up? Recently, I was doing one of my regular visitations. I was at Christ Church in Redondo Beach. Among the seven people I was confirming that day was a lesbian couple, one of whom was nine months pregnant. They had both grown up in the Roman Catholic Church, and they had learned that in that church, it wasn't okay to be homosexual.

I preached a sermon that day on the renunciation of evil. There are three kinds of evil. The first is cosmic evil. The second is systemic evil—I talked about racism, sexism, homophobia. And the third is personal evil, which we call sin and individual temptation. But we are all God's children. God loves us as the people we are.

I'm not out there being a militant about anything except about the love of God. God's covenant with us is that God has given us more love than our hearts can hold; we simply need to respond. I am passionate about the Gospel. I continue to grow in the Christian faith, and I take Scripture very seriously. It informs my faith. I learn from it daily. It has authority over me. But we are going to disagree about interpretation.

It seems to me that it's a heterosexual analysis to think it's all about sex and not about relationships. But what are we really talking about? We're talking about issues of power and authority. This is a culture where men are dominant over women. There's something so profoundly threatening to men in the idea of two women who can have a relationship without them. And they see gay men as effeminate. The real issue worldwide, underlying the sexuality issue, is the gender issue. This is about control.

# A HOUSE OF PRAYER FOR ALL PEOPLE

## The Metropolitan Community Church

*San Francisco; Las Vegas*

In October 1968, a Los Angeles man named Troy Perry started a new church. Perry, a North Carolina native who had been preaching since his teens, had married young, had two kids with his wife, went to seminary, came out as a gay man, and divorced. He had tried to ditch his faith when he left his straight, married life. "I said, 'God, don't bug me. I don't care anymore. I won't bother you. It's not important. They tell me you can't love me and I can't love you, so let's just call it quits.' But it was not that simple," he says. "It's like that famous remark from *Brokeback Mountain*: 'I just can't quit you.' It was like that."

Perry was working as a division manager at Sears when he felt a pull back to ministry. It was a ludicrous notion—no major denomination in America was then ordaining openly gay people.* "I said in my heart of hearts, 'God, if you want to see a church, just let me know when,'" he says. "And that still small voice in my mind's ear said, 'Now.'"

---

* The first openly gay minister in a major American denomination was William Johnson, ordained in 1972 in the United Church of Christ.

One day at work, he wrote the word *church* on a piece of paper. Then he thought to himself, What kind of church should this be? "I wanted to go out into the GLBT community, but it was also open to everybody. So I wrote 'community.'" Then he thought about what area he hoped to reach. The answer: metropolitan Los Angeles. "So I wrote 'Metropolitan.' And it just seemed right: Metropolitan Community Church."

The Metropolitan Community Church met for the first time on October 6, 1968, in Perry's Los Angeles living room. Twelve people showed up—nine friends and three strangers who had seen an ad that Perry bought in a local gay paper.

That Sunday, Perry preached on Job, who the Bible says was "the greatest man among all the people of the East." There has never been a greater humbling than that of Job, who, in chapter 13, Perry's key passage, is batting 0-for-infinity. He has lost his home, his seven sons and three daughters, servants, 7,000 sheep, 3,000 camels, 1,000 oxen, and 500 female donkeys (which, because of their milk, were more valuable than male donkeys). The only thing he has gained are painful boils "from the sole of his foot to the crown of his head."

Perry built his sermon on Job 13:15, when, amid crazy loss and "what else could go wrong?"-level tribulation, Job says: "Though he slay me, yet will I hope in him." His faith is shockingly constant. Perry's message to his nascent flock was at once humble and all confident: "I don't have all the answers, but I know that God loves me, and if God loves me, he loves you, too." (He certainly did love Job, who eventually was rewarded with seven new sons, three new daughters, 14,000 sheep, 6,000 camels, 2,000 oxen, 1,000 female donkeys, a whole book of the Bible, and several bonus mentions elsewhere.)

One of Perry's goals has been to bring joy to a marginalized population that craves but lacks it. "I've always believed in the joy of salvation. We don't have to look like the Missouri mule eating briars to be Christian," he says. "I really do believe that Christians must remember that joy."

Today the Metropolitan Community Church, the world's first and only predominantly gay denomination, has more than two hundred congregations, in thirty-seven countries. It's hard to say what a typical MCC looks like, because it's so diverse, especially theologically. Some of its member churches are extremely liberal, some are quite conservative, and most are somewhere in the middle. "My big fight is always to keep the five percent on each end from killing the rest of us, just as in any denomination," jokes Perry, who retired as the moderator of the MCC in 2005 but still retains considerable moral authority as its paterfamilias. "Everybody is welcome."

Everything you need to know about the ethos of the Metropolitan Community Church of San Francisco is contained in a stained-glass window in its Castro District sanctuary. Titled "A House of Prayer for All People," the window was created by the designers Roy Little and Jim Raidl in 1995, for the church's twenty-fifth anniversary. The design centers on a simple cross made of panels of clear glass, each of which contains a symbol of a different belief system—a menorah for Judaism, a mask representing African tribal religions, a yin-yang symbol for Taoism.

"Our tagline: 'No matter who you are, no matter where you came from, you're welcome here. All of you,'" says Glenn Stover, a board member at MCC-SF. "The only thing we absolutely insist on is that everybody be permitted to find their own way to go." A number of members and attendees don't even identify as Christians. There's a Druid, a Jew, and a large contingent of agnostics and atheists. "Some of the best Christians I know call themselves atheists," Stover says. I must have looked confused, because he added quickly, "They have rejected the man-made constructs of Christianity, but they follow the principles of Christ. Each person must find his or her pathway. It's not up to me or to us to tell them what practice to engage in or not to engage in."

It's an ecclesiastical version of an M. C. Escher brainteaser: Is the common thread that there is no common thread? Organized religion as I've experienced it has to be organized around something. I always thought church pointed in a particular direction toward a particular divine, whether through architecture or music or sermons or liturgy. Mustn't there be some rules and standards? What is this church's identity—a word that comes from the Latin *idem*, meaning "the same"?

MCC-SF's resistance to existing dogma makes sense in one context: As the second-oldest Metropolitan Community Church congregation, it has always gone its own unorthodox way. The church's first formal services, in April 1970, were held in the upper room (biblical) of a North Beach bar (not so biblical) called Jackson's. In its early years, it evangelized aggressively, if unconventionally; one invitation read: "Bring a trick to church."

The church's first decade was nomadic—it met in a dozen different buildings in the 1970s—and its leadership no more steady, with eight different pastors at the helm. Even in San Francisco, it encountered hostility. In 1973, an arsonist burned down the building on Guerrero Street where the small congregation was then meeting. Finally, in 1980, the congregation bought a turn-of-the-century church called Voice of Pentecost, now repainted a pale pinkish purple, on Eureka Street in the Castro. "When that church found out it was a gay church trying to buy the building," Stover says, "they tried to rescind."

Perhaps the defining experience of the church's life has been the AIDS epidemic, which decimated San Francisco's gay-male population in the 1980s and the early 1990s. The first MCC-SF member to die was named Jackie; he passed away in 1983, less than a year after the term *AIDS* replaced the unfortunate terms *GRID* (gay-related immune deficiency) and *4-H disease* (because the syndrome seemed to hit homosexuals, heroin addicts, hemophiliacs, and Haitians). Some weekends, the church was a house of perpetual mourning, holding eight or ten memorial services.

AIDS transformed MCC-SF's demographics. "The majority of the church is women," says interim pastor William Knight. "The lesbian community really stepped up and accepted the responsibility to care for the men. They cared for the people and they buried the ones who needed to be buried." It didn't matter whether they were Christian or not—this was a mercy ministry of the purest kind.

Today the church holds five types of services. Each Sunday morning, the liturgy is rooted in high Protestant tradition. Sunday evenings, the service skews more low-church and Pentecostal. On Tuesdays, there is the meditative, Buddhist-inspired Q-Sangha service—the Q is for queer, and *Sangha* is Sanskrit for "assembly." (For a time, the church had on staff a "minister of Buddhist spirituality.") Wednesday is Taizé night, a candlelit, chant-filled service in the spirit of the French monastic order. And one Saturday a month, there is a lesbian Catholic Eucharist.

Ninety-nine percent of the MCC-SF congregation is gay. Sexuality is exalted in this congregation, which calls itself a "home for queer spirituality." "If you're not gay, maybe it isn't for you," Stover says. "We talk *a lot* about gay issues." The online bios of MCC-SF's board members cite, for instance, that biff wilson (as his name is given on the church website) "is actively involved in the imperial/leather/bear/dyke community, holding the titles of Bay Area Cub 2001, Imperial Crown Prince [San Francisco Imperial Court], and Mama's boycub."

The core audience for this kind of messaging? "People raised in religious traditions who were told they weren't worth anything if they weren't traditional, fundamentalist believers. Those people who felt badly treated in their traditions. Victimized," Pastor William says as he shows me around the church. "This congregation is full of people recovering from religious abuse."

At times, it seems as if MCC-SF will do anything that isn't traditionally done in old-school church. Take its online Queer Book of Hours, a modern iteration of the prayer guides popularized during medieval times. It almost seems intended to be an antidote to a conventional Bible-centric church culture. Unlike traditional Books of Hours, which include psalms and passages from the Gospels,

MCC-SF's contains no Christian Scripture at all—though there are Navajo prayers on Sunday and Monday, thoughts from the Tibetan Buddhist nun Pema Chödrön on Tuesday, and a passage by the Zen Buddhist monk Thich Nhat Hanh on Friday.

At one point, Pastor William and I stop in the sacristy, which is hung, packed, and stacked with the things of worship—all kinds of things and all kinds of worship. There are cushions for the Taizé service, robes and vestments in different fabrics and hues, and a score of Buddhas of varying sizes. I spot a small bottle marked "blessed oil" and ask Pastor William where it came from. "We don't know who blessed it," he says jovially, "or who it was blessed to!"

The day after my visit to MCC-SF, I fly to Las Vegas to visit the MCC congregation there. The Strip, the touristy heart of Las Vegas, is a neon-lit diagonal of casinos, resorts, and all manner of exuberant ersatzity that slashes through the rest of town, an unremarkable and orderly Tetris board of suburban subdivisions and strip malls. MCC-LV lives in its own blah strip mall, tucked behind a Taco Bell and a car stereo shop, about a mile east of the old Sahara Hotel and Casino. The only concession to form on its facade is a series of arches, but even these seem clumsy and inelegant.

Wayne Lindsey, MCC-LV's tall, lanky senior pastor, could be the better-looking, more earnest older brother of *Seinfeld*'s Kramer. He has a similar, slightly awkward manner, cut by Southern warmth and gentility that frequently bubbles up. One wall of his small office contains more crucifixes than I saw in the entire MCC-SF complex—he has been collecting them for twenty years, and he points out a few with personal significance: the one a boyfriend in Dallas gave him; a wooden one with pink triangles; one from England, made from nails pulled from the wreckage of Coventry Cathedral after it was bombed by the Luftwaffe during World War II.

On another wall, he has a collection of Christian icons. A print of an icon-like painting of Jonathan, David, and Jesus was a gift from his friend Roger Corliss, who cofounded the field of Buddhist-Christian studies and taught for years at Duke Divinity School. "I do like that one," Pastor Wayne says of the print, which features Jonathan and David holding scrolls that read "Keep sacred your promise. Be loyal to me" and "How wonderful was your love for me." "You have these Old Testament figures with Jesus looking down at them."

I ask for Pastor Wayne's help placing MCC-LV on the denomination's theological spectrum. "Every single church is going to be a little different in the MCC. It usually reflects the individual pastor and the individual congregation. It's not like a Catholic thing, where they say, 'This is it!' and you just have to believe it," he says. "This church is not as liberal as some—but then Las Vegas is not as liberal as people think. The Strip is like Disneyland, and the town that surrounds it is much, much more conservative."

I can see a need for a gay-friendly church in a city like Vegas—in other words, a non–San Francisco. Pastor Wayne notes the strong Mormon influence in the state—both of Nevada's U.S. senators are Latter-day Saints—and the city's sizable Hispanic population. Within the congregation, he says he leans more liberal and much of the congregation skews more conservative—later, I meet one woman who proudly proclaims herself a "lesbian fundamentalist Christian." While he pushes for inclusive, gender-neutral language in all the readings, preaching, and hymns, "it goes over the heads of a lot of people.

"There's this one blood song they always want to do—'O the Blood.'" He rolls his eyes. "When they sing that, the congregation goes wild! It's the whole sacrifice and redemption thing—the fact that someone had to die to forgive me. Well, if God's all-powerful, someone didn't *have* to die, did they? That substitutionary-atonement theology is not something I really buy into, but it's important to a lot of people here."

Pastor Wayne's own background is eclectic: He grew up Methodist, attending a conservative country church in the upper-right-hand corner of North Carolina, near the Outer Banks. When he went off to study at North Carolina State University in Raleigh, he stuck with his denomination, joining the Wesley Foundation, the Methodists' campus ministry, but this was the 1970s and it was college, so "it was more liberal," pushing him to examine some of the givens of his childhood faith. "One day in Sunday school, we were questioning the Virgin Birth," he says. "I couldn't believe they were doing it! It was just different and a little uncomfortable at first. The main thing was that I was surprised it was okay to question that in church."

After graduation, he dabbled in Episcopalianism and then was invited to a new MCC church that was meeting in a United Church of Christ building. "We could fit in two pews on one side of the church," Pastor Wayne says. "It immediately felt like home: It was a small group, which reminded me a lot of the Wesley Foundation, and we all went out to eat together after church." A few years later, he began his studies at the Southeastern Baptist Theological Seminary. "The Baptists then were not as conservative as they are now," he explains. "Plus, it was close, and it was cheap." After serving his church in Raleigh and then a much bigger one in Dallas, he became head pastor of MCC-LV in 2006.

Before the 5:30 p.m. Saturday "Rainbow" service at MCC-LV, I stop at In-N-Out Burger, a key refueling point on the Western portions of my pilgrimage. In-N-Out prints tiny Bible references on its drink cups and burger wrappers. The verse I get with my hamburger is Revelation 3:20. I don't know this verse, so I fold the wrapper and tuck it into my notebook for later.

MCC-LV holds three services each weekend in its sanctuary, a dull, boxy, windowless room with a low acoustic-tiled ceiling and rows of gray, padded meeting-room chairs. The Saturday evening service targets Hispanic congregants. Everything is bilingual—from the worship songs to the sermon, which feels doubly long because the words of the Filipino-born pastor, George Balgan, are translated into Spanish. There are abundant Catholic influences, too, from the priestly procession at the start of the service to the shout-out on this evening to the Virgin of Guadalupe to the sign of the cross that Pastor George makes at the end of prayer.

The 9 a.m. service the next day hews more to traditional Protestant practice. There's a small but enthusiastic choir, and Pastor Wayne wears simple vestments. For the 11 a.m. service, which is meant to be more contemporary, he ditches the robes, and the choir gives way to a worship band.

The sermons dwell largely on gay themes, reinforcing positivity and God's promises. On Saturday evening, Pastor George preaches on one of his favorite Scriptures, Jeremiah 29:11: "For I know the plans I have for you, declares the Lord, plans to prosper you and not to harm you, plans to give you hope and a future." Pastor George emphasizes the part of about hope and a future, and he spends a while talking about the calling of this congregation. "It was quite different forty years ago when we were not welcome in church," he says. "It has changed. . . . But still, we have this special call, having experienced being shut out." On Sunday morning, Pastor Wayne's sermon is titled "Get Your Joy Drag On!" "Lots of us have been prisoners or captives to our pasts," he says. "God is offering us a new suit of clothes—an opportunity to be different, an opportunity to think differently. . . . Let us choose this day to put on and wear a spirit of joy."

I can see the promise of a joyful future for this congregation. We all desire these things, but how much more so among a population of the traditionally excluded? How much more meaningful is the appeal not just of acceptance but also of embrace?

On Sunday morning, I meet Orlena Rascon and Claudia Sanchez, a warm couple who are raising two teen sons and have been attending MCC-LV for the past three years. "We're Catholic, but we often struggled with the fact that we couldn't be ourselves in the Catholic Church," Claudia says. Trying a non-Catholic denomination was a momentous, difficult step. Catholicism "is not only spiritual and religious—it's a way of life," Orlena says. Then she pauses, and at the same moment, the two women say in unison: "It's a *culture*."

Cultures can feel oppressive to those who don't hew to their norms—say, a lesbian with progressive politics who is helping to rear her partner's two sons. "I couldn't handle that I felt so out of place in church. I couldn't focus," Orlena says. "But here, you can focus on your relationship with God." "We can't stay away," Claudia says. "Even if we're tired, our whole week is thrown off if we don't come to church. It's like home here."

The concept of full embrace is expressed beautifully in the way the church serves communion. It's something common to all MCC churches: Communion is open to all, and it is served personally, intimately, with warmth and prayer and more often than not, hugs. When I go forward at one of the Sunday morning services, Pastor Wayne places the wafer in my mouth and then says gently, hands hovering around my shoulders, "Come and see how good our God is, my brother Jeff. I pray that God may bear you forth and that you may go in peace."

After church, back at my hotel, I riffle through my notebooks and find the burger wrapper from In-N-Out. I look up Revelation 3:20. "Here I am!" the verse says. "I stand at the door and knock. If anyone hears my voice and opens the door, I will come in and eat with that person, and they with me."

Of course. MCC-LV is nothing if not welcoming. And it's appropriate to its setting: It is a very Vegas spiritual buffet with a little bit of something for everyone, an element borrowed from here, a tradition pulled from there—a table set for all. But the reason it feels off to me goes back to something the Apostle Paul discusses in his Letter to the Galatians. Christianity was especially radical in his time because it defied the Roman Empire's strict hierarchies, and in Galatians, Paul addresses the question of converts from non-Jewish backgrounds. "In Christ Jesus," Paul writes, "you are all children of God through faith, for all of you who were baptized into Christ have clothed yourselves with Christ. There is neither Jew nor Gentile, neither slave nor free, nor is there male and female, for you are all one in Christ Jesus. If you belong to Christ, then you are Abraham's seed, and heirs according to the promise."

This is one of many verses that speak of equality in the church, and by extension, unity. In reality, of course, the church isn't unified, and believers aren't equal. But still, in the twenty-first century, the question remains: Should there be a separate church for gays and lesbians?

"I personally don't believe that this is a gay church," Donna Robinson, an ebullient member of the MCC-LV church board, told me. "We're Christians and that's the bottom line. We welcome all people and we preach the love of Christ." But the MCC was started by a gay man to serve gay people and has attracted an almost entirely gay membership, so it *is*, by some significant measures, gay. And it has long struggled with its identity as a gay church, so much so that Troy Perry seemed exasperated when I asked him about it. "I don't try to convince people it's not a gay church. The perception is out there," he said. "One famous Protestant minister used to say, if you can't fix it, feature it."

This has been problematic. In 2006, the Cathedral of Hope, the Dallas congregation that had been the largest in the MCC, left for the United Church of Christ and took with it nearly a tenth of the MCC's annual revenues. The Cathedral of Hope had gone through a season of debilitating internal political strife. But one of the main concerns that surfaced during debates over its future was the worry that MCC was too narrowly focused on gays and lesbians.

This denomination was a child of the 1970s and 1980s, when fledgling MCC congregations were attacked and activists like Anita Bryant, the former Miss Oklahoma turned pop star and orange juice icon, said, sometimes convincingly, things like "[homosexuals] cannot biologically reproduce children; therefore, they must recruit our children." The MCC guards its heritage fiercely, and sometimes its people get defensive about it: When I referred to the gay Episcopal bishop Gene Robinson as a pioneer, Pastor Wayne corrected me.

"Troy Perry was a pioneer. Gene Robinson is more of a settler who came after the pioneer," he says. "We've been dealing with this issue longer than anyone else and keeping it in the forefront."

This is true not only in the United States but overseas, and much of the Metropolitan Community Church's foreign work supports gay and lesbian believers in nations where gay rights are either not codified or anathema or both. Each Easter, the denomination takes an offering for a handful of specially chosen ministries. In 2011, the funds were split among Uganda, to help contribute toward safe housing for gays and lesbians in a country that keeps toying with the death penalty for homosexuals; Russia, where a church elder is working with LGBTQ Christians; and the Philippines, where the handful of MCC congregations needs organizational help and basic training. "Those are interesting follow-the-money things," says Barbara Crabtree, the denomination's operations director. "We are doing fabulous, incredible, life-changing work."

But Christianity in the MCC's homeland has changed radically over the last twenty years, along with American society and culture. Pastor Wayne notes that gay ghettos in urban centers are crumbling, with gays and lesbians integrating geographically. "Whether it's West Hollywood or Christopher Street in New York or Cedar Springs in Dallas or Hillcrest in San Diego, there's just a lot more straight people in those neighborhoods. Everything is more gentrified and less concentrated."

All this has pushed the MCC toward obsolescence. "Younger folks don't have some of the same issues. They didn't grow up with the same opposition. It's something about which we have yet to come up with a real plan," says Pastor William. "Part of the issue for them is, Why can't we just go where we want to go?"

Exactly. One common argument among MCC clergy is that the denomination continues to be relevant because American Christianity, even on the liberal side, isn't as welcoming to gays and lesbians as we might imagine. "There's still a place for a truly affirming voice, a congregation where people can feel at home and themselves, and they're not just a token presence," Pastor Wayne says. "Even the Episcopalians, they elected Gene Robinson, but they split over that. And the UCC is open and affirming, but not everywhere."

Pastor William puts it in more strident language. "Many churches say that they're open and affirming, which means, 'We're so open-minded, we'll let you infected people come be part of our congregation!'" he says. "Instead of honoring and celebrating who you are, they tolerate you. And I don't accept toleration. It's like you're somehow less-than, thereby *requiring* their tolerance."

One of the wonderful things about the Metropolitan Community Church is that it has always focused on those (many) people whom the broader church alienates. Pastor William explains it beautifully when he describes his approach to those who have been alienated by the community of faith. "You give them constant doses of the truth, the truth that is based in love that is unconditional," he says. "You love them until they can hear that they are lovable. You love them until they know nobody else can define who they are. You love them until they can process their pain without reliving that pain." The MCC home page affirms this, boldly proclaiming: "Empowerment." "Hope." "Bridges that liberate and unite voices of sacred defiance."

Yet this plan never mentions God. While the denomination has clear roots in Christianity and most MCC congregations are more overtly Christian than the San Francisco one, faith does not seem to be its unifying element—sexuality does. Perhaps it has become more a network of community centers, where gays and lesbians can gather and talk about the things of the spirit and the soul, whatever religious system they may subscribe to. Which is nice, but for me, it's not church. And while I don't want alienation or exclusion when I'm in the pews, I'm also not there to celebrate other people. I thought the whole point was to celebrate God.

We each choose our churches through unscientific, highly personal processes. Some people spend their whole lives worshipping in the same parish—just as their grandparents did and just as their grandchildren will. Others are ecclesiastical butterflies, flitting from congregation to congregation, feeding a little here and a little there. Some people must visit a church for weeks or many months until they decide it's a good fit. Others know instantly that a church is not for them. A bad experience with one congregation can color a person's sentiments about an entire denomination forever—or not.

As I traveled around the country interviewing gay and lesbian Christians, many of those on the more conservative end of the theological spectrum said that they had attended MCCs but had been turned off by the theology ("theology lite," "bastardization of church"). A significant minority also reported an oversexualized atmosphere. "Everyone was just macking on each other during the passing of the peace," one gay acquaintance told me, although I thought he was just being a little oversensitive, or, perhaps, slightly boastful.

Then I get hit on myself, twice, during the passing of the peace at the church in Las Vegas—the only time this happens during my entire pilgrimage. First, an elderly man who shakes my hand says, "My, you have a firm grip." Pause. "Are you a wrestler?" Wink.

*What?!*

Before I can conjure some kind of reply, I'm grabbed into a hug by a big fiftysomething, with a gold chain, hairy chest, shirt unbuttoned nearly to his navel. "So glad you're here," he whispers into my ear as he holds on for just a second too long. Perhaps I wouldn't think much about this hug, except that he'd barreled his way across the entire sanctuary to get to me. And it's his second hug of the service. He'd been handing out programs at the door, and rejected my attempt at a handshake in favor of a hug then, saying, "We don't do that here."

Church should be a place where one can safely feel vulnerable. I've always thought of this vulnerability being spiritual and theological—a posture of questioning and hoping and examining. But in Vegas, the passing of the peace turned into the passing of the profane. And later, as my immediate discomfort from those incidents faded, I thought more about how such isolated misuses of church by even a few members does such a disservice to them all. It plays right into the stereotypes of gay people as hypersexualized. It confirms the suspicions of many people—including my parents and some of my childhood churchy friends—that gay men think first with their penises and then with their brains.

The biggest problem is that these two men reinforced my own suspicions that the MCC is more focused on people than on God. As I was reflecting on these church visits, I came across a tweet from Tullian Tchividjian, a grandson of Billy Graham and the pastor of the influential Coral Ridge Presbyterian Church in Fort Lauderdale, Florida. "By reading the Bible as if it were fundamentally about us," he tweeted, "we'll totally miss Jesus." And by building the church as if it were fundamentally about making ourselves feel better, I wonder if we also totally miss God.

# FEELS LIKE HOME

## Highlands Church

*Denver*

---

Occasionally, someone will ask me where "home" is. I never know quite how to answer that question. Some people say it should be New York, where I have lived for the past seven years, but I've always felt I'm in an NYC phase, not settled here. London was where I became an adult—paying my own bills (financial and otherwise), coming to terms with my debts (emotional and otherwise), and figuring out who I am, as opposed to who others want me to be. Miami was where I spent the last seven years of my childhood, but other than a love for Cuban food and a smattering of Spanglish, I never felt entirely at home there, either. Sometimes I say "home" will always be the San Francisco Bay Area, where I lived until I was nine and spent every summer growing up. That explains my near-religious love for the 49ers, but I often think the Bay Area of my memory moves farther and farther from the reality, to the point that if I ever moved back, I imagine I might be horribly disappointed.

My rootlessness applies to church as well. I've been to all kinds. In California and in Miami, my family went to Chinese Baptist churches. When I was in junior high, my parents decided that my sister and I needed friends at church—we had none—so we started going to a

Presbyterian church that some of my classmates went to. In college I did the nondenominational thing. London was my Anglican phase—mostly what people in England call the "happy clappy" strain, not "smells and bells," because as much as I liked the bells, the smell of incense always nauseated me. Today my boyfriend and I go to a mainline Reformed church; we adore our pastor and we like the building, but I wouldn't say we necessarily feel spiritually settled there, either.

In some ways, this year of pilgrimage, of spiritual searching, hasn't just been a search for God in America. It has also been a quest to find a church that feels right to me, a congregation that can begin removing the emotional and spiritual barnacles of the past years: the cynicism, the doubt, my insecurities, my fears of letting people know who I am and what questions I have.

Since I was a child, I've been told that God created humans for community, that it is important for faith not to be purely an individual thing. But church is one of those places where I've always felt like I am wearing an invisibility cloak. (Another was any high school dance, which evoked a similar sweaty-palm-and-racing-heartbeat anxiety.) The passing of the peace, for instance, always feels so rote: repeatedly, "Peace be with you!," except for some of the lazier people, who barely manage just "Peace." It has become the "How are you?" of Sunday worship—almost devoid of meaning, something that you say because you are supposed to, not because you actually mean the words. We shake hands, but they don't see me.

When I get to Highlands Church in Denver, I do what I always do when I visit a church for the first time: I don't go in.

I was especially nervous about Highlands because of my past experiences with churches that emphasize inclusion of gay people. But I'd read—if not quite believed—that Highlands somehow balanced an evangelical bent with full embrace of gays and lesbians without being a totally gay church. One of its copastors is a straight, married man, the other a partnered lesbian. They are nominally in charge,

but in some ways, the church's nonhierarchy seems designed to re-
semble a socialist community, with various functions—prayer, hospitality, worship—devolved to standing committees. How did any of
this work? I wanted to find out.

Highlands is located in a Denver neighborhood of the same name,
about ten minutes by car from downtown. In the late 1800s, this was
a separate town on the northwestern edge of Denver, west of and
uphill from the Platte River. The higher ground proved appealing
after an 1864 flood that destroyed lower-lying sections of the city.

The neat, tree-shaded streets are lined with bungalows, Victo-
rians, and Craftsman-style homes, many of them from the early
twentieth century, when waves of strivers—first Italian, German,
and Irish immigrants, then quickly followed, starting in the 1920s,
by Mexican-Americans—began settling in the neighborhood. Today
it's the kind of urban area being repopulated and gentrified by young
families who, ten or twenty years ago, tended to flee to the suburbs.

On the morning of my visit, I walk up Lowell Boulevard, past
the building—imposing, big and brick, respectably churchy. A good
twenty yards down the sidewalk, I do a quick U-turn and walk past
the church again. Toward the end of the block, I pull out my Black-
Berry and pretend to read an email, not that anything new has landed
in my inbox at 8:55 on a Sunday morning. Then I do the whole bit
all over again.

Visiting a new church always has an infantilizing effect on me.
It's the religious equivalent of the first day at a new school. Given
that my mom is not there to walk me in the front door, I want a sign
that God is there. And just before the 10:15 a.m. service begins, I
get one: Pre-church mimosas are being served. Do you even need to
know anything else?

Highlands was founded in 2009 by Colorado native Mark Tidd, a
short, animated man with bushy, mobile eyebrows. He and his wife,
Leanne, invited me to stay in their home during my visit to Denver,

and over a series of conversations, Mark tells me about his long journey from his Roman Catholic, church-hating youth to the ministry.
"I first heard someone talk plainly about Jesus in high school. I was
probably stoned at the time," he says. The messenger was a street-
corner preacher in Boulder. "He wasn't a kook. He'd just stand on his
soapbox and reason with people. And the name of Jesus just pierced
me."

At times, Mark seems like a big kid, so it seems natural that once,
he wanted to study dinosaurs when he grew up. Married young, he
ended up at Kent State University, pursuing a Ph.D. in paleontol-
ogy. But he changed course after a mentor suggested he consider
seminary. He went to Calvin Seminary, the Reformed nerve center
in Grand Rapids, Michigan, and then returned to Boulder to pastor
a Reformed church.

In 2006, Mark, who was living in Denver near his wife's work
and commuting to Boulder, had major surgery, and afterward, as he
was coming off the Versed, he had "this really vivid . . . well, I want
to say vision, but there were drugs involved, so let's just say dream."
He was lying on his back, eight stone tablets were piled on his chest,
and each was gradually revealed to him. The first said, "Your neighbors need to know God." The second said, "Your neighbors need to
know God." The third said, "Your neighbors need to know God."
And the fourth and the fifth and the sixth. The seventh said, "Love
your good wife." And the eighth one said, "Your neighbors need to
know God."

After much thought, prayer, and withdrawal, Mark went to his
congregation to share his feeling that he needed to minister to the
community around his Denver home. And in January 2007, he and
a small group of friends started a once-a-month spiritually focused
get-together. A large evangelical church in Denver called Pathways
heard about his initiative. It had been thinking of starting a new site
in the Highlands neighborhood and asked Mark whether he would
like to partner up. On Christmas Eve 2008, the first service of Pathways in the Highlands took place.

Everything would have been fine if it weren't for the gays—or, more precisely, Mark's take on the gays. He had told Pathways early on that his thinking had been shifting as he studied the issue. "I was reevaluating my entire hermeneutic, asking, 'What are the implications? Are there certain verses I've ignored or thrown out?' But what happened was I was not just scrutinizing God's word but also scrutinizing God's world."

What it comes down to for Mark is an acknowledgment that when we read Scripture, we are always filtering it through a lens—or perhaps multiple ones. What does "love" mean to me? How is "justice" interpreted? What cultural biases do I impose when I read about biblical rules for women, or laws about food, or regulations about sex? What societal mores existed then? Mark explains, "I run into people all the time who say, 'The Bible says . . .' They never say, ' . . . as it has been translated and interpreted.' There is no hermeneutical awareness, and you shouldn't be able to get away with that. We are all interpreting."

Mark's differences with the more conservative Pathways leadership over homosexuality led him to walk his fledgling congregation away from its mother church. "In the course of a week, half of the people interested in starting this church—and two-thirds of the financing—said, 'We just can't do it,'" he recalls. "It was an ugly delivery, but a beautiful baby." This theology also cost him personally. The denomination that had ordained him in 1984, the Christian Reformed Church, defrocked him for violating doctrine with his views on sexuality.

New churches are not much different from small businesses: Eighty percent of them fail within the first two years. But since the first service of the independent Highlands in September 2009, the church has grown and grown and grown. On the Sunday of my visit, Highlands is thronged with hundreds of worshipers, and I'm trying to figure out what it has done differently.

For the first little bit, the service seems normal, American, non-denominational, contemporary—standard big screen with the lyrics to the worship songs, band, people standing and singing and doing what passes for dancing in church. But then the worship pastor, Rachael McClair, begins praying, my first indication that this will be a church experience unlike any I've had. "We are grateful to have a community where we can bring our whole selves," she says, "both the part that's experiencing hope and the part that's experiencing despair."

What? I thought. Who's going to show off their despair at church? That would be undignified!

For me, church has always been a place where you not only have to wear your Sunday-best clothes but also your Sunday-best face. That isn't how things are done at Highlands at all. Look at the church ethos, which Mark wrote and is recited every Sunday:

> Married, divorced or single here, it's one family that
>     mingles here.
> Conservative or liberal here, we've all gotta give a little
>     here.
> Big or small here, there's room for us all here.
> Gay or straight here, there's no hate here.
> Woman or man here, everyone can here.
> Whatever your race here, for all of us grace here.

Yes, it's cheesy and kind of kumbaya, but in his sermon, Mark develops this theme, drilling at the importance of fearless transparency. Referring to 1 John 4:18, he says: "When you know you are being loved and not judged, fear has nothing to control. . . . Perfect love is the multivitamin every Highlander should take. Perfect love drives out fear, because fear has to do with judgment."

The default setting for most of us, he continues, is to believe that God is judging us. "The epic tragedy is that the organization on earth that is supposed to represent the Good Shepherd is better known for sacrificing the lambs or scattering them. This bigotry in the name of Jesus must end!" Across the auditorium, there's a smattering of amens.

"We are not a two-year-old gay church!" he says. They say, "Amen!"

"We are a Christ-centered church!" he says. And again they say, "Amen!"

Later, during communion, something unprecedented happens: I start tearing up. This part of the service was led by Mark's co-pastor, Jenny Morgan, whose voice is the silk to his sandpaper. She tells the congregation that it is open to everyone—"whatever denomination, whatever faith tradition you come from, even if you haven't darkened the door of a church for years, you are wel-come." And then the people come forward to take a morsel of home-baked bread (or a gluten-free cracker) and dip it in grape juice. They are young and they are old, gay and straight, singles and couples, in jeans and T-shirts and chiffony frocks and biz-casual khakis, strappy sandals and flip-flops and killer heels. One tall, blond guy comes to the table barefoot. A mom approaches with her toddler son riding her shoulders. Another mom, a white woman, carries her Asian baby forward. All of them come to eat the body and drink the blood. They write words of thanksgiving on little strips of paper. They light candles on the altar; one boy, surely a child after my own pyromaniac heart, lights candle after candle, until the table is ablaze.

From the start, Mark Tidd felt that the church didn't need just good leadership; it also required symbolic leadership, and so he invited Jenny Morgan to be his copastor. If Mark is the church's expansive, enthusiastic vision, she is its tender, theologically obsessive heart. Right after church, we sit on a pew in a darkened corridor, and she tells me about her long, twisty road from Roman Catholicism to this pastorate.

Jenny grew up in Pittsburgh, and you can still hear its open vowels in her speech. When she was nine, her beloved grandmother died. The loss prompted some childhood soul-searching. In church one Sunday soon afterward, she looked up at a crucifix, saw Christ's body hanging there, and just knew: *If Jesus did that for me, he must love me.* "It filled this gap in my heart that my grandmother had been holding," she says. She still says this with wonder filling her warm, heart-shaped face.

When she was a teenager, she began to read the Bible, over the objections of several nuns and a priest. Their opposition puzzled her. "I thought, Why wouldn't you want me to read it?" she says. "I do understand it now—I think they were just trying to protect people—but that's when the Bible became foundational for me. It still is."

When Jenny was sixteen, she had what she now calls a calling, "though that's not what I would have called it then. I was a band geek, and I was standing at the back of the band room, behind the timpani. I had a vision from God. I'm looking around, thinking, I wonder if he knows how much God loves him. And him. And her. I didn't even know the word *evangelism*, but I felt called to it. It was God saying to me, 'Talk to people about me!' "

At Northwestern University, she joined Campus Crusade for Christ. After college she went to seminary, but her newfound brand of evangelicalism told her as a woman, she shouldn't preach or teach. She could evangelize, but that was different. It was fine with her at the time. "I just wanted to share the gospel," she says. "I didn't want to fight that battle."

The battle she had to fight instead was against her lesbianism. She was a serial monogamist, finding girlfriend after girlfriend—six in all over thirty years that she spent working for the evangelical organization Youth for Christ. She went to ex-gay ministries. She spent countless hours in prayer, asking God's guidance; always, she said, she would hear God saying, "Stop lying," not "Stop being with women." She spent thousands and thousands of dollars on counseling—fifty thousand, by her best estimate.

"I don't regret a penny of it," she says. "None of it changed my sexuality, but all of it drew me closer to Christ."

The breaking point with Youth for Christ came when she was accused of living in a lesbian relationship. The funny thing, she says, was that "I wasn't. Not yet. During my last week there, the president calls me in. He is crying. He says to me, 'I need to know what is going on.' I say, 'Dan, I know the boundaries, and I am not violating them.' I wasn't lying. I was living within the boundaries."

She looks down at her lap. "Most people in Youth for Christ despise me," she says. "They think I have been deceived and that, as a preacher, I am deceiving other people. They think I have fallen so far that I can't come back."

With her partner, Kristy, the newly out Jenny Morgan visited more than two dozen churches. None felt right. Then one day, a friend mentioned that a new start-up congregation needed a drummer once a month, and would she be interested? More than she could have realized. "I would cry every time I watched all these gays go forward for communion and serve communion," she says, remembering her early visits to Highlands. "It just undid me. There are a lot of great mainline churches out there, but here is another option: a deeply Christ-centered, deeply biblical church that is okay with the gays. A church where you can come as a drummer and end up a copastor."

Mark Tidd started Highlands in this neighborhood and gave the church this name because it's where he has lived since 1999 and he wanted it to be a church for and of the community. But it's also a remarkably appropriate name for a congregation of its purpose and mission.

The name Highlands strikes me as particularly apt given an accusation often directed at more liberal churches: that they go for lowest-common-denominator, people-pleasing theology, something that Mark and Jenny have strived to avoid. "This church is deeply

Christo-centric," Jenny says. "What I mean by that is that the foundation of this church is the person, the work, and the teaching of Jesus Christ. His death. His resurrection. The belief that he is coming back. That he was and is God."

I challenge her on this point, because nearly everyone says that they focus on Christ; it's just that they differ on what this means and what this demands. None of us reads Scripture as it has always been read—that is impossible. We all impose our cultural constructs, our individual lenses, our biases and prejudices and wants and desires.

But what's compelling is their argument that they are not trying to build a community of convenience. For instance, the church has so far declined to start a second service. "It just makes it a more consumer environment," Jenny says. Instead they have talked about how, when the church outgrows its space, they'll divide and plant another, thereby creating another church community rather than bifurcating this one and potentially weakening it.

They also are unafraid to ask the congregation for contributions—not money, but time and prayer and physical and spiritual investment. "We want our people participating in worship first, but by that, we don't mean sixty-five minutes of Sunday morning. We do not want to be a drive-by church," Jenny says. "It's volunteering maybe once a week or for some, once a month. It's spiritual development and what God is doing in your life. It is *not* feeling guilty."

In some ways, this is much more demanding than your typical new church, and yet new people have kept coming and coming and coming, proving that the more-is-more model may be the ticket.

After church, I drop by the Neuroth-Howard home, about a mile away. Kirk Neuroth, his husband Eugene Howard, and their two kids, Benjamin and Isaiah, have been attending Highlands for the past year, and while Eugene distracts the kids, Kirk and I sit on their patio and chat.

Kirk grew up in Michigan. Early in his childhood, his family went to what he calls a "tiny little in-the-middle-of-the-cornfield, non-denominational, freaky Pentecostal church." A graduate of Wheaton College in Illinois, he has lived in Japan, Chicago, the San Francisco Bay Area, and Denver—and his spiritual life has been about as peripatetic.

At times he didn't go to church at all. He has also tried MCCs. The one in Chicago "felt like a cruisy bar where we happened to sing praise songs." The one in Denver "felt like theology lite. The pastor there is wonderful. He lets people know that God is crazy about them. People need and want to hear that, but I wanted more. The biblical exegesis is something I was missing."

He notices me noticing his hands, which move nearly constantly. "I'm a sign-language interpreter and I do sign language to remember things—pardon me," he says, as if he had been excluding me from the conversation. "Of all the places I have called my spiritual community or faith home, [Highlands] is the only one I've been to where they do not throw the theological baby out with the bathwater, saying, 'None of this matters. It's all about inclusion.' It's the only place where I've felt people wrestling honestly with a lot of tension. It stays in the tension and lets people ask the hard questions," says Kirk, who is thirty-six. "Church is an uncomfortable place for a lot of people, but it seems like at Highlands, there are a lot of people who are ready to be uncomfortable together."

Highlands is too young a church to have had any members who grew up in the congregation, and it strikes me that, like Kirk, everyone else in the church has come from somewhere else. This is and will long be a church of denominational immigrants, and during my days in Denver, I meet former Baptists and Presbyterians and Methodists and Catholics and MCCers and even one ex–Berean Fundamentalist, people who would call themselves theological conservatives and those who would identify as liberals.

There's Joe Song, a single, gay, twentysomething Korean-American Web designer. His grandfather was a Methodist minister and his parents attended a Presbyterian church, but the relevant facts were that the churches were always Korean—in some sense, more community centers than congregations—and that Joe always disliked church. "I still don't like church, but I like Highlands," he says. "Highlands is radical inclusivity. It's Christ-centered and justice-oriented."

There's Scott Wolf, raised Lutheran, and his wife, Jamie, who grew up a Chreaster* Christian. Scott and Jamie met as students at Northwestern. They are teachers, soft-spoken and earnest, and Jamie leads the prayer team at Highlands. "This church has given me a bigger picture of God," she says. "When Jenny gave her testimony, she said at the very end that we need to grapple with the question 'What if we're wrong?' It takes a lot of humility to be able to ask that at a church that has declared a position! To hear her say that the cross is big enough for all our misconceptions—Jesus covered it!—that was a transformational moment in my understanding of God." When she pauses, Scott adds: "I think that Highlands is just really committed to the process of trying to listen to what God wants."

There's Stacy Price, who attended a Southern Baptist seminary. Without Highlands, she says, "I might have been dead." She has struggled with suicidal feelings for a long time, but integrating herself into the community at Highlands—where she met her girlfriend, Chrissy Folken—has helped enormously. "This," she says, "is me choosing life."

There's Christina Gradillas, who didn't grow up going to church and works at a Denver not-for-profit, and her wife, Tara Moxon, a lifelong evangelical who is a police officer. "Highlands really tries to live out unconditional love," Tara says. "We're all human and we all fail." Highlands, says Christina, "is what church should be."

There's Deb Saint-Phard, a Baptist-preacher's kid and former Olympic shot putter who currently heads the University of Colorado's women's sports medicine program, who isn't even sure about

---

* Christmas + Easter.

the divinity of Jesus. "For me, theology is philosophy," says Deb, forty-seven, the single mother of two daughters. "There's a spirit and an essence to the Bible stories that we need to follow, but I don't think it's a master plan."

By the time I get to Scott and Nina McVicker's house for dinner one evening, I'm thinking that there really is something different about Highlands. When I ask Nina and Scott why they chose Highlands, Scott, who grew up in Iowa, attending a Reformed church, says simply: "We just wanted that feeling of normalcy. We wanted our church to be a place where it just feels like you should be there. This is a church that is not crazy."

From the beginning, the McVickers have recognized that homosexuality is a key social justice issue at Highlands. "In the back of my mind, I don't want it to become a gay church," says Scott, who runs the data team for a mutual fund company. Yet they appreciate that their two sons are growing up in a congregation that fully accepts gay people. "It's important that our kids grow up without this being an issue," says Nina, a Colombian-American who was reared Roman Catholic. I spot a Celtic cross tattooed on her right calf, and I ask about its significance. "It's a never-ending loop," she says, "because God's love is never-ending."

Nina reflects on their first visit to Highlands and smiles. "Honestly, I did not want to like it. *Evangelical* to me means those crazy guys on TV. But I've found myself telling my running buddies about my church and inviting people. I am kind of shocked at us, because we are not those people!" says Nina who works as a Web designer. "This is faith I never knew existed. We believe Jesus wanted everyone to come—not because if you don't, you're going to hell, but because you're part of the family."

Progressive evangelicals from around the United States have begun to visit Highlands, hoping to replicate its model. Some of them have fixated on Highlands' embrace of gays and lesbians, and if this is what they take away as the core of the model, I think they will likely fail. What I find to be unique about Highlands is less its theological position on homosexuality than its stance on humanity. While remaining committed to deep and constant engagement with the Bible, it encourages people not just to come to services but to bring their whole selves, not just their sacred stances but also their profane fears and insecurities. They are called to do what is uncommon in the church: question boldly, without fear and in confidence. "Can we live and love without labels?" Mark Tidd asks. "Can we help each other do justice, love mercy, and walk humbly with our God?"

On my last morning in Denver, I meet a special-ed teacher named Joey Torres for breakfast. He has sandy hair and a lightly bearded, wide-open face that somehow seems smiley even when he isn't smiling. "Highlands is weird," he says. "We're having conversations that the broader church is having—hard conversations that can break up churches—but it's the ethos that is different. We're not in pursuit of people. We're in pursuit of God, and through that pursuit, people like us end up coming."

Up Joey's right forearm runs a tattoo that proclaims in big script: "There could be love." The phrase comes from Lois Lowry's book *The Giver*, which is about a kid who grows up in a bizarre utopia that, he comes to realize, totally lacks love. "It reminds me to constantly be pursuing love and putting more love into every situation in my life," Joey explains. "It's compassion and sensitivity and listening and just being present in the life of a person who maybe hasn't had that before."

That spirit is what I found at Highlands. And if I could find it in more churches in America, the pews would be more full, *evangelical* might not be such a polarizing word, and more people might still believe that the Gospel really is good news.

from: Gideon Eads
to: Jeff Chu
date: Mon, Oct 3, 2011 at 1:38 AM
subject: My meeting with the counselor

Hey Jeff,

I hope that you had a good weekend. I met with my appointed counselor last Thursday. It was a long meeting, and a frustrating one. I
was defeated in that office before I walked into the room.

We started the visit off with a simple prayer asking God for wisdom.
I almost visualize Jesus responding to that prayer, trying the door-
knob only to find that it's locked by the chains and padlocks wrapped
around my counselor's mind. Not that Jesus, being God Himself,
couldn't have broken through the door, but we all know He often
responds to our humble willingness.

"First of all, I would like to tell you that everything you say today goes
without judgment on my part," he started. "You can be totally open,
and it stays in this office."

"OK," I responded.

"Why don't you tell me why you're here?"

I decided to find out what he already knew. I had expected the pastor
to share the details. "Well, I'm sure Pastor has already filled you in on
my situation . . ."

"Not really." *Really?* I thought.

"Well, I'm gay. I've always known I've been this way. Even when I was
a child, I knew there was something different about me from my dad
and my brother."

He interjected, "Now you say you've always felt like you think you're
gay." Did you catch that? He changes my words to I *think* I felt gay.

"But you're sitting here in my office, which suggests that some part of you thinks this lifestyle is wrong."

To quote one of my favorite characters, Winnie the Pooh, it was an "Oh bother" moment. We'd been talking for less than five minutes, and he already defined my position as a practicing sinful homosexual under the term "lifestyle."

I began to tell him how my opinions matched his and the pastor's for most of my life. That way of thinking only caused me grief and pain. I shared my experience of my prayer life, searching for God under the stars. If it was so wrong for me to be gay, then I wanted to figure out why. If, however, there was some way I could be happy in my sexuality and continue in God's Word and Ministry, I wanted to find that option.

He stopped me. "Can I suggest that maybe, you felt grief and pain because the lifestyle you wanted is wrong and against God's will?"

"The grief and pain was felt *before* I came to these conclusions," I responded.

"Well, let's take a look at the scriptures, shall we?"

"Absolutely," I said, and I pulled out my phone with the Bible app I use.

"Let's go to Genesis 19:4–5." It's the famous Sodom and Gomorrah story where the men of the city commit homosexual rape against the guests (angels). After some discussion, we both agreed that this passage was not even about homosexuality. I wondered why he brought this passage up, if he agreed the story was not about homosexuality.

We moved on to the verses in Leviticus that state "lying with a man as with a woman is an abomination" (Leviticus 18:22–24 and Leviticus 20:13). He began to talk about how holy and perfect the union between one man and one woman was. I agreed, but said, "This is not a verse about homosexual love, or being gay. This command is there with all kinds of connotations of adultery, promiscuity, and idol worship from the surrounding nations."

"Let's move on to 1 Corinthians 6:9–10," he said, the passage which lists the types of people who will not inherit the kingdom of God, the "unrighteous, sexually immoral, idolaters, adulterers, or men who practice homosexuality."

Once again I asked to bring the context and cultural influences into play, but he interjected, "In every instance of scripture, homosexuality is spoken of in a very disapproving way. There is no 'good' homosexual mentioned. If we let ourselves think that way, does that mean there are good thieves? Good liars?"

If I had been allowed to finish the thought I started before he moved us on, I would have pointed out that this is what I was trying to get him to see—the pictures of that homosexual and the ones I'm talking about are not one and the same. There are no good thieves . . . but there are generous giving people. There are not good liars . . . but there are people who are truthful. There are no good promiscuous homosexual encounters, there are no good homosexual prostitutes, and there are no good homosexual idol worshipers. There are, however, gay men who are sexually responsible/celibate, who don't exploit their bodies but treat them like the temple of God, who don't have anal sex at a shrine, but rather go to church, pray, seek God's will.

Next we read the passage in Romans 1: 26–27, out of context from the chapter, as, if you've noticed, we did with all the others. This passage speaks of God giving up the people to dishonorable passions, men and women committing "shameless" acts with their own sex. He paused to form a thought, so I tried to take advantage of that. "Could I propose that the men were actually giving up their natural desires in order to perform pagan sex rituals?"

He cut me off again. "This is speaking of the perfect nature of marriage, the union of one man and one woman. God created only Adam and Eve, and they physically fit together, becoming one."

I was overwhelmed by where we were going. He was setting the definition of every aspect of our discussion, and not letting me finish my thoughts.

I tried one more time. "I'm not arguing any of that. I think God's creation was perfect. Sin has messed everything up, and humankind has had to make all kinds of coping circumstances." Surprised that he had not cut me off yet, I continued. "God is amazing at being the same and having the same standards, yet allowing cultures to change, and even rules to change. There are several kinds of marriages, different from that of Adam and Eve, that were blessed by God. God declares punishment on the ones that did not honor him, for example, King David. He was blessed by God with many wives and concubines, because of his faithfulness to God's will and righteousness. When did God get mad at him for taking another woman? When he lusted, stole, lied, and murdered for sex with her."

This was the only moment he actually considered what I said. "I honestly don't know why God didn't do anything about all David's wives, but I do know it was not God's intention for him. I can't explain all the reasons God lets things go sometimes."

Finally! Some real critical thinking! Unfortunately it was cut short.

"Now you say you think you've always felt gay," he paused. "Have you ever been abused or molested?"

Ah . . . so this is where this was going! We were going to figure out what happened to make me gay.

"Never," I said. "I know these questions, I know the classic Christian ideas of what causes homosexuality . . ."

Cut off again. "Well let's just get through this."

"OK," I said, already knowing the next question would be about my father.

"How was your relationship with your father growing up?"

*Ding ding ding! I bet the next one is about my mother.*

"He was an awesome dad, one of the biggest influences to my faith. He taught me awesome things. He was and is always there for me."

"OK," he said, and if you could read his facial expression, it would have said, "Hm, well that's not it."

"What about your mom?"

"She has always been a very strong Christian lady, a faith much different from my dad's, much more emotional. She let us be sociable, but did her best to keep us 'unstained' from the world. They've created one of the strongest families, and I am blessed to be a part of it."

"I'm assuming you haven't told them yet?" he asked.

"No, they hold a very traditional view."

"Have you ever had a girlfriend?"

"No, I've never even been attracted to a girl. Ever."

He scratched his chin. "I've never even seen you with a girl . . . So has there ever been a strain on your relationship with the parents?"

"I've always been close to them, despite my feeling different. In recent years I feel some distance only because I feel like they don't know the real me."

He leaned forward. "So this issue is putting a strain on your family? Don't you think that's a telltale sign that this is not of God?"

"That's not exactly right," I corrected. "The distance is one-sided, *my* side. I can see how it will cause strain when I come out, but as of right now, things are the same on their side. They just don't know how I feel on the inside."

"Hm." The next question, I guessed, would be about sex, with the slightly embarrassed body language he started to exhibit. "My next questions are even more personal, they are not meant to embarrass you, and again not for me to judge you."

"OK," I responded.

"Have you been sexually active . . . and by that I mean . . . any form of . . . of . . ." He was struggling with the words.

"Yes," I said, and he seemed relieved that I responded before he had to mention anything specific. "I'm not proud of it, but I have been active a few times. I got to a point of trying so hard, pretending so much, that when temptation came along, I easily caved."

"How did you feel after you engaged in sex?"

"Um . . . guilty?"

"Don't you think there is something to say for the fact that you felt guilty?"

"If you're asking why I felt guilty, it's because those acts were fueled by lust, and acted out in release, not trust in God."

"Don't you think you were feeling guilty because this is a lifestyle God does not want you to live?"

"Of course *that's* not the lifestyle He wants. I've repented from those acts, and come to trust in God, but not until *after* I accepted my sexual orientation, reconciling it with my faith."

"You say you felt guilty though when you became one with those other men. Is not that a sure sign that God does not want that life for you? The gay life?" he asked.

"I did not feel guilty because it was *gay* sex. I felt guilty because it was *sex.* I had sex out of the boundaries that I believe God lays out in His word. It doesn't matter if I had sex with a man or woman. That's why I repented."

"But you see," he leaned forward again, "you already took that step towards all those things. If you continue forward, you are stepping into a such a dark, dark, dark, pit of deception that Satan has cre-ated within the gay movement, inside their communities." I wondered if he ever spent any time with gay Christians. "Satan has his claws very deep inside you right now, and he's waiting for you to make the choice so he can drag you down into that pit, from where you won't be able to return."

I began to protest, but he continued, "You're ignoring the strain on your family, the guilt of your lifestyle, and the loss you will experience when you make this choice, based on nothing more than you feeling like you're gay. I'm telling you, if you go down this road, nothing good lies ahead. Your family, the relationships you love the most, your integrity, your ministries, a chance to ever have a family or a wife—you will lose it all."

I thought it was very bold of him to say I would lose things like integrity. Shouldn't my integrity be based on how I've lived my life? The love and respect I treat people with? The way I serve faithfully? I might have made a few bad sexual choices years ago, but I'm betting that since I've come to trust God in my acceptance of my sexuality, I've been far better at sexual temptation than 90% of the straight men who attend our church, who look at pornography, who have cheated, who have been divorced several times. The fact that I'm gay makes every other item in my life a sin by association? Oh . . . and a wife? Really? For someone who's never been attracted to a woman, why would that matter?

I should have said all this, but I was dumbfounded.

"What if you're wrong?" he asked after he finished.

"Wrong about . . . being gay?" I asked.

"About everything. What if God's Word is right?"

I made a mental note that he implied I was opposed to God's Word by being gay.

"I always ask that. I was very surprised to arrive in this place of acceptance; I thought for sure God's Word would lead me to the traditional point of view."

"So what does it mean if you are wrong?"

"Then I'm stuck being wrong, being gay, and trying to live my life pleasing to God as a gay person."

He seemed caught off-guard by this.

"I've prayed hard, studied hard, had faith, and tried my hardest not to be this way. So if I'm right or wrong, I'm stuck either way."

"You've been so passionately involved with viewing this from the *other side*, that you've lost your biblical perspective."

I protested, "No, my studies *started* with scripture, and *remain* on scripture . . ."

He cut me off. "I would like you to come back to scripture for three months. Study only God's Word . . ."

I tried to cut him off. "But that's what . . ."

"And sources that confirm a biblical perspective. I have some material for you from a few books."

He held up a stack of papers. The first page read "Homosexuality" and he had my name written across the top.

"Now wait," I said loudly. "I can't read anything that disagrees with *your perspective*? How am I supposed to critically think and cross-examine what I'm reading, if all I can read is material that agrees with each other?"

"You've spent so long on the other side of the issue, that you need to refocus on this side for a while. God will open your eyes."

Feeling humiliated, I began to consider doing this just to hold up my biblical integrity. If the truths I've discovered really are the truth, then they would withstand three months of one-sided opinion.

"OK," I said.

He snatched that answer up, grabbed a pen and began to write on the front of the materials he was going to give me. "OK, let's write these rules . . . No . . . let's call it a covenant, let's write down the covenant between me and you."

"OK?" I wasn't even sure if I was agreeing or questioning.

He wrote down the first thing we talked about.

"Number two, I don't want you having any contact with anyone who is gay, struggling with being gay, or any online chatting or emails to gay people. No reading gay theologian materials or pro-gay teachings."

I agreed, not fully considering what that would mean. His last rule was the easiest to agree to, which was simply to meet with him and the pastor at least one more time before the three months were up.

As he finished writing, the room was fuzzy. I was in a daze. I had no idea what to feel other than frustration. We got ready to pray, but he gave me a warning. "Oh, and I need to mention that if you think rumors are going around about you, and your lifestyle, you need to tell your family right away, in person, to their faces."

Wow. He began to pray, but I could not focus. All I could think about were those last words. He implied that I was living such a sinful secret lifestyle that it was bound to get out. This would be understandable if I had come to him with a sexual addiction, or was a gay-party-scene lover. But simply being gay? A lifestyle?

Let's take a look at my gay lifestyle: I go to work. I come home. I eat. I study my Bible. I hang out with friends. I watch movies. I go to church. I go jogging, and on occasion when I have the extra cash, I give rides to homeless people and feed them.

All I could do was muster up an "OK" and bow my head for prayer. I cannot remember a word he prayed; I was so frustrated in my spirit! We ended and I shook his hand. I walked out to my car, pulled myself in and sat at the steering wheel for a moment. What did I just agree to do?

I picked up the papers to read the rules again. That's when I noticed rule number one: "Come back to God."

Nice.

Everything in me tells me this three-month challenge is not for me. I know now if I decide not to do it, it will only be a sign to them that I'm so depraved I couldn't even last one month. I have no idea what to do.

---

from: Jeff Chu
to: Gideon Eads
date: Mon, Oct 3, 2011 at 7:41 AM
subject: Re: My meeting with the counselor

Dear Gideon,

I guess by corresponding with me, you have already broken the covenant! I am sorry. This was hard for you, I know. Thanks for sharing with me. Keep me posted.

Jeff

---

from: Gideon Eads
to: Jeff Chu
date: Sun, Oct 9, 2011 at 9:18 PM
subject: (no subject)

Hey Jeff,

I hope you've had a great weekend, I was certainly glad to be off work for a couple days!

Just wanted to give you a heads up, I've scheduled another meeting with the counselor. After some prayer I feel I need to do a better job of communicating, so I'm basically doing a do-over meeting LOL. I felt that the challenges he gave me were unbiblical, so I'm going to try to show him again what the situation is.

God bless, have a great Monday!

                                                              —Gideon Eads

_____

from: Jeff Chu
to: Gideon Eads
date: Wed, Oct 12, 2011 at 12:12 AM
subject: Re:

Gideon,

Good luck with your meeting with the counselor. Let me know how it goes.

                                                                        Jeff

_____

from: Gideon Eads
to: Jeff Chu
date: Wed, Oct 12, 2011 at 11:55 PM
subject: Update

Hey Jeff,

What a couple days on the coming out scene! I ended up buying a cocker spaniel puppy, which I couldn't really afford, but I needed something to cuddle with as I go through all these things lol. He's the cutest sweetest thing.

I made the decision earlier in the week to finally meet with some good friends of mine, a couple who joined the church with their 7 children about 10 years ago. I've always felt really comfortable around them, but just never had the opportunity to try to contact them about this, they are always surrounded by people and kids lol. Last night I met them at Starbucks. I told them that I was gay and everything I had been dealing with, and they immediately started understanding my position. They hugged me and prayed for me at the end, and said, "We're so impressed with the way you've handled all this on your own. We love you and are always there for you." They assured me our fellowship was only made stronger by entrusting my sexuality to them. There was so much joy in me on the drive home.

Fast forward to today. I had my meeting with the counselor, the one I requested to talk about the things I felt were wrong in the last meeting, and the terms of our "covenant." This time I made him listen, but he was still unaccepting of anything I said. We parted on disagreement, not hard feelings (I hope). He basically said that he had done all he could do to save me from making a disastrous life choice, that he was grieving for me already. I'm pretty sure that's my last meeting with him.

I'm not sure what's next. I think I'm gonna just enjoy the new puppy the next couple weeks and save up my money in case anything unexpected happens and I find myself in need of a place to stay. . . .

So . . . That's the freshest info lol. I hope you're having a great day! God bless

—Gideon Eads

---

from: Jeff Chu
to: Gideon Eads
date: Sun, Oct 16, 2011 at 9:28 PM
subject: Re: Update

Hey, congrats on the new dog! That's really exciting. What did you name him?

So glad that your good friends were kind to you when you came out to them. Have you had any conversations with them since? Did they say anything concrete about how they feel about the issue of homosexuality?

Sorry to hear about the counselor, although I guess I am not super-surprised. I really hope that he doesn't do any damage.

How was your weekend?

---

from: Gideon Eads
to: Jeff Chu
date: Mon, Oct 17, 2011 at 1:13 AM
subject: RE: Update

His name is Bailey, and he's the cutest thing in the world. Very smart too, learns really fast :)

I haven't had any more conversation with that couple. I've been around family and friends most of the time since, and it's more of a private phone conversation at this point lol. They did not outline their exact beliefs about the issue of homosexuality, but they were very clear that they understood this not to be any kind of choice, much less any kind of sinful choice. His wife did mention being much more liberal then her surrounding Christians.

On one hand, I'm not surprised with the counselor. I expected his views. I was surprised at how he treated me. This guy judged me as the worst type of homosexual sinner, and he would constantly tell me how things "really" were or even what he knew deep down how I was "really" feeling. His theology didn't surprise me, but his method did.

This weekend had its ups and downs. Had some good time with the family and a few friends, and I worked on a small cake order.

Take care :) God bless.

from: Gideon Eads
to: Jeff Chu
date: Tue, Nov 15, 2011 at 10:17 PM
subject: RE: hey

Hey Jeff!

I just got a new job at bakery, finally! Getting to do what I love, decorate cakes, and I also will be working a few overnight shifts a week so I can get a full 40 hours. Gonna mess my body clock up a little bit lol, but it's all been good so far!

The pastor just called to schedule a meeting a couple weeks from now. The tone in his voice sounded disappointed that I didn't repent at my meetings with the councilor lol.

I hope all is well for you.

God bless!

---

from: Jeff Chu
to: Gideon Eads
date: Tue, Nov 22, 2011 at 9:32 AM
subject: Re: hey

Congrats on the new job! How are the hours? Are the overnights tough?

I was wondering, what would you think about meeting up in person? I know your schedule is tough, but let me know what you think.

from: Gideon Eads
to: Jeff Chu
date: Tue, Nov 22, 2011 at 7:58 PM
subject: RE: hey

Hi Jeff,

Thanks, I'm really enjoying the new job. I like the decorating hours better then the overnight doughnut hours, but it's all good. Pretty tired today. It was supposed to be my day off, so I stayed up late watching a movie, but then they called me to cover an overnight shift, so I didn't get to go to bed. It's great though. It's like a little family back there that has adopted me into the team.

I think that would be so cool to meet you in person! You'd really fly out just for that?

Have a great day!

# HOPING

---

"Be ye watchful, and cast away fear; be sober, and hope to the end."

–PART II, THE EIGHTH STAGE, *THE PILGRIM'S PROGRESS*

# I THINK GOD UNDERSTANDS

Gideon Eads

---

*Kingman, Arizona*

A couple of weeks before Christmas, I go on my last trip of this long journey, flying west to meet my email pen pal, Gideon. Kingman, where he has lived all his life, sits in the northwestern corner of Arizona, far closer to Las Vegas than Phoenix. The road from Vegas south to Kingman (population: 28,800) twists through a biblical landscape of devilishly craggy, ocher mountains and flat, scrubby lowlands. Just before you descend into the valley where Kingman sprawls, you pass a strange collection of pockmarked outcroppings and cartoonish boulders. It's as if God experimented with sculpture in rock and left his discards atop that last line of hills.

The valley floor is as dull as the hilltops are diverse—strip malls, double-wides, an entire flattish city assembled from the kinds of buildings that writers too often describe as "nondescript." The most notable thing about the town is one of the roads that delivers most visitors—Route 66—and just as quickly whisks them out.

Gideon is waiting for me in the parking lot of my motel. A short, pimply guy with an open, boyish face, he's still wearing his supermarket name tag and uniform. He wears markers of his cake-decorating work: His black polo shirt, half-untucked from his baggy black slacks, is flecked with sugar and icing.

It's nearly 3 p.m., and neither of us has had lunch. "Let's go get something to eat. I'll buy. What's the best place around here?" I say. He seems stumped, confessing that almost every eatery in town comes from either the fast-food or cheap-chain part of the culinary spectrum. Finally he picks a sandwich shop in the same shopping center as his store.

Even though we've been corresponding for months—or maybe because of it—it's weird to be sitting across from him, and we don't quite know where to begin our conversation. It feels awkward to start from scratch, as if we've never met, and yet it seems equally incorrect to pick up where our emails left off, because in some ways, he's still a stranger. This is the first time I've heard his voice.

I ask him about his work. "I taught myself how to make cakes," he says. "My brother likes working with wood—my dad has a cabinet shop—but I like food stuff. I was always helping in the kitchen. When I was around ten, a friend of my family's gave me a cake-decorating book. It's been trial and error and practice."

Gideon was homeschooled for his entire childhood, and his parents never encouraged higher education. "They think if you go to college, you're going to lose your faith," he explains. "They feel like you'd be paying tons of money just to learn worldly things."

The Eadses value the work of one's hands—and yet it's cake decorating we're talking about. It is not the career a strict, Southern Baptist, cabinet-shop-owning father would choose for his son. Gideon admits that his dad "wanted me to be more boyish like my brother." At first he didn't approve. But Gideon felt a turn "when I started making three-D stuff that doesn't look like cake." He made a *Little House on the Prairie* house. There was a fashion-themed cake for which he crafted blue gems and white pearls out of sugar. He did a *Toy Story* cake, complete with Buzz Lightyear and Woody. "Buzz Lightyear's head looked almost exactly like him. But only almost. I was not one hundred percent happy," he says. "There was just something I couldn't figure out, and I still remember all the imperfections."

After lunch, we go over to the supermarket so that he can show me some of his latest designs. On a typical day, Gideon is expected to make and decorate thirty-five traditional, rectangular cakes—some quarter sheets, some half sheets. Atop the cake display case are a few standard themed cakes that you can order. The most popular: a fifty-dollar, tiered princess cake featuring Tinker Bell. The least: "Sesame Street. I have never sold a Sesame Street cake."

When he's done filling his quota and any special orders that have come in, his manager lets him freelance. For Christmas, he has made one shaped like a Christmas present, beribboned and wrapped in shiny blue "paper." Another looks like a mug of hot cocoa. But his favorite is shaped like a snowman, part of a recent series of experiments with spherical cakes. It's three tiers of white cake carved into globes, covered with buttercream, and adorned with a red-and-green icing scarf. "If I ever had enough snow here, that's the snowman I'd like to make for real," he says. "Oh, and his name is Jeff, by the way. I don't know why."

The sky is shooting daggers of icy rain when we come out of the supermarket, but despite the weather, we drive around town. As we speed past the church in which he has worshipped for nearly his entire life, he tells me it might be time to find another church. His parents have already moved to another Baptist church in town, and I wonder silently whether the negative response from his pastor about Gideon's sexuality might end up being a push factor for him. But if it is, Gideon won't say so. Instead, he says, "I don't like that the pastor has been recycling the same sermons. I've heard each one maybe ten or fifteen times. He has one about children, one about marriage, one about homosexuality. For the holidays, he has one about Baby Jesus and one about saying Merry Christmas, not Happy Holidays. But the gospel is rarely preached, and there's nothing challenging. Nothing you can pull from and say, 'Wow, that was amazing.'"

Some of his other complaints are pretty standard-issue and also have nothing to do with sexuality. "The focus is on how much money we're bringing in, and how many people are coming. Well, there used to be a total of three hundred for both services, and now it's down to about one hundred and fifty. They're obviously not doing what they're supposed to be doing, which is loving people and telling people about Christ. There is definitely not much love going on there right now."

From the church, Gideon speeds north. As we head toward his house, he tells me about the strictures of his family. On the list of things that his family is against: tattoos, alcohol, and Harry Potter. "I used to be against things because they were, but I never understood why. I used to just have standards or rules for no reason that I knew of. Like, what's wrong with someone getting a Bible verse tattooed on his arm? They would consider it backsliding for a Christian to get a tattoo. Or if you went to watch Harry Potter, they'd say it's reminiscent of paganism and we need to pray for you. But now I understand that parents are taking kids to a movie because it is entertaining, not because they want to worship the devil or go home and cast spells. A lot of my faith has been my parents' faith, but now I'm finding out what I believe. And thinking about all this stuff has opened a door to loving people for who they are, as opposed to for who we expect them to change into."

Gideon still regards his father as one of his spiritual role models. "He's so humble. I love when he prays," he says. "It's so personal." Yet Gideon has also gradually begun to see inconsistencies in his family's faith and practice. His brother, for instance, disapproves of Christmas. "One year, my mom did consider not celebrating Christmas on Christmas, mainly because of the commercial stuff. My brother just goes around saying, 'Christmas trees are pagan! Christmas lights are pagan! Christmas trees were an idol in some culture!' But he still celebrates. So then he likes pirates, and he'll watch *Pirates of the*

*Caribbean*, which is full of mysticism and legends and bad words and sensuality. I don't bring it up to him, but I see it. You say this, but you do that."

This season of exploration has also redefined what "gay" means to him. A few weeks before we meet, Gideon went to a gay bar for the first time. There isn't one in Kingman, so he drove the forty miles to Laughlin, across the Nevada border. "I wasn't sure what to expect. Other people think anything gay is dirty or raunchy or sex-driven, so I guess that's sort of what I expected," he says. "I sat there for like six hours, and I just listened to the people talk. If I hadn't known it was a gay bar, well, I wouldn't have known! Because there was nothing sex-related! It wasn't dirty or perverted at all! I was surprised how regular the people were."

We pass a dull, brown ranch-style box squatting on our left, in the foothills of the Cerbat Mountains. "That's my house," he says. "My dad built the whole thing." Of course we can't go in. His mom will be at home, and how would he explain who this random guy is?

Anyway, his mom doesn't like having gay people in the house. She has two gay relatives who live elsewhere—Gideon says he's actually not sure where—and not too long ago, they came to Kingman to visit. They stopped by the Eadses' one afternoon, and afterward, "things were just getting Febreezed and wiped down with bleach, right after they left," Gideon says. "She walked them out, and then right away, she was using those sanitizing wipes and making snide comments. She'd say things like 'You never know what they're doing.' She just seemed disgusted. I think she does love them, but just enough to have contact with them and hope they change. It's not the unconditional kind of love. And when my brother got home, he was like, 'They were in our *house?*' That makes me hesitant to tell them about me, because I don't want them to think of me that way. I'm still the person they grew up with and had fun with and made memories with."

Imagine if she knew about the books that Gideon hides in his bedroom: theological tomes about sexuality. He has spent countless hours reading online, too, and studying and restudying the Bible. "I've been thinking about how we look at the context of when this stuff was written," he says, "and how the words have been translated. I've been investigating a lot. And there's been no guilt, which was a little surprising to me."

The Eads home sits on twenty acres, and the outdoors have always been Gideon's refuge. "Being homeschooled was nice, because whenever I was done with my work, I could just go for a hike. When I got a little older, I'd go for four or five hours, just by myself. Now I don't have as much time, but when I am frustrated, I usually try to go for a long hike."

He lifts his eyes to the hills. "The one with the point on the top, we call that Doughnut Mountain because it has a hole in it," he says. "I don't know what it's really called."

A minute or so down the road, he turns left onto a dirt track. We bounce about half a mile, and finally he stops his SUV.

"I push out my frustration by climbing to the top as fast as I can. Actually, I've never been all the way up, but when I get close to the top, I stop and I can talk out loud to God," he says, pointing at a peak. "Up there, I can see how big everything is. God is keeping it all running, with the animals and the trees, and it's so vast. It's very rocky, and there's tons of weeds and different varieties of cactuses. There aren't a whole lot of trees, but some places there are Joshua trees. And as you go up the mountain, it changes—there are sandy parts and there are rocky parts. Small rocks give way to big ones.

"When I am up there, I think about my frustration, not knowing how to express what I want to say. I vent, and I think God understands. Up there, I feel extremely peaceful. There is such a sense of beauty. When I look at my own life, I tend to focus on the problems, not the beautiful things. Up there, you realize that even the bad stuff you go through is small, compared to God and what he does on a daily basis. I look at what God has created. How much more beautiful is he, if he has made such beautiful things?

"You think about how good we have it. You think about all the people who have worked and pushed for the freedom to be a gay person. Thirty or forty or fifty years ago, I don't think I would have had courage to say anything at all. When I am up there, it's crystal clear. You can see so far. Everything feels like a painting. When I look out, there's so much clearness that it's almost fuzzy."

The spot where we've stopped is separated from the hill by a collection of large boulders. I can't see a path, so I ask him how he gets up top. It seems to be a question that nobody has ever asked him. He shrugs.

"There isn't really a trail," he says. "If there is, I don't go on it. I don't follow it."

That night, I spent some time reading about the biblical Gideon. The Hebrew name Gideon means "mighty warrior." If you were to meet Gideon Eads, you might appraise his slight build, his soft edges, and think his name was a bit of a joke. But the Book of Judges provides no physical description of Gideon. It's all about his evolution as a leader, the development of his faith and character.

We meet Gideon in the sixth chapter of Judges, when God instructs him to call his fellow Israelites away from their idol worship and back to faithfulness. Gideon demands proof that this is his divinely appointed mission. First, God sends an angel to Gideon. But Gideon doubts. "You say that you have decided to use me to rescue Israel," he says to God. "Well, I am putting some wool on the ground where we thresh the wheat. If in the morning, there is dew only on the wool but not on the ground, then I will know." That's what happens. Again, Gideon doubts. "Please let me make one more test with the wool," he says to God. "This time let the wool be dry and the ground be wet." That's what happens.

So Gideon destroys his community's altar to the god Baal and pole dedicated to the goddess Asherah. Then, with an army of just three hundred men, Gideon defeats the Midianites. His people ask him to become their king, but he declines, reminding them that God is their one true sovereign. And for the rest of his life, the Israelites are faithful to their God.

The twenty-first-century Gideon picks me up at my motel at noon the next day—he'd spent the morning hiking in those hills—and we go into downtown Kingman for lunch. His faith is much on his mind. "The one thing I do want is to follow God," he says. "I want to do that with integrity. Some traditional Christians make it seem like every gay community or event is filled with terrible people and lifestyles, but I've learned that the majority of people just want to live like everybody else. They don't want bad relationships or bad things."

Recently, the couple with whom Gideon has shared his secret invited him, his brother, and his sister over for dinner. The wife mentioned that she'd seen one of the *Twilight* movies, and cited a few parts that she especially liked. In the car on the way home, Gideon's sister shrilly said: "I can't believe she would go see that movie."

"I'm kind of surprised they even go to my church," Gideon says to me. "It's not that they're very liberal, but when I told them, they just said they knew who I am. They told me, 'We've got your back, no matter what. If you need a place to hang out, let us know. If you need more advice, let us know.' They said, 'We're honored you told us.' And they treat me exactly the same as they did before. That's all I want from people: to treat me exactly the same as they did before."

After lunch, we walk a couple of blocks to an empty storefront at 402 Beale Street, where Gideon hopes to open a cake shop someday. The facade is glazed white brick, and the windows are trimmed in green. Above the front door is a green-and-white stained-glass transom that hints at past prosperity—the space once housed a bustling general store called Central Commercial.

Peering through the dirty shop windows, he tells me what he imagines. Where I see chipped, dusty mosaic tiles, he sees "a little bit of seating, some cases for the cakes. In the back, I'll have my cake workshop. In the front, I think I would do green on the bottom of the walls, and black on top. There will be some old-fashioned wood and brass."

I ask him why he seems so intent on staying in Kingman, and he shrugs. He has traveled a little bit. "I've been to Phoenix. It was all hot and dirty. I went to Kansas City once, and that seemed so big to me," he says. Once, when he was too little to remember, his family road-tripped to Southern California. "But we haven't been to Disneyland since then, partly because Disney supports gay and lesbian people. When I was thirteen, we boycotted Disney movies because of that." Another time, his family piled into the car—"my mom and dad could drive forever," he says—and headed for Northern California, to see the redwoods. "We drove through San Francisco, but we didn't stop," he says. "I kind of wondered why. It seemed kind of cool.

"I just like this town. I like the landscape. I can be down in the desert or up in the mountains," he says. "There are gay people who live here who are still alive! It's not as bad as it seems. It's not as bad as it could be. I think it's medium—it's not completely gay-hating."

He seems worried yet hopeful. "Is it going to hurt my business to be gay? All my customers right now are church people and friends of church people," he says. "They'd probably say, 'We're not going to give you business until you change.' Or maybe not. I don't know."

It's a bright day, but breezy, and the wind and a stream of cars whip past us. I consider the things that encourage me about Gideon, the building blocks of the kinship I feel with this guy who comes from a world quite different from mine. I think it's the way he asks questions—big and lonely and difficult questions that would be easier not to ask, because the answers could mean so much loss. I think it's his fearlessness, his open stance to the future—it's his faith.

"I'm a little naïve in this town but I'm praying for what the right thing is. There's still so much to investigate," he says. "My motive is just to live a life that's not contrary to the Gospel of Jesus Christ. It's to live according to the same standards you'd expect of straight people in the church."

Then he says with a half smile: "It's been quite a journey, but I am the same person I always was." I know what he means, but I totally disagree. Even in the months I've been corresponding with him, I've seen how he has grown into a Gideon worthy of that name: a mighty warrior fighting for his own life and faith. And his openness, his eagerly curious spirit, is what I want for myself—a prerequisite to being a work-in-earnest progress, seeking, trying, struggling, challenging, and hoping.

"I'll be okay," he says.

I have no doubt.

# CONCLUSION

Midjourney, I was out for drinks in L.A. with Derek, a friend from high school. We were talking about the book, and of course the name of our outed Bible teacher came up. "Whatever happened to Byers?" Derek asked. I said I didn't know, but I'd been wondering the same thing since my pilgrimage began.

What I had learned—what our principal had not told us—was that Mr. Byers's wife had caught him with his boyfriend, and Byers had been forced to resign. But what then?

A few hours of googling told me that he'd lived all over the place: Charlotte, Atlanta, Fort Lauderdale, Washington, D.C. Eventually I discovered that the reason it was so hard to find him was that he wasn't Mr. Byers anymore—he was Mr. Russell. He had married and taken his husband's name. He was now living in Vermont.

I friended him on Facebook and sent him a message: Could we meet up? He said yes. So one sunny afternoon several weeks later, I walk into a Friendly's just outside Burlington and scan the booths. Finally, I spot him, his hair grayer and his face creased, but with the same smile—warm and welcoming, with slightly melancholy eyes.

We make nervous small talk for a few minutes, and then I tell him about my journey and ask if it's all right for me to take notes and write about his story. He says it's okay, and after we order, I invite him to go back and tell me the whole thing: "What happened?"

He sighs heavily, and then begins speaking, slowly and softly at first. He was twenty-four, "the age when most people came out back then," he says. His wife, his college sweetheart, knew he'd struggled with homosexuality, but he'd gone to counseling—even did a residential program. "She'd been given the spiel and believed it: People can change! People can live a heterosexual life! I didn't question it, either, because the alternative is that you believe God created you to put you to hell."

Having a son built his confidence—"I fell in love with my son. And it was okay! I was doing the best I could with what I had"—as did teaching. He never felt hypocritical or lost in the classroom. "It was not a class where I was supposed to be teaching people how to think. It was teaching what the Bible thought," he says, his voice turning slightly defensive. "I think I did that pretty well. Even now, I look back at how I taught. I don't feel like I was a fake."

The guy's name was Mike. "We met at Bally's. I intended to forget something in my locker so I'd have a chance to talk to him." While his wife was away, Mike came over, and when she came home, "the neighbors confided to her that somebody had stayed the night, but they didn't know who." One day, he even brought Mike to school, to show off his classroom. Mr. Byers recalls that the school chaplain saw them. "I think part of me did want to get caught," he says. "I had always been a goody two-shoes, and I was such a bad liar. I couldn't have possibly lived very long with that kind of internal conflict."

He didn't have the chance. When his wife confronted him, she was pregnant with their second child. He confessed, both to her and to the school administrators. "They gave me the option to resign," he says, emphasizing the word *option* to emphasize it was no such thing. "So I resigned. I know what I did was wrong. I was lying. I was having an affair. Something definitely had to happen. How could I be an authentic teacher?"

At first, he and his wife tried to make it work. Our church gave him a thousand dollars to move to North Carolina and attempt a reboot of their life. His wife and son stayed with his aunt and uncle while he moved into another relative's apartment, but things quickly deteriorated, especially after their daughter was born. "They made me out to be the bad guy," he says. "I mean, I was the bad guy, but supervised visits with the kids?"

Eventually they divorced. After she remarried, he gave up his parental rights and the new husband adopted the kids. He hasn't seen either child in more than a decade, though his son recently friended him on Facebook. His brother no longer speaks to him, though his parents do. "Humans survive because parents commit to their kids and kids commit to their parents. It's very biblical—honor thy father and mother—but it's also evolutionary. What good is it to shun them?" he says. "I would lose something if I didn't have my parents going into their old age. Anyway, my dad compartmentalizes things, and things have been fine with my mom since I told her, 'Your lifestyle is just as despicable to me as mine is to you, so we need to find some common ground.'"

He says he no longer believes in the God he was raised with, the God he once taught me about. At one point, he took an online faith-diagnostic quiz, which told him he was nearly either Unitarian or Buddhist. While he occasionally attends the Unitarian church where his husband grew up, he says he "can't stand the liturgy." "I am not a Christian and I am not trying to be a Christian," he says. "For a long time, I had the Sunday morning guilt, but I'm finally able to not think about church or religion."

This statement is not entirely true. A few minutes later, he confesses that he occasionally catches himself humming hymns or sometimes a little ditty that he learned in vacation Bible school. Suddenly he begins to sing, a wistful look on his face: "'Climb, climb up Sonshine Mountain, faces all aglow. . . .'" He quickly stops himself, and as if by way of apology, he says, "It's my parents' legacy, imprinted on me. They invested their entire lives in spiritual concepts and missionary work." He shakes his head. "I'm finally at a point where I'm not put out by all that Bible stuff. I just think Christianity was a bad idea. Now I would say I'm a pantheist or Unitarian Universalist with pagan tendencies and earth-centered rituals. I feel integrated now. I feel at peace."

I don't believe him. During lunch, I've gotten quieter and quieter, asking fewer and fewer questions as he has exposed more of his wounds. I don't believe him because he doesn't seem at peace, although that could be because he's sitting across from a guy who keeps asking him invasive questions. I also don't believe him because I don't want to believe him. This is how it ends? I am thinking. Where's the redemption? Where's the endurance of the faith? Where's the perseverance of the saint?

He jolts me back to the present. "Life's a little more complicated than we can wrap up in a Bible class." Then a moment of silence. "So what happened after I left?" he asks. "What did they tell you guys?"

I told him I didn't remember. It was a long time ago.

Most Sundays at my church, we recite the Apostles' Creed, which includes a line about our belief in "the holy catholic church"—catholic, with its small *c*, meaning "universal" and "singular." It's a nice idea. But the first major lesson of my pilgrimage is that the church in America is neither holy—by which I mean entirely devoted to God's work—nor catholic; in other words, one.

"The church" here is at least unified in this sense: As a whole, it's an institution that has shown itself to be incapable of dealing with who we are and where we are—and a church that is ill-equipped for honesty is not a church worthy of the Jesus of the Bible. I visited dozens of congregations in a host of denominations. There were warm churches and cold ones, big and small, welcoming and standoffish, formal and intimate, congregations of thousands and those of tiny bands of believers. What I never found was unity in what Jesus taught. If the church is supposed to be the body of Christ, then what I saw on my trip were our Lord's dismembered and terribly dishonored remains. Those of us who care at all about the concept of "the church" should look at these ruins and weep.

As I've sought to explore the whys of the diminution of my faith in the church, three key elements—not necessarily reasons—came to the fore.

1. PASTORS: Once, I believed in pastors. I was raised to believe in them, to honor them, to buy them meals in homage to their life of sacrifice and godly devotion. I was taught that they had special insight, some heavenly hotline that gave them wisdom and knowledge and all these things that I did not have. I did meet ministers who were humble, thoughtful, courageous, and kind, all across the theological spectrum, and I've already shared some of their stories. But what I encountered more often was cowardice.

In the introduction, I mentioned that I found pastors to be more sheep than shepherd. If you were looking for examples of that in the following chapters, there were few, because with nearly all the pastors I contacted, we never even got to the interview stage. So many of the pastors I approached were afraid even to discuss the h-word. It's not that they don't have opinions—in fact, many of them have preached on the subject. No doubt some of them feared that I, as a member of the "liberal media elite," might somehow twist their words. One Midwestern pastor, who is the president of a major evangelical group, happily corresponded with me via email until he learned that I wanted to talk about homosexuality; at that point he said that he would not have *any time in the next eight months* to talk. Another influential minister emailed me after months of courtship to apologize for his unwillingness to talk. Speaking out about such a controversial issue, he said, would jeopardize some funding he needed for a homeless ministry. Bad timing!

How do we proclaim our faith courageously if our pastors refuse to do the same? Why are these men and women afraid to state what they believe? Did Paul fear being misquoted? I'd rather be told by a principled pastor that I'm going to hell for my homosexuality than to have him think that but keep it to himself. But I certainly want nothing to do with a church where the leaders fear the hard work at the front.

*My* fear is that the people who pay the greatest price for pastoral failure are not those like me who flit in, ask a few questions, and then move on our way. The real unfortunates are those who do not get the nurture they hope for and need, and then find themselves marginalized from the family of faith, believing that there is no place for them in it.

2. LANGUAGE: We don't know how to speak with one another anymore. We think we speak the same language, yet we find it nearly impossible to communicate—not to mention commune—with one another. Forget about salvation or sin. Let's talk about love. What could be simpler and more essential? God is love! For God so loved the world! The greatest of these is love! And yet there is no word that is more complicated, more confusing, more divisive, more multiply defined.

The late Polish roving correspondent Ryszard Kapuściński, one of my favorite journalists and travel writers, observes upon landing in India for the first time that "language struck me . . . as something material, something with a physical dimension, a wall rising up in the middle of the road and preventing my going further, closing off the world, making it unattainable." That is the power of language, of words. Actually, I'd tweak Kapuściński's metaphor slightly. Words are bricks, which, depending on how you use them, can pave pathways or build high walls.

3. THE PEOPLE: There are a number of compelling reasons that the word *Christian* has taken on such negative connotations in our society, and we have to be humble enough to acknowledge that one of them is that Christians have behaved badly. If those of us who align ourselves with Jesus don't seek to understand more deeply *his* language and what *he* meant by love, we'll fail. If those of us who have some loyalty to this thing called the church do not consider what that requires of us in terms of openness and hospitality, we'll continue to alienate and shut off conversation when we should be doing the opposite. We can—really, must—be firm in our faith and

yet kind and open. We must personify grace. We must recognize our limitations and leave to God what is God's.

When I was in Nashville, I had coffee with Matthew Paul Turner, the wonderful, thoughtful, occasionally impish writer and blogger. I told him about my story and what I was trying to do on this journey, and he gave me a souvenir, a few words that have remained a touchstone for me. "It's not my responsibility or my job to push people out of God's story or tell them there's something they have to overcome to be part of it," he said. "They are part of God's story—as they are."

And yet God can redeem all this. Once, when I was exasperated at some church-related shenanigan, a pastor friend of mine posted a note of encouragement on my Facebook wall: "The most amazing thing is that even though God has seen all the nonsense in the church, he still loves it and works through it. And I might add, that despite all the nonsense in my own life, he still loves me and works through me. And Jeff, despite all the nonsense in your life, he still loves you and will work through you."

It would be nice to believe that.

My favorite psalm, the 121st, begins: "I lift my eyes to the hills. Where does my help come from?" So often in my life, I've fixed my gaze on the church and its people. But over this pilgrimage year, I learned how important it is to distinguish between the church and the God that it purports to represent. Especially for those who stand outside the church, whether as a disillusioned ex-member or as a curious bystander, that's perhaps the most crucial thing to understand.

My faith in my God has only strengthened—He has become, more than ever, the refuge and the strength mentioned in Psalm 121. But I've also learned how crucial it is to have that qualifier *my* before the name of God. This is not because I am so important but because I know I am not. I know that my God differs from your God and his God and her God and their God, and as I searched for God in America, I came to see that, even if we still call ourselves Christians, we do not worship the same Christ. Indeed I did find God on this trip—many of him (and some of her).

I have heard people say that what I have seen are simply the many faces of God, that he is so complex and enormous that all around us we just get glimpses, as if he were a majestic painting. Well, you can view the *Mona Lisa* from a gazillion angles, but it's still the *Mona Lisa*. But the Gods that Americans describe are as different from one another as the Mona Lisa and Lisa Simpson— just about the only thing that links them together is some ineffable aura of mystery.

It's as if we have all Hinduized our Christianity—is your god more a god of bellicosity and war, or does he look more like the god of prosperity, or perhaps the god of social justice? At least the Hindus aim for clarity by calling them by different names, yet we insist on using the same word—God—and identifying our priorities as his. We have taken a God of many names and hand-selected our favorite few. A vast and mysterious yet intimate and personal God has been reduced into something small and manageable and comprehensible. Whereas the Scripture says that we were created in God's image, we have remade him in ours.

So does Jesus really love me? It depends on whom you ask. If you ask me, I would say that He does, but after my year of pilgrimage, I understand that love differently. A year ago, I would have said that it can be a private love, something I keep tucked away in my heart, like a spiritual blankie that's there to make me feel better when I need it. Now, after hearing the stories of so many, I would say that my old conception of the love of Jesus was the mark of a selfish fool. It's not to be kept private. It's to be shared. It's not just for me. It is for all. It's not a luxury. It's a necessity, especially in a world where so many have been told that the love of Jesus is off-limits to them.

In some ways, my faith has shrunk, but much of what I lost was imaginary anyway—illusions and dreams and wishful thoughts. From those I feel liberated. I can now try to be a more productive and constructive part of the body of believers that does exist. I now know, more than ever, that my faith is not about buildings. It is not about elder boards. It is not about any of the bureaucratic, extra-biblical bullshit that we sometimes mistake for church.

I have come to value skepticism more than ever as a key part of faith. It's important because it can bring clarity. In his book *The Genesee Diary*, Henri Nouwen muses on the example of Thomas, the doubting apostle, who asked to see Christ's wounds after the resurrection: "Although Thomas did not believe in the resurrection of the Lord, he kept faithful to the community of the apostles. In that community the Lord appeared to him and strengthened his faith. I find this a very profound and consoling thought. In times of doubt or unbelief, the community can 'carry you along,' so to speak; it can even offer on your behalf what you yourself overlook, and can be the context in which you may recognize the Lord again." So I see the church now for what it is, not for what I once wished it could be. And I see my faith now for what it is, not for what others wished it would be.

This pilgrimage is not over, but then what journey, if it is of any true and lasting significance, ever is? Always, you'll carry something of it with you.

It has taken me this far to reach a beginning, not an end, of a re-newed faith in God—my God—who is bigger than I ever imagined possible. And perhaps this has been the most significant lesson of this journey: My God isn't simply the God I believe in but the God I *want* to believe in and *need* to believe in. A God of unimaginable grace, a God of patience, a God of justice, a God of unconditional love, a God whose wisdom and mercy are incomprehensible to our feeble minds. This trip has reinforced my hope in that God and my desire to live out those virtues as best as I can. My faith may be too small, my misunderstandings too great, but my God is a big God.

Believing that, I will keep doing what I've done on this journey, exploring the aspects of Him that may not be exactly as I wish them. And if therefore I am one day damned to hell, all I can say is that I have tried my best.

As I was finishing this writing, I had one last exchange, by text message, with Gideon Eads.

1/24

Received @ 7:27 PM Update: my mom just found out I'm gay

Sent @ 7:57 PM Oh my. What happened? Are you ok?

Received @ 7:58 PM I'm ok, she is disgusted though

Sent @ 10:24 PM How did she find out? What did she say?

Received @ 10:25 PM She found a beer in my fridge so she snooped through all my stuff, and found my homosexuality study books. So she confronted me about both so I told her I was gay

1/25

Sent @ 7:10 AM Did she seem mad? Sad? Angry? And did she tell your dad?

Received @ 9:20 AM Very mad, and she's been acting depressed since. Though she's made forced small talk, I'm not sure if she told him everything, but I know he's aware something big is up. However he has not treated me differently yet

Sent @ 10:15 PM How are you feeling? Sorry, I left my phone at home when I went to work.

Received @ 10:20 PM No worries, I feel ok, not bad or good, just curious what is to come.

Amen.

# ACKNOWLEDGMENTS

Bylines lie. There may be just one name after the word "by," but this book isn't really my own. It exists because of the testimonies of hundreds of people—a few identified in the preceding pages, but many more not—who opened their hearts and shared their heartbreak and voiced their hope and revealed their pain to me. Their stories were my building blocks. For those gifts, I'll always be grateful.

Perhaps it's appropriate that the genesis of a book about a journey came during a road trip. Beth Adams, I blame you. Without you, your nagging, your friendship, and your irreverence, this book would never have happened.

My day job provided the safety net, health insurance, and journalistic anchor that made my travels possible. Bob Safian, my boss and friend at Fast Company, gave me the time and the freedom to wander far off the FC reservation as well as unfailing support throughout my adventure.

The book world was an alien land to this nervous newbie, so I am indebted to Todd Shuster at Zachary Shuster Harmsworth as well as to Gail Winston, Maya Ziv, and the rest of the team at Harper-Collins not only for all of your deft surgery and editorial advice but also for holding my hand.

The reporting process is usually fun, but writing can suck.

Throughout the joy and the drudgery, so many people helped—with meals, double cappuccinos and G&Ts, laughter, suggestions, enthusiasm, wise counsel, listening ears, their guest bedrooms, prayers, and joyous distraction—including Wayne Adams, James-Olivia Avigail and Luke Esposito, Sara and Roy Bahat, Paul Bartoloni, Theunis Bates and Ruth Margolis, Michael and Simone Green, Ryan Kull, Ellen McGirt, Dana and Tim Meinch, Martin O'Connell, Sharon Sampson, Adam Shepard and Jessica Taraski, Gabriel Sherman, David Van Biema, and my "family" at the Seminar on Debates About Religion and Sexuality at Harvard Divinity School.

Three people in particular deserve special honor for being my readers, absorbing chapter after unpolished chapter. Rachel Arndt, Stephanie Schomer, and especially Denise Martin: you sharpened my writing and made this book better than it ever could have been without your keen eyes and probing questions.

Daniel Meeter and J. Al Lacour, faithful pastors and shepherds to me at two very different but superformative junctures, offered prayers, thoughtful advice, gentle guidance, and honest feedback, leaving their marks not only on the words I've written but also on the path I've chosen.

To Gretta Adams, Ryan Won, and Caleb Won, I am so grateful for you and to you, for not caring about any of this madness at all, for just being normal. May the world embrace you for whoever you are and for whomever you grow up to be, and may you never, ever doubt the love of God—or the love of your Uncle Jeff.

My mother used to say, "Well, you were born into the wrong family." No, I wasn't. To my parents and to my sister: I am grateful for your love and for your prayers. I am thankful to be your son and your brother. Neither life nor I turned out the way you expected, and I know that has often been hard. Still, I hope and pray that you can see the good that has come of it. I would not be who I am without you.

Finally, my Tristan: Your patience, understanding, and love have been infinite and far greater than I deserve. Thank you for letting me make the journey I had to make. Truly, truly, truly: Tristan is the best!

# ABOUT THE AUTHOR

**JEFF CHU** grew up in Berkeley, California, and Miami, Florida. He graduated magna cum laude from Princeton University, earned a master's degree from the London School of Economics, and received French-American Foundation and Harvard Divinity School fellowships. He has written and edited for *Time*, *Condé Nast Portfolio*, and *Fast Company*, winning Deadline Club and German Marshall Fund awards for his work. He lives in Brooklyn, New York.